IREDELL COUNTY PUBLIC LIBRARY
www.iredell.lib.nc.us

W9-ALX-128

THE LAST
UNICORN

ALSO BY WILLIAM deBUYS

*A Great Aridness: Climate Change and the
Future of the American Southwest*

The Walk

River of Traps: A New Mexico Mountain Life
(with Alex Harris)

Salt Dreams: Land and Water in Low-Down California
(with Joan Myers)

*Enchantment and Exploitation: The Life and Hard Times
of a New Mexico Mountain Range*

Valles Caldera: A Vision for New Mexico's National Preserve
(with Don J. Usner)

Seeing Things Whole: The Essential John Wesley Powell
(editor)

THE LAST UNICORN

A Search for
One of Earth's
Rarest Creatures

WILLIAM deBUYS

Little, Brown and Company

New York   Boston   London

Copyright © 2015 by William deBuys

All rights reserved. In accordance with the U.S. Copyright Act of 1976, the scanning, uploading, and electronic sharing of any part of this book without the permission of the publisher constitute unlawful piracy and theft of the author's intellectual property. If you would like to use material from the book (other than for review purposes), prior written permission must be obtained by contacting the publisher at permissions@hbgusa.com. Thank you for your support of the author's rights.

Little, Brown and Company
Hachette Book Group
1290 Avenue of the Americas, New York, NY 10104
littlebrown.com

First Edition: March 2015

Little, Brown and Company is a division of Hachette Book Group, Inc. The Little, Brown name and logo are trademarks of Hachette Book Group, Inc.

The publisher is not responsible for websites (or their content) that are not owned by the publisher.

The Hachette Speakers Bureau provides a wide range of authors for speaking events. To find out more, go to hachettespeakersbureau.com or call (866) 376-6591.

The epigraph taken from "Revolution in the Revolution in the Revolution" is quoted by permission of Gary Snyder. The epigraph from *The Night of the Iguana* is drawn from the film of that name and does not appear in published versions of the play.

Portions of material appearing in chapters for March 14 and 15 were previously published in "A Glimpse of the Wild," introduction to *The Jungle at the Door: A Glimpse of Wild India* by Joan Myers (photographer). George F. Thompson Publishing, 2012.

Unless otherwise noted, all photographs are from the author's collection.

Maps by Deborah Reade

Library of Congress Cataloging-in-Publication Data

deBuys, William.
   The last unicorn : a search for one of Earth's rarest creatures / William deBuys.—First edition.
      pages cm.
   ISBN 978-0-316-23286-9
   1. Saola—Laos—Nakai–Nam Theun National Biodiversity Conservation Area.   2. Endangered species—Laos—Nakai–Nam Theun National Biodiversity Conservation Area.   3. Wildlife conservation—Laos—Nakai–Nam Theun National Biodiversity Conservation Area.   4. Nakai–Nam Theun National Biodiversity Conservation Area (Laos).   I. Title.
   QL737.U53D434 2015
   591.6809594—dc23   2014020923

10 9 8 7 6 5 4 3 2 1

RRD-C

Printed in the United States of America

For

Art Ortenberg
1926–2014
who set the standard for commitment

and

Mary Elizabeth Burford
1957–2011
rarest and bravest

The Unicorn is captured
And presented to the royal court in the hunter's snare.
Creeping, it frees itself from the snare pole
And heals itself with viper's venom.

> —*Engelberg Codex 314, fol. 150v–152, ca. 1400*

Shannon: On the side, Shannon has been collecting
   evidence.
Hannah: Evidence of what?
Shannon: Man's inhumanity to God.
Hannah: What do you mean by that?
Shannon: The pain we cause Him. We've poisoned His
   atmosphere; we've slaughtered His wild creatures....

> —*Tennessee Williams,* The Night of the Iguana

"From the masses to the masses" the most
Revolutionary consciousness is to be found
Among the most ruthlessly exploited classes:
Animals, trees, water, air, grasses...

> —*Gary Snyder, "Revolution in the Revolution in the
   Revolution"*

CONTENTS

Prologue   3

Maps

    Laos, Vietnam, and Selected Provinces   5

    Nakai–Nam Theun National Protected Area   6

I. Entry   7

II. To the Far Nam Nyang   97

III. Circling Back: Nakai, Again   227

IV. Upriver: The *Poung* of the Nam Mon   263

Epilogue   325

Acknowledgments   330

*Appendix: Pronunciation, Nomenclature,
and Acronyms*   333

Notes   336

Index   343

THE LAST
UNICORN

Prologue

S trange paths lead to unexpected places, and sometimes the world opens up. Early in 2009 I researched efforts in central Borneo to protect a forest where captive orangutans were freed and reintroduced into the wild. Months later, I gave a brief talk on the project to a roomful of strangers in Washington, DC. One of those strangers, Jack Tordoff, telephoned the following week. He asked, "How would you like to write about saola?"

"About what?"

I had never heard the word *saola* spoken.

Tordoff explained that saola (*Pseudoryx nghetinhensis*) were among the rarest large animals on Earth and that they became known to Western science only in 1992. He said they constituted the sole species of a unique genus of bovids—grazing animals that include antelopes, goats, cattle, bison, and other ruminants. He added that they lived under constant threat, mainly from illegal snaring, in their limited range in the Annamite Mountains that divide Vietnam and Laos. He also said that they were beautiful, enigmatic, and, for him as well as many other conservation biologists, inspiring. Tordoff invited me to attend a meeting of the Saola Working Group, or SWG, a subunit of the Asian Wild Cattle Specialist Group of the International Union for the Conservation of Nature, in Vientiane, Laos, in August of 2009.

The meeting's energetic and dedicated coordinator was Bill Robichaud, a field biologist experienced in Southeast Asia, particularly

Laos. Robichaud and I began a conversation that continued stateside. Eventually, in February and March of 2011, I was privileged to join Robichaud on a journey, recounted here, into remote corners of the Nakai–Nam Theun National Protected Area in Laos, hard by the international border with Vietnam. Our expedition had multiple purposes, principally involving reconnaissance of potential saola habitat and evaluation of poaching pressure. Our mission was also "diplomatic" in the sense that it was intended to build support for wildlife conservation among indigenous villagers living or hunting where saola might be found. Overall we hoped to advance priorities identified by Robichaud and his SWG colleagues and to contribute in some way, no matter how small, to the group's paramount goal, which was—and remains—to save the saola from extinction.

Joined by two Lao university students, and later by a staff member of the agency responsible for the protected area, we traveled by car from Vientiane to Nakai, a frontier town roughly hewn from the forest of central Laos, and thence by boat across the vast reservoir of the Nam Theun 2 Hydroelectric Project. We continued upriver into the Annamite Mountains, which are known as the Sayphou Louang in Laos and whose crest forms the international border with Vietnam. We hiked overland to the village of Ban Tong and procured new boats to take us up another river, the Nam Pheo, to the farthest village reachable by boat. There we lingered several days before hiring guides and porters to accompany us on a trek into the vast backcountry, beyond the frontiers of the village world. Our destination was the canyon-cut watershed of yet another river, the Nam Nyang, a land where we hoped to find evidence of living saola and upon which blue Western eyes like Robichaud's and mine had never gazed.

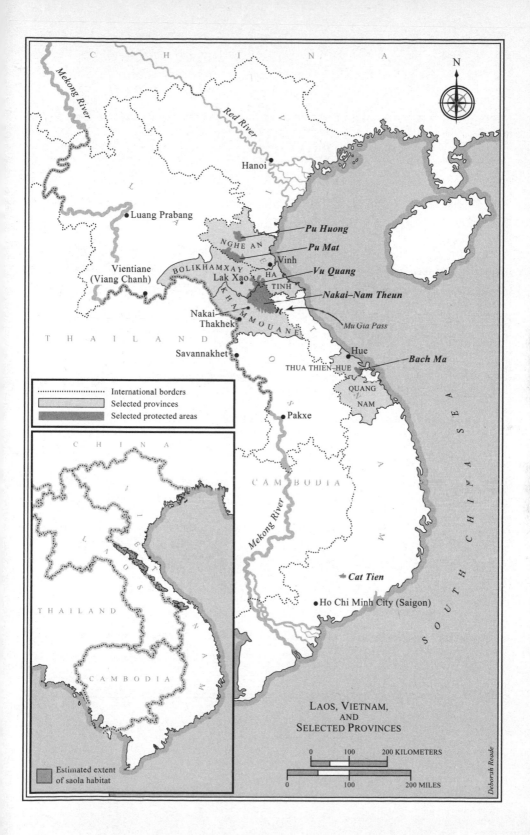

LAOS, VIETNAM,
AND
SELECTED PROVINCES

International borders
Selected provinces
Selected protected areas

Estimated extent
of saola habitat

Mekong River

Red River

Hanoi

Luang Prabang

Vientiane
(Viang Chanh)

BOLIKHAMXAY

Lak Xao

Nakai
Thakhek

Savannakhet

Pakxe

NGHE AN

Vinh

HA
TINH

KHAMMOUANE

Pu Huong

Pu Mat

Vu Quang

Nakai–Nam Theun

Mu Gia Pass

Hue

THUA THIEN–HUE

QUANG
NAM

Bach Ma

Cat Tien

Ho Chi Minh City (Saigon)

CHINA

THAILAND

CAMBODIA

Mekong River

SOUTH CHINA SEA

0   100   200 KILOMETERS

0   100   200 MILES

CHINA

THAILAND

CAMBODIA

Deborah Reade

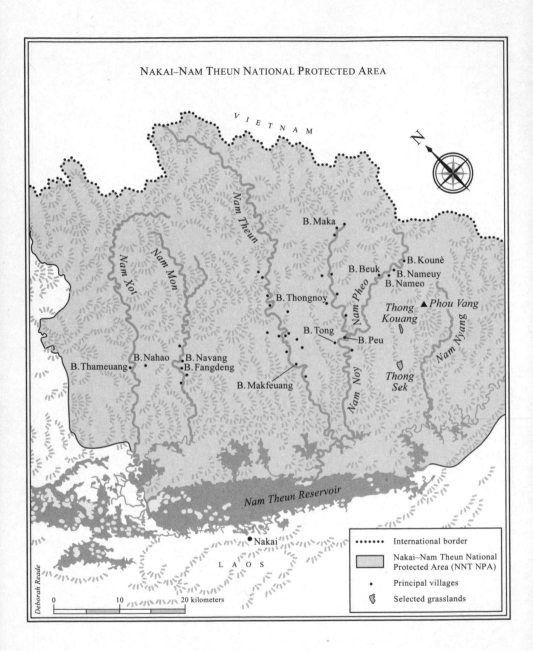

NAKAI–NAM THEUN NATIONAL PROTECTED AREA

VIETNAM

N

Nam Theun

Nam Xot

Nam Mon

B. Maka

B. Beuk

B. Kounè
B. Nameuy
B. Nameo

B. Thongnoy

Nam Pheo

Thong Kouang

▲ Phou Vang

B. Tong

B. Peu

Nam Nyang

B. Thameuang

B. Nahao

B. Navang
B. Fangdeng

Thong Sek

Nam Noy

B. Makfeuang

Nam Theun Reservoir

Deborah Reade

Nakai

LAOS

0   10   20 kilometers

••••••• International border

         Nakai–Nam Theun National
         Protected Area (NNT NPA)

•   Principal villages

         Selected grasslands

I
Entry

February 24

Nam Theun Reservoir

We strike out across the drowned forest in a narrow, battered launch that draws no water except when heavily laden, as it now is with our camp gear and food. A white sky silvers the surface of the water. We squat in silence among the bundles, wrapped like Bedouins against the sun. There is no point in talking. The chainsaw racket of the engine drones tonelessly, incessantly.

Our quarry is an animal known only in a small, remote patch of the planet, an animal known mainly for being unknown. We have no idea if we will find it. The odds, we know, are against us.

The boatman steers through treetops that puncture the surface of the reservoir, down lanes known only to him. We skim the forest at bird level, scraping the edges of canopies whose branches supplicate the sky in a final leafless gesture. We pass a copse of bamboo, its stems arcing upward like antennae. The woody shafts dance and clatter in our wake. Farther along rises a solitary dipterocarp, a hardwood tree considered majestic even by the standards of this timber-rich region. Its thick trunk is charred by fire from years earlier, before the forest was drowned. I shout a question to Robichaud. He yells back, "Not much lightning around here. Probably villagers collecting resin started that one, and it got away from them."

Robichaud sits against a bag of rice in the bow, binoculars at the ready. A rule of expeditions like this one holds that the best observer goes first in line, on water or on land. You never know what you might see. Maybe the next bird in the sky is the last white-winged duck in central Laos. Maybe it's a fish eagle never before reported

9

for this particular place. Maybe you will have no more than a second to bring up the glasses and make the ID. For the habitat where we are headed, you can count on a carpenter's hand the other people in the world who might have a quicker or more knowledgeable eye than Robichaud, and none of them is in the boat. Robichaud has been wandering the forests on the far side of this lake for decades. We are days away from saola habitat, but he is tense with pleasure on this morning of new beginning. Behind him in the boat, I see only his back, but he is sitting as straight and attentive as a bird dog on its way to a hunt.

I am next in line, assigned to a low, bare thwart, vainly seeking comfort among the backpacks and bundles piled fore and aft. There is no extra room and precious little freeboard. The boat is tippy, easily rocked. I am learning that if I stretch out a knee, my back soon complains; if I bring in my leg and lean back, the knee begins to ache. The only thing to do is move the pain from place to place.

Crossing drowned forest, Nam Theun Reservoir, William Robichaud in the bow.

We have two, maybe three hours to cross the reservoir and ply our way upstream along a narrow river to Ban Makfeuang. *Ban* means "place" or "village." *Makfeuang,* to me, is indecipherable, a mouthful of sound without meaning. I have never been there, nor, I imagine, anyplace like it. From Ban Makfeuang, we will hike some hours to another village, Ban Tong, where we hope to hire other boats to take us up a second river to Ban Nameuy, beyond which we will sleep in the forest. The names of these places sit on my tongue like the seeds of an exotic fruit. I do not know whether to swallow them or spit them out.

Behind me, side by side on another thwart, are the boys, Olay and Touy, both of them Lao. They are not boys, really, but young men, one just out of university, the other in his last semesters, though both are younger than my own children. Jammed together in the narrow boat, they have zipped their rain jackets to the chin, although there is no threat of rain. They are as new to each other as they are to me, and it is good to see in their glances and gestures that they are becoming friends. While Touy hails from a royal family of prerevolutionary Laos, Olay is the son of a man born with no social advantages. Now they pass a small camera back and forth and smile modestly when I twist around to look at them.

Behind the boys is Simeuang—lithe, athletic, and ever smiling. Also Lao, he is nearly as young as they are yet possesses a soft and centered gravitas. His presence makes our journey official—and permissible. Hailing from Pakxe, a city on the Mekong River in the south of Laos, he works for the Watershed Management and Protection Authority, the WMPA, which came into being as part of the colossal hydropower project that inundated the forest and created the reservoir we are traversing. The WMPA decrees what may and may not be done in the forests on the far side of the reservoir, which stretch away to a mountainous, cloud-hung horizon we cannot see, past which lies Vietnam. These forests are rich with wildlife and also with people.

Last of all is the boatman, whose face, shrouded by a towel he

11

drapes beneath his hat, is as grave as Charon's. The din of the engine hammers upon him; the long tiller vibrates in his hand. His work is to ferry people and their freight from the dusty town of Nakai, possessed of electricity and a cacophonous market, across the glassy lake and up its tributaries to villages that perch on sandy riverbanks, their houses built on stilts even where floods are not in prospect. These are the homes of "hill tribes," in the terminology of an earlier time; the people of the villages are nowadays—and no more helpfully—referred to as "ethnics" or "ethnic people."

The boat that carries us is a blunt-nosed pirogue, about twenty-five feet long, with a squared stern, where the engine hangs. In design, it is a direct descendant of the dugout canoe, good for navigating the twists and turns of shallow rivers. Sturdy planks have replaced the tree trunk of the original, and a gasoline engine endows the new creation with speed, commotion, and a name: this kind of craft is called a *chak hang*, which translates as "motor tail," a term that aptly describes the long driveshaft slanting backwards from the engine, which ends in a two-bladed propeller hardly bigger than your hand. The shallow slant of the driveshaft keeps the propeller only barely submerged, the better to avoid the rocks and sandbars of the riverbeds. When the boatman opens the throttle, the engine screams, and the prop shoots up a gleaming rooster tail of water, which is the first thing you see when you sight a *chak hang* at a distance.

Once upon a time, certainly years before the dam was closed and the forest flooded, our *chak hang* sported a handsome coat of royal-blue paint, which age and abrasion have since faded to the color of worn-out jeans. The color seems not so much painted on the boat as infused into the fibers of its wood. Were an artist to paint this scene, with its hard-boiled sky, the mirroring water, and forlorn treetops, the weathered boat would give the canvas its only life. Chased by our rooster tail of spray, we are a lone dash of color advancing into the dissolving distance. Soon we, too, will be absorbed by the hazy land.

. . .

As the trees grow fewer in number, the watery prairie opens. The reservoir has now deepened past the height of even the tallest dipterocarps; or, more likely, the trees that used to grow here were felled and hauled to a sawmill before the waters came. In the shimmering distance, the outline of a wooded shore begins to emerge.

The river that was dammed to form the lake is the Nam Theun. *Nam* means "water," also "river." Saying "Nam Theun River" is redundant, like saying "Rio Grande River." *Theun,* in one reading, expresses a wry humor. The word is ancient, coined by some long-vanished ethnic group, and its original meaning may have vanished with them. Among the subsequent connotations that have attached to it over the centuries are "opposite-flowing" and even "wrong way." Nam Theun: Wrong Way River. Before it was drowned, the Nam Theun flowed roughly northwest across the Nakai Plateau, a direction opposite that of the region's other major rivers, which trend southeastward, including the great Mekong, sixty kilometers to the west. The Mekong marks most of the boundary between Thailand and Laos. Or not *Laos:* officially we are in the Lao People's Democratic Republic — Lao PDR. Along with China, Vietnam, North Korea, and Cuba, it is one of the world's last self-described Communist governments.

Past where the Nam Theun spills from the plateau and bends west to flow into the Mekong, it changes its name. It becomes the Nam Kading. *Kading:* the sound of a pretty bell, although this is probably another false etymology. Many place names in Laos go deep in time, bringing a sense of romance and lyricism to the present. By no means are all of them, or even a majority of them, derived from the Lao language. Lao PDR's 6.5 million people, by most counts, are divided among more than 150 distinct ethnicities, speaking scores of different languages. As a result, Laos is one of the world's most culturally heterogeneous nations. Perhaps nowhere else on the planet is extraordinary biological diversity so well matched by ethnic and linguistic variety.

Days earlier, on our way from Vientiane, the capital, to the frontier town of Nakai, we stopped just short of the bridge over the mouth of the Nam Kading and visited a roadhouse. It was just Robichaud, the boys, and me; we would rendezvous with Simeuang later in Nakai. The boys got soft drinks, and Robichaud and I bought cans of chilled coffee and bags of Thai snack food. Then Robichaud disappeared next door. He came back with a half dozen oranges that were the size of limes and almost as green. They looked unappetizing, and I wondered why he had bought them. A few hundred meters down the road, as we approached the bridge over the Nam Kading, he passed them out. It is important, he explained, to make an offering to the river spirits as you cross the river. You give them something, and maybe you get good fortune in return. "Try not to hit any fishermen," he added. And so as our vehicle sped across the bridge, we rolled down the windows and pitched the little oranges over the railing. The water—and any fishermen—lay far below. We could not see where our offerings landed, but I confess I did not think about fishermen—the river gods were much more on my mind. I prayed for the kiss of luck. On the trek that lay before us, it would be a welcome thing, perhaps essential.

The Nakai Plateau, now submerged beneath our boat, was once legendary for its beauty and wildlife. Lao princes and the French colonialists who succeeded them hunted its tigers from the backs of elephants. Unspoiled forests of dipterocarps and stately pines resounded with the gabble of monkeys, the ethereal hoots of gibbons, and the chatter of birds of every hue. Rhinos snorted in the wetlands. Herds of elephants and wild cattle—banteng and gaur (which would dwarf an American bison)—and the rare and regal Eld's deer grew fat in the savannas.

Years before the dam was conceived, but still in living memory, the tigers and rhinos were largely hunted out, and the herds of wild cattle had dwindled. Even so, the grand forests and nearly all their lesser denizens remained.

That such a land should be drowned for a tepid reservoir is a function of three things: the thirst of the world (in this case, Thailand) for electricity, the hunger of Laos for foreign currency, and the confidence, questionable though it may be, of the highest echelon of the globe's economic and financial mavens that a defensible balance of loss and gain might be devised. (Flood control, a common rationale for the building of dams, did not apply.) The masters of the global economy determined to trade the wonders of the Nakai Plateau for the commensurate glories of the sprawling mountain slopes that drain into it, sacrificing the former for the assured protection of the latter. Those slopes are the land to which we are headed—the upper watershed of the Nam Theun, which lies beyond the lake and stretches eastward for many kilometers to the crest of the Annamite Mountains[1] and the border with Vietnam. Designated the Nakai–Nam Theun National Protected Area, it is a patch of planet as pristine as any in Southeast Asia, naturally rife with wildlife, rich in aboriginal culture, and dense with undiscovered marvels. At more than four thousand square kilometers (1,544 square miles), the Nakai–Nam Theun watershed is either the largest or among the two or three largest protected areas (depending on who is doing the counting) in all of Laos, Vietnam, and Cambodia—the region the French called Indochina.[2]

Of course, the wonders of Nakai–Nam Theun have existed through the ages. Exchanging development for preservation does not bring them into being. The purpose of the trade was to make possible the actual protection of those wonders, which were otherwise considered doomed by the usual forces of exploitation. Before the dam came along, Nakai–Nam Theun already enjoyed special status as a "national biodiversity conservation area," but it was a park only on paper, like so many others in the developing world. It received little in the way of management or funding to defend it from hunters, chain saws, and bulldozers.

Development offered an alternative. With cash from a giant hydropower project to fund the watershed's defense, all that would change. Nakai–Nam Theun, it was promised, would be actively patrolled and protected. A dedicated stream of revenue taken from the sale of the electricity—roughly one million dollars a year out of a much larger total, adjusted for inflation—would be directed to protecting the environment and to improving the social and economic well-being of people living in the affected area. A new agency, the Watershed Management and Protection Authority—Simeuang's employer—would come into being to achieve those goals.

This time around—and by many reckonings, for the first time ever—a large-scale, internationally funded hydropower project would be *done right*. Multiple levels of checks and balances would assure quality and accountability, making the project corruption-free, compassionate to native people, and environmentally conscious. The World Bank and its peer agencies were acutely aware that virtually all the large hydropower projects they had funded in the past had produced environmental and cultural calamity. In the wilds of central Laos, they would start afresh and produce a new model for the world. In funding one of the largest construction projects then under way on the planet, they would demonstrate how economic development and environmental protection might be made not just compatible but synergistic. At least, that was the hope.

The construction cost of the Nam Theun 2 Hydroelectric Project, or NT2, as it came to be known, ultimately reached $1.3 billion. Construction began in 2005 and involved as many as eight thousand workers on-site. NT2's army of laborers built two main dams and fourteen saddle dams (to keep water from spilling off the side of the plateau), plus two power stations, ten bridges, six kilometers of tunnels and shafts, and 140 kilometers of roads. They also erected 180 kilometers of high-voltage transmission lines, batched half a million cubic meters of concrete, and installed ten thousand tons of steel. The gates of the dam finally closed in 2008.

NT2 has a capacity of 1,070 megawatts, which puts it in the big leagues of world hydroelectric generation but not at the highest level. (Hoover Dam, on the Colorado River, for example, has a capacity almost twice as great, and the largest individual projects in India, Brazil, and China are five times larger than Hoover.) NT2 exports 95 percent of its power to Thailand, with the remaining 5 percent consumed at home in Laos. Its gross annual sales approach $240 million.[3] No one can doubt the project's value to the Lao economy: NT2 accounts for roughly 5 percent of Lao PDR's gross domestic product.

Motor howling, sun glaring, we leave the expanse of the lake and enter what appears to be a cove. But it is not a cove: the water narrows between encroaching stands of flooded trees and slaloms into the forest. We follow. This is the channel of the Nam Theun, carving its way eastward. Soon we pass a checkpoint maintained by the WMPA, part of the security apparatus for the watershed. A speedboat is tied to the crude dock, but no one is visible in the shack it serves. We neither stop nor slow down.

Raptors perch in a high treetop. Crested serpent eagles. Commonplace. Like red-tailed hawks at home. Robichaud gives them a sidelong glance, no more. Then a shrill call pierces even the drone of the engine. We scan the shoreline eagerly but cannot locate the source and so keep going. Minutes later, Robichaud waves urgently to the boatman to stop. He has seen two birds, nearly as big as pigeons, in trees on the left bank. The boatman cuts the clamorous motor, and the breeze of movement stops. Heat pools around the boat. An insect whine rushes out from the forest to embrace us. The birds Robichaud has spotted have reddish bills and a suggestion of white on the wings. Possibly dusky broadbills, new to the protected area. But no, he says, lowering his binoculars. Just dollarbirds. No big deal.

As we continue, I have the sense of entering a doomed land, like the forest of William Faulkner's bear. The night before we departed, writing notes in my guesthouse room, I had asked myself, what are my fears about the expedition? The first thing I wrote down was that I might not stand up to its rigors. The next was that the forest might prove to be empty of all but tragedy and loss. The unfortunate reality within Nakai–Nam Theun is that the protected area is largely unprotected. Much of it is heavily hunted — by local villagers, by Hmong entering from the north, and by Vietnamese who cross the mountains from the east. The villagers have obvious rights to the forest, and their "take," aside from certain species, may well be sustainable. Not so the others. But the WMPA's enforcement of prohibitions against hunting and trapping by outsiders has so far proved notoriously ineffective. The impacts of the Vietnamese are especially damaging, for they are market hunters, harvesting all manner of wildlife, large and small, for sale in Vietnam and China. The demand in those countries for status restaurant foods, including wild meats of all kinds, and for animal-based medicinal treatments is both voracious and insatiable. It places a price on the head of nearly every mammal and reptile in the forest. And the price keeps rising. As the economies of the expanding East grow wealthier, more and more money chases fewer and fewer animals, and the ransacking of the forest intensifies.

Many of the seemingly wild places of the planet are lamentably empty. The old trees may still tower, and the touch of machinery may be light, but no wild animal larger than a cocker spaniel remains. Nearly all the four-leggeds of any size, along with the monkeys and apes, have been hunted or trapped or starved out. They may have been eaten in a nearby town or sold down the line to a stylish restaurant. They may have been killed for the putative medicinal power of their antlers, scales, skin, bones, or gallbladders. Or they may not have been wanted for any of those purposes but may have met their ends because they stepped into a loop of wire that was waiting for something else. A lucky few, possibly some of the big cats, might be smart enough to bypass most snares but not so lucky that they can avoid perishing from hunger (or failed reproduction, which is starvation at a species level) when the deer, sambar, and wild pigs they depend on exist no more. Robichaud has borne witness to the effects of poaching in Nakai–Nam Theun (NNT) for fifteen years. Notwithstanding the policies and good intentions of the WMPA and related organizations, the depredations of poachers threaten to empty NNT's forests of their wildlife wealth. We would soon find out whether matters had lately grown better or worse.

A second, even stronger purpose motivates this journey: one of the rarest creatures on the planet inhabits the forests to which we are bound. Or, rather, it has inhabited them until recently. Whether the clock of extinction now reads two minutes before midnight or two minutes after no one can say. Perhaps we'll know more when our journey is over. Perhaps, having learned to mistrust something we thought was certain, we'll know even less.

We do know, however, that the creature is extraordinary. It is as big as a carousel pony, striking in appearance, and as elusive as a ghost. It is a grazing mammal with cloven hooves and long tapered horns that curve ever so slightly backwards. According to Robichaud, who once spent two weeks closely observing one of these creatures in a crude menagerie not far from the boundary of the protected area, it possesses a disposition both singular and mysterious. The animal that Robichaud watched did not survive its captivity, but he was with it long enough to understand that it was strangely serene and unlike any other animal he had known, domestic or wild. It allowed him to touch it, to pick ticks from its ears, to tend it. It seemed Buddha-like in its calm. Compared with other animals, this one had a different sense about it, a different way of being in the world. The little that biologists like Robichaud have learned about it suggests that its habits may be unique. It does not feed in the same way as the deer and wild goats that share its dank habitat. Nor does it respond to danger as they do. It may travel along paths of its own or along no paths at all.

The creature is called *saola,* a word borrowed from both Lao and the closely related language of the Tai ethnic minority in the mountains of Vietnam. It is the only Lao word that has been imported into English. *Sao* (rhymes with *now*) means "post"; *la* is a small spinning wheel used in the Annamites: *sao la* are the tapered posts that support a spool for winding thread. The posts of the spinning wheel resemble the horns of the animal.

Beyond the forest villages of the Laos-Vietnam border, no one knew that saola existed until 1992, when scientists spotted strange horns on the wall of a Vietnamese hunter's shack. Suddenly the scientific world had before it proof of a large, new, *living* creature, previously unimagined. The news raced around the world.

Robichaud remembers exactly where he was when word of the discovery reached him. He was relaxing in a café in Vientiane, reading the *Bangkok Post*. A photograph caught his eye. It showed a scientist holding a pair of long, straight, sharply pointed horns. The scientist was John MacKinnon, then working for the World Wildlife Fund and a leader of the survey that had made the find. The word *saola* had not yet entered general use, and the unpoetic name initially given for the animal was Vu Quang ox, after the Vu Quang Nature Reserve (now a national park) in Vietnam, where the discovery was made. An inset map showed the location. It was just across the border from Laos, up from the Nakai Plateau, not far away. Robichaud, a naturalist still finding his path, was thrilled. At that moment, little else seemed more exciting or more splendid.

He had come to Southeast Asia in 1990 with the International Crane Foundation, assisting in a search for the rare sarus crane in Vietnam's Mekong River delta. After the project concluded, he had time on his hands. It struck him that Vietnam and Cambodia frequently made the news, but he never heard much about Laos — so that's where he went. He obtained a two-week visa, settled in, and soon found that he liked the people, the pace, and the feel of things. When his visa ran out, he returned to the States and began looking for a way to get back to Laos. In those days his main focus was hawks. He landed a small grant that allowed him to return in 1992, ostensibly to explore ways of conducting conservation and bird studies in Laos. When he read about the discovery of the saola and saw the proximity of its habitat to Laos, his instinct was to bend his steps in the saola's direction.

He scrounged up provisions, a jungle hammock, and other gear and rode the bus south along the Mekong. He disembarked at the foot of the Nakai Plateau and hiked up the escarpment. At that time Nakai was hardly a town. He plunged into the forest.

Brazenly, Robichaud had decided to go walkabout toward saola country. His adventure did not start auspiciously. On the first night, he'd barely settled into his jungle hammock when he felt something stinging his face. And stinging his neck. And crawling in his hair. He bailed out of the hammock. Red ants clung to his hands and fell like dandruff from his head. A column of them had climbed the tree he'd lashed the hammock to, and the advance guard was marching down the lash rope, through an eyelet, and into the screened sleeping compartment. He shook out the ants as best he could and anointed the lash rope with shampoo or some other ant-repelling lotion. Then once more he attempted sleep.

The next morning he set out through a majestic pine forest. For days he walked through the pines. He stayed away from villages and slept in the forest. His solitary ways spared him contact with local police and village officials, who would have had no idea what to make of him. A lone American wandering through rural Laos? Was he a spy? A prospector hunting gold? Or was he searching for the downed pilots the Americans called MIAs? Because he had no knowledge of the country and little in the way of maps, he ultimately elected not to head up-mountain, toward the Vietnamese border and into whatever the saola's habitat might turn out to be. Instead, he stuck to the plateau proper, the very land that NT2 would later inundate, which proved unspeakably beautiful and marvelous enough. In the days before the plateau was logged and drowned, it supported one of the finest primary pine forests left on the planet.

Robichaud exited the forest at the crossroads town of Lak Xao, the same town where years later he would encounter the captive saola. He had three days left to return to Vientiane and catch his plane to the States. He inquired after the bus. Alas, the rainy season had begun, and the next bus, he was told, would not call at Lak Xao until the dry season, four months hence. Robichaud was stunned: four months! He *had* to get to Vientiane. Quickly.

On the way into town he'd passed an impressive private compound with a big Soviet-built Mi-8 helicopter parked inside it. This was the headquarters of General Cheng Sayavong, satrap of the region, who would loom large for Robichaud in later years. Robichaud had not quite screwed up the courage to turn around, go back, and knock on the door of the compound to ask if the helicopter might soon head to Vientiane, when a man stepped forward. He had observed Robichaud's disappointment about the bus. He said, I have to deliver my son to school in Vientiane; I will take you, too. And so by the luck that attends those who have nothing else, Robichaud joined the man on a journey by foot, truck, and boat that eventually brought him to the main highway running to the capital. He waited, caught a bus, and narrowly made his flight in time.

Early reports of the saola's discovery asserted that the last large mammal previously identified to Western science had been the kouprey, a species of wild cattle similar to banteng and gaur. It, too, was native to Indochina and had been named from the forests of Cambodia more than a half century earlier, in 1937. The last before the kouprey was the giant forest hog, which joined the bestiary of the world in 1904, and before that, the okapi, a forest-dwelling cousin of the giraffe whose existence was confirmed in 1901. The saola was deemed to have revived this impressive succession of discoveries, suggesting that the world might be younger, newer, and more blessed with marvels than anyone dared hope. The claim wasn't precisely true: a half dozen species of whales and porpoises, mammals of the sea and unquestionably large, had been identified to science in the years since the kouprey's discovery, as had more than a half dozen largish land mammals—a pig, a peccary, four species of deer, a gazelle, and a wild sheep.[4] But not many observers lingered over that roster. Sure, new whales might churn the waters of the sea, and new variations on old mammalian themes might manifest themselves from time to time, but saola were not just a new species. They were a new genus, and some taxonomists continue to think their singularity might go even further than that—to the level of tribe. Saola were more than a surprise. They were a mystery drawn from a largely uninventoried habitat that promised still further surprises. They were the embodiment of a land of marvels.

In short order the saola's presence in Laos was confirmed, again by the presence of trophies on hunters' walls—not by live sightings. As more scientists began to probe the Annamite Mountains, a series of stunning additional discoveries ensued. Within years of confirmation of the saola, more new mammals were identified, including several new species of muntjac, or barking deer. The taxonomic validity of one of these, *Muntiacus vuquangensis,* the large-antlered muntjac, is beyond question; other proposed species are still debated because not much evidence about them is available, and the little that exists fails to fit in neat categories. The effort to solve the riddles of the Annamites' biology continues undiminished to this day; indeed, that is why we are here.

One reason the saola so captured the imagination of scientists is its "phylogenetic distinctiveness." That's a fancy way of saying that the saola has no close relatives in evolutionary or genetic terms. It is not a late-branching twig on the tree of life; it is a stub off a major limb, and it grows close to the trunk. From the large, strange scent glands on either side of its muzzle to the bands of color on its tail, the saola resembles no other animal. Classifying it was a puzzle. Was it an antelope? A goat? It looked more like an Arabian oryx than anything else, hence its genus name, *Pseudoryx.* Another datum in favor of the antelope hypothesis was its habitat, which was similar to that of the duiker, a small, furtive antelope of African rain forests. DNA analysis of the bone of its horns, however, indicated a greater affinity with wild cattle and suggested that the saola was a very ancient kind of ox that had diverged eons ago, perhaps in Miocene times, from the ancestors of aurochs, bison, and buffalo. In the subsequent seesaw between moist and dry environments, the saola's cousins grew ponderous and spread through the region's grasslands, savannas, and dry forests. The saola, meantime, remained physically nimble but environmentally cramped. As the moist evergreen forests on which it depended ultimately retreated to the Annamites, the saola necessarily retreated as well. Today, among the large mammals on Earth, few, if any, possess so small a habitat.

So distant is the saola from the lumbering ruminants with which it shares the greater part of its genes that it seems closer, at least in a metaphorical way, to a creature of myth. In its spirit—or perhaps only in the spirit that the Westerners pursuing it imagine it to have—the saola seems kindred to the fabled unicorn of medieval lore. Like the unicorn, it is as rare as the rarest thing on Earth. It is shy and elusive, hard to find and harder to capture, the same as the unicorn was said to be. Also like the unicorn, it seems to possess an otherworldly disposition, different from that of other beasts. And its horns, up to half a meter long and elegantly tapered, are as beautiful as the unicorn's. When seen in profile, the saola's horns merge into one, and the animal becomes single-horned—a unicorn by perspective. Like that other one-horned beast, it stands close to being the apotheosis of the ineffable, the embodiment of magic in nature. Unlike the unicorn, however, the saola is corporeal. It lives, and it can die.

Robichaud and I have been joking: we acknowledge a problem inherent in our efforts. In the year 1250, when the high vaults of Notre-Dame de Chartres were still under construction, it was common knowledge that none but a virgin of impeccable purity might approach a unicorn or persuade one to approach her. It was believed, in fact, that only the pure of heart might hope to glimpse a unicorn. I will not speak for Robichaud, but if the same purity of heart applies to saola, I am immediately disqualified. Besides, unless some army ranger glimpsed one decades ago along the Ho Chi Minh Trail, no Westerner has ever seen a saola in the wild.

Robichaud says he is detached from the idea of being the first, that it is not a particular goal he pursues, yet I am certain he would very much relish it. As for me, I would like nothing more than to behold the glint of horns and the flash of a white-splashed muzzle through a weave of lianas, but the odds of finding buried treasure are better. I will be thrilled simply to make it into saola habitat. I want to be where saola are. Once there, we'll set up camera traps — stations near trails, water holes, and salt licks where we'll strap cameras equipped with infrared sensors to trees. If the equipment works correctly, the body heat of passing animals will trigger the shutter, and the resulting photographs will constitute a record of the wildlife of the area. Our expedition has additional goals: we will discuss saola protection with the village elders, evaluate various conservation schemes, and collect DNA samples from the saola heads and horns that hunters have saved as trophies. Most important, we will survey a little-known watershed — that of the Nam Nyang, which no Westerner has previously explored — for saola and other wildlife. Possibly in the Nam Nyang, possibly elsewhere, we will leave the cameras behind to do their work unattended after we are gone. We are hunting not just scat and other marks of saola passage but also the animal's lasting digital image.

We are at a disadvantage, however, compared to the unicorn hunters of yore. We have no bait. Leonardo da Vinci, a man of his time, knew that the best way to catch a unicorn was not to beat the bushes but to lure it in and let the unicorn come to its seeker. According to Leonardo, the lure of choice was a virgin: "The unicorn, through its intemperance and not knowing how to control itself, for the love it bears to fair maidens forgets its ferocity and wildness; and laying aside all fear it will go up to a seated damsel and go to sleep in her lap, and thus the hunters take it."[5]

Leonardo does not explain how the virgin simultaneously preserves her purity while also betraying the unicorn, yet in the classic

25

accounts, betray him she does, although she weeps sweet tears for doing so. Her remorse comes after the fact. From the start the beatific maiden has been in cahoots with the hunters, plotting against the unicorn. In oft-told tales, her malice aforethought goes unexplained.

Logic and unicorns, however, seldom inhabit the same domain. The Greeks wrote of unicorns when writing was still new. For them the beast was not a mythological creature but a denizen of natural history. It lived beyond the horizon and even further beyond verification. The Old Testament, in the King James Version, mentions unicorns at least eight times, although each appears to be a mistranslation. The Hebrew word *re'em* probably referred to aurochs, the now extinct ancestor of domestic cattle. But the translators found the word *unicorn* more evocative, so unicorn it was. By the time of the King James Bible, unicorns had bowed, pranced, and laid their heads in virginal laps for centuries, and no one doubted their existence. A brisk and long-standing trade in "actual" unicorn horns had attested to their physical reality—notwithstanding that the horns were in fact narwhal tusks gathered from northern waters by Vikings and their successors and sold into the same eager market that gobbled up saints' bones and pieces of the True Cross.

Not even Marco Polo, upon his return from Asia in about 1300, managed to dampen enthusiasm for unicorns when he described them as "ugly brutes" with hairy legs, prone to wallowing in mires. In all likelihood Polo had glimpsed some species of Asian rhinoceros. (Indian and Javan rhinos have one horn; the Sumatran has two, but the second horn is small and often hard to see.)

The image of the unicorn adorned innumerable coats of arms as an avatar of courtly love: the noble lover was irresistibly attracted to his lady as the unicorn was drawn to the virgin. Because a unicorn's horn was believed to neutralize poisons, kings and queens (and others with reason to fear those close to them) paid handsomely to obtain cups made from the miraculous material. In Christian iconography the lamb may have stood for the baby Jesus, but the unicorn, in its goodness and transcendent power, became an animal analog of the adult Savior, a symbolism evident in its devotion to the Virgin and its sacrifice at the hands of hunters.

Vietnam has its own tradition of something near to a unicorn — the *ky lan,* which seems to have revealed itself to a number of ancient rulers when their victories over enemy armies were particularly impressive. Most depictions of the *ky lan,* however, more closely resemble a dragon than any creature of flesh and blood. The same might be said of its antecedent, the Chinese *qilin,* which in Japanese became *kirin.* The logo of the beer of that name looks like a mescaline-induced vision of a fiery quadrupedal demon.

The unicorn remains a marketing tool for more than beer. These days, on Amazon.com, you can buy a 5.5-ounce tin of "unicorn meat" from "Radiant Farms" for $14.95. Inside is a stuffed toy. Don't expect to eat it.

The river we are following has narrowed but remains slack. It is an arm of the lake, its water the color of cola. A palisade of slender trees crowds the shallows. Behind this scrim extends the enfolding forest, which we feel as a brooding presence. Now we spot another raptor, and Robichaud takes interest. It is an osprey, a new arrival to Nakai– Nam Theun. Its presence is another indication, albeit an unsurprising one, of the changing habitat the lake has produced. Ospreys elicit Robichaud's admiration. Excluding house sparrows and European starlings, which spread and thrive in humanized environments, ospreys, together with peregrine falcons and barn owls, may be the most widespread bird species on the planet.

The boat wails onward. Din and discomfort have numbed us, and the sun is a heavy drug. Another half hour passes. Finally the water begins to clear. Bubble lines on the surface suggest the beginning of a current. The river begins to look like a river. A pod of water buffalo lazes on a sandbar, their gaze stupid and faraway. A *chak hang* much like ours heads past us downstream. Its passengers watch us deadpan, without a smile or nod. Then we round a bend, and a fresh swidden—a patch of newly cleared forest—appears on the right bank. Piles of slash smolder. The smoke rises in wisps, the air suddenly acrid. Another turn of the channel, and three sun-dark boys in midriver pause from fishing to stare at us gravely, their wet nets gleaming in their hands. Swiddens now line both sides of the river. Trails angle to the river's edge. Then more buffalo, one of them on its back, legs up, rolling in sand, another one shitting. At a boat upturned on a sandbar, a boy kneels, caulking. The river bends again, and in the flat water of an eddy, a slender woman, hair long and straight, wades thigh-deep in an eddy, hitching up her sarong, which is as green as the forest. She is bathing, the water calm around her, and she stares back with dark eyes.

The river, now shallow, flows on a gravel bed, the current strong. Past another bend the boatman suddenly kills the engine and glides onto a spit of sand. Robichaud and Simeuang speak in Lao. I hear what might be "Makfeuang." On cramped legs I hobble to shore. No buildings are in sight, just sand and scrub. After three hours, we have escaped the boat, but there is no time to savor our relief. We still have far to go.

A trail leads up a sandy bluff. I grab a pack and follow the others.

The first sign of the village is a stack of twenty-five yellow crates of empty Beerlao bottles, freight awaiting a downriver trip. Amplified music blares in the distance, a new thing in Ban Makfeuang, says Robichaud, thanks to the arrival of photovoltaics. While Simeuang goes to recruit a hand tractor—another new arrival—to haul our gear to Ban Tong, the rest of us hump the remaining packs, duffels, and bulging rice sacks up the bluff. We stow the gear nearby in a shack on stilts that is half filled with bags of rice—perhaps it is some kind of warehouse, but before I can ask its purpose, Robichaud beckons me to come along. He wants to see a friend.

We walk rapidly down a village lane between houses raised on stilts. Unsmiling women lean from the windows to watch us pass. I imagine that they and their mothers have been frowning at passing visitors for centuries. Yellow dogs growl in the shadows beneath the houses, and weird Lao music throbs up ahead. At a solitary spigot, a mother washes her naked daughter. Gaunt cows, under clouds of flies, shuffle from our path. More houses, more windows, more solemn women leaning out, their small children peering over the sills, craning to see. Two paces back, beyond range of a kick, dogs trail us, teeth bared. A pig squeals. I realize I am walking closer to Robichaud than I mean to.

Paa Ket—Auntie Ket—is not at home, but we are invited by persons I cannot see to come in and wait for her. Ket's house, like every other one here, is raised off the ground, a neat separation of the domain of humans from that of pigs, dogs, and other critters, both wild and tame. It is reached by a five-foot ladder of thin poles. Seeing Robichaud kick off his sandals at the top of the entry ladder, I shed mine at the bottom and climb the rails barefoot, a decision I instantly regret because my shoe-spoiled feet are soft and the skinny rungs shoot stabs of pain up my legs. The word *tenderfoot* lights up in my mind like a neon sign, adding embarrassment to the anxiety I feel as an alien on a new planet. Inside, the house is dark and cool. We sit on a bare, swept floor in an unadorned room. Someone has gone to fetch Auntie. Robichaud chats easily in Lao with a youngish man. A little girl toddles over to inspect me. With her standing and me sitting, we meet eye to eye. I softly say, "Sabaidee," hello, one of my few Lao expressions. She stares at me with a blend of incomprehension and disapproval.

Robichaud has told me about Paa Ket. He saw her in action at an economic development meeting in Thakhek, the provincial capital. Dozens of big shots and professionals, both Lao and Western, filled a modest hall. Paa Ket was the village representative of the Lao Women's Union. When it was her turn to speak, everyone expected the usual shy, mumbling deference that hill country "ethnics" typically show their lowland "betters." Instead Paa Ket strode to the lectern and stood at stiff attention with her shoulders back. Unblinking, she surveyed the room, and in a loud, confident voice began, "I am so *happy* to be here and I want to *thank* everyone. I am almost fifty years old, and this is my first visit to the capital of the province...." In seconds her intrepid warmth won over the room. She went on to speak frankly about the difficulty of small-scale economics in the villages and the failings of development projects designed from afar. Against their instincts and inclinations, the jaded audience embraced both her and her message.

Now we hear movement on the ladder outside. Paa Ket enters. She is graceful and sinewy. Rapid of gesture. Gray hair tied back. A sculptured face. Her black eyes light up as she greets Robichaud: "Sabaidee, Wil-yam!" Introductions are quick. Her warm, dry hand feels fleetingly sensuous. The genial young man Robichaud has been talking to turns out to be her husband. He is easily twenty years her junior—and there is no surprise that the lively Paa Ket, widowed by her first husband, sought youth in the second. Paa Ket explains that a *hiit*—some kind of ritual celebration—is under way at another house. She must return. And we must come, too. There can be no objection. Oh, and we should make a small contribution for the hosts. Twenty thousand Lao kip—about $2.50—would be appropriate. We dig out the money, and with the bills balled in her fist, she is gone.

Robichaud slips on his flip-flops and skitters down the ladder before I have touched the first painful rung. At the bottom, rushing to keep up, I hop on one foot to pull a sandal on the other, yanking so violently that I break the loop that is supposed to help me pull it on. Then I hurry behind Robichaud, and reinforce, with every step, the anthropological cliché of the bumbling white neophyte newly arrived in the thrumming village. A hundred meters down the lane, the giddy Lao music reaches a crescendo. Another entry ladder, another sandal shedding. The porch is crowded with glassy-eyed men sucking rice wine through bamboo straws from a giant urn. They gesture for us to join them. We slide past and enter the house.

There is one large room. Thirty hard-drinking men are on one side. Twenty shy women, some of them also hard-drinking, sit with their children on the other. Between them, Paa Ket kneels at a line of large beer bottles arrayed as a low fence across the floor, dividing the sexes. Robichaud and I have entered on the men's side, and we pick our way through the crowd that is seated and lounging on the floor. Everyone reaches up to shake hands. Like a politician at a barbecue, Robichaud has a warm word for everyone. I stumble behind, trying not to step on anyone, a task made harder by the inexplicable little judo tugs that come with the handshakes. "Sabaidee." "Sabaidee." Finally we settle on cushions at the head of the room.

I find myself next to an old man with sunken cheeks who seems not at all disappointed that I am incapable of understanding a word he says. Evidently he is hosting the *hiit,* and by the look of his bright eyes, he has abundantly enjoyed his own hospitality. Notwithstanding my incomprehension, he has much to say to me, and his openmouthed animation affords many a glimpse of his gums, which are toothless except for a single, bulbous, coal-black object, smooth as a river stone, that appears to have erupted from his lower jaw. It gleams like onyx. I can't tell if it is an actual tooth or a perversely located jewel. He is amused when I take his picture and delighted when I show him his image on my camera. He reaches out and takes the eyeglasses from my head. He puts them on. I take another picture. His delight is unrestrained. He rustles out a jug of homemade whiskey from the forest of bottles at his side. Dark things marinate in the bottom of it. The liquid tastes like lamp fuel. "Delicious," I say. *Drink more,* he gestures, and the music blasts on. Someone makes a loud statement. Laughter. Paa Ket makes a reply. More laughter. She is the only woman on the men's side of the beerbottle fence. I try to capture her angular beauty in a photograph, but the room is dim and she is swaying, gesturing, always a blur.

Then comes the food tray, a flat-topped mushroom of woven rattan. It is the nearest thing to furniture in the house. On it are plastic bags of sticky rice, bottles of beer, and bowls brimming with brown lumps in brown puddles. A chorus rises from a dozen voices: "Kin khao, kin khao." "Eat, eat," they say, although the literal translation of *kin khao* is "eat rice," which is a redundancy in Laos, where all eating involves rice. It would be an insult not to taste something, and I am searching for the lesser evils among the brown puddles when a figure looms, backlit, in the doorway. It is Simeuang. He has found a hand tractor. Our journey mustn't wait. Robichaud rises to his feet. I retrieve my glasses from the old man, bidding him thanks and good-bye. The mysterious bauble in his mouth gleams anew. I say good-bye as well to Paa Ket. After a dozen jujitsu handshakes crossing the room, we are out the door, past the drunken veranda, and quickly down the ladder.

A hand tractor is an engine on two wheels. New to the watershed, it recently joined the water buffalo—and partly replaced it—as a source of pulling power. It has a single axle, and were it not for the cart hitched behind it, it would tip forward on its nose. The operator steers the vehicle by means of handlebars of prodigious length. Our operator is in a hurry. He wants to get to Ban Tong, dump our stuff, and make the return trip home before dark. The instant our last sack is thrown in the cart, he cranks the engine and roars down the yellow clay track. Olay, Touy, Simeuang, Robichaud, and I, each carrying a light pack, follow hurriedly on foot, but the tractor, which jolts along at five or ten miles per hour, is soon out of sight.

Simeuang sets the pace, a fast one. He moves lightly, as though his pack weighed nothing, as though he weighed nothing. When we met a few nights ago in Nakai, I was struck by his bright, quick energy. He wore a nylon jacket, fire-engine red. I said to myself, That's the color for him, as bold as a siren. Now he seems to glide down the trail.

We soon enter forest, and the trail becomes a tunnel through stands of vine-hung trees. Chain saws, tools as new to the watershed as hand tractors, have recently felled many large trees close to the trail, rendering the forest as scraggly as a badly barbered head. Most of what we see is second or third or umpteenth growth, for this portion of the watershed has been cleared for swidden cultivation not once but repeatedly over generations, possibly over centuries. Patch by patch, it grows back.

After two or three kilometers, we come to a village. As in Ban Makfeuang, the people are Brou, the largest ethnic group in NNT. Again, stony faces watch us from windows. Robichaud calls out a greeting in the Brou language, "Banchouan," and our observers crack the makings of a smile. Maybe the novelty of hearing a Westerner speak a word of Brou amuses them. Maybe it is the way he pronounces it. A young man pushing a motorbike stops to shake hands. Seeing we are not dangerous, others step away from their laundry or carpentering to experience the exotic visitors up close. We exchange greetings and keep moving, soon reentering the forest, our pace never slowing.

I do not know how far we have to go, and I am determined not to ask. Don't measure, don't count, don't look at your watch, I think. Just go. But the early weariness in my legs—we have been walking only an hour—prompts the thought that the cumulative age of my two lower limbs runs to nearly a century and a quarter—122 years, to be exact—which makes the weariness more amusing if not tolerable. As Simeuang skims blithely ahead, I ask his age. He is twenty-five, although he is broadly experienced in the watershed and has traveled here with Robichaud before. The boys are each twenty-two. Touy asks my age—his English is good but limited—and both he and Olay register shock when I tell them. "Oh, you are doing well. You are strong," says Touy. I thank him and, without much confidence, hope that he is right. Olay nods assent, smiling meekly. He can follow most of an English conversation, but partly out of shyness speaks less than Touy. His stiff, cowlicked hair and sleepy eyes give him a perpetually just-awakened look, but he has the lean, leathery constitution of a coyote. In a long march he would match Simeuang stride for stride. This is his second trip in NNT with Robichaud; he came along on a similar trek in 2009. Touy, meanwhile, seems indomitably cheerful. His name, which is really a nickname, is a common one in Laos. It means "chubby," in an affectionate way.

True to his name, Touy is fat-cheeked, but although his face is round and full, he is not at all heavy. By the way he strides down the trail, he appears more than fit.

The same might be said of Robichaud, who is fifty-two. His heritage is Acadian on his father's side. Not Canadian or French Canadian, he would tell you, but Acadian. In the eighteenth century, the British masters of Canada expelled the French from Acadia, which included Nova Scotia and other maritime lands. Some of them went to Louisiana, where the word *Acadian* was shortened to *Cajun*. Others, including Robichaud's forebears, took refuge in New England. His mother's stock includes Irish. On both sides, he inherits pale skin, as do I, and notwithstanding his translocation to the tropics, he never courts exposure to the sun. He is blessed with ruddy good looks and a rugged constitution, which in Southeast Asia is as much a prerequisite for a field biologist as a sharp eye.

Our route winds through forest, in and out of ravines, along the rough path taken by the hand tractor. We cross the intermittent

William Robichaud.

creeks and seeps on foot logs and occasionally a plank. We pass more swiddens and more ragged forest. We pause in our brisk march only when we encounter travelers — two kids on a motorbike, a family walking, all of them bound back the way we've come. Another hour passes. At last even Simeuang betrays fatigue. His pace slows. Then we hear a roar. It is the hand tractor coming back on its return to Ban Makfeuang. The driver nods to us as he roars by. Ban Tong cannot be far now.

Robichaud grew up in Wisconsin. He was the youngest of six children, all but one of whom were boys. Family life was more than turbulent. He was the silent one, the one who could hide in plain sight, the little observer perched at the fringes of the perpetual vortex, where tides of strong emotion and extreme behavior surged among the big people. The currents that ran in his veins were less destructive but no less powerful. They carried him to safety, away from the vortex, pulling him toward birds. As adolescence took hold, the attraction to wild birds — raptors, especially — grew ever stronger, and he gave it full expression: he *wanted*, no, he *would have*, he *must have*, a hawk, a bird of prey. He *would be* a falconer. No other path would do.

He identified three nests of red-tailed hawks not far from his home. He went with his father to one, but his father forbade the attempt to retrieve a chick. The climb was too dangerous. He went to another, but the young had already flown. He persisted. He was sixteen, newly licensed to drive. Days later he fit his mother's laundry hamper into her car and drove to the third and last nest. It was raining. He was still scrawny, not yet grown into the body of a man, and the oak tree was tall. Yet hamper in tow, he climbed the slippery trunk and out onto the swaying, wind-lashed upper branches. Fear tightened his throat until he could scarcely breathe. He kept on. Only one chick remained in the nest. It was small and scrawny, like Robichaud. A battle commenced amid the rain and wind. It was runt versus runt, as Robichaud fought the chick into the hamper.

35

He named the red-tail Genghis. "What else is a sixteen-year-old going to name a hawk?" he will say. There was a railroad near where he lived, and he hunted the bird along the tracks, walking the ties. Genghis became the scourge of rabbits dwelling by the right-of-way. The partnership was long-lasting.

The bond between boy and hawk rarely went astray, but when it did, *sweet Jesus,* the results were spectacular. One day, not on the railroad tracks but on a street, Genghis cruised the treetops, and Robichaud, whose mind had wandered, suddenly sensed that the tinkle of the hawk's bell was headed the wrong way. The Doppler effect wasn't right. Genghis should have been coming. He was going. Robichaud turned to see the hawk diving, laser-locked on a kill. An old lady was walking her shih tzu or Lhasa apso. Genghis was on final approach, targeted on the dog. There was no stopping him.

The tableau of assault is etched in Robichaud's memory. The bird slammed into the dog and sent it rolling. The old lady shrieked. The panicked dog scrambled upright and leapt like a salmon into its mistress's arms. Genghis wheeled and pursued, wings flailing, and clawed at the woman's coat sleeve, grabbing for the dog. Robichaud slid into the scene and pulled off the bird barely in time to avert physical harm. And then stood there, taking his medicine, enduring the righteous intervention of the old lady's daughter, the bawling out, the dressing-down, the aggrieved search for wounds on the dog, the lecture about "wild animals in the city." A crotch-tightening fear tinged his abject apology: What if she calls the cops?

Robichaud survived, as did Genghis. As did Robichaud's fascination with birds. Fresh out of high school, he volunteered at the Cedar Grove Ornithological Research Station, home to a legendary bird-banding operation. The station occupies a gap in the forest close to the western shore of Lake Michigan, where migrating raptors funnel through a narrow patch of airspace. Volunteers trap and count the birds flying by. Trapped hawks are then banded, measured, and set free, each one adding to a cumulative record of raptor movement across the inland core of North America. Robichaud has helped out at Cedar Grove for more than three decades, and he has written of the magic that keeps bringing him back: "It's the potential to see in a day a hundred Merlins (one of nature's most spectacular fliers), or a thousand Sharp-shinned Hawks floating on a fresh northwest wind in a single morning (a record flight day in 1983), or a single Harris's Hawk (in 1994, the only Wisconsin record). It's the possibility of trapping 75 Northern Goshawks in a day (during an invasion of those gray ghosts in 1982), or finding Northern Saw-whet Owls hanging in the mistnets in the morning like Christmas tree ornaments. These are minor miracles. Some go to church on Sunday, some to Cedar Grove."[6]

Robichaud refuses to call himself a birder. For him, birders are hobbyists who lavish fortunes on exotic trips and acquire sightings the way others collect beer mugs or stamps. Robichaud does not collect. Something different motivates him. He likes to quote a scrap of graffiti someone scrawled long ago on the wall of the Cedar Grove trapping blind: THE INFINITE PASSION OF EXPECTATION. The phrase is still there, he says. No one would dream of removing it.

It is midafternoon when we arrive in Ban Tong to find our gear piled beneath a tree outside the house of the headman, whose name is An. He is a short, slim, stoical man no more than thirty-five years old. And no, he says, he cannot arrange for boats to take us upriver to Ban Nameuy until tomorrow. Robichaud grimaces at the news. Today there is a *hiit*, or some kind of house ceremony, or perhaps a ceremony has to be prepared—the details are unclear, and I am not inclined to press Robichaud for explanation, as he is dismayed and disinclined to talk. Time matters. We have a long distance to travel, a considerable number of tasks to accomplish, and a limited store of time and cash with which to get them done.

Robichaud's frustration stems not just from the present delay but because the tractor driver charged an exorbitant six hundred thousand kip (seventy-five dollars) to ferry our goods here, and now An is quoting equally extortionate prices for the boats we will need, when we finally get them. The costs are more than the expedition's small treasury (funded by a modest grant from a US foundation) can bear. Price inflation, like a new virus, has evidently infected the watershed, and Robichaud did not budget for it. Mr. An, however, is not hard-hearted. He offers to let us sleep on his porch — provided we make a gift to him of a T-shirt. In this particular, Robichaud believes that An is not shaking us down. He says it is reasonable that a gift should be offered to please the house spirits, which must not be slighted.

We settle in, bathing in a nearby creek and lingering over a dinner we have brought from Nakai: sticky rice, pickled fish, a paste of eggplant and chili, and dried meat skewered on tough strips of bamboo. Sticky rice, also called glutinous rice, is grown in thousands of varieties in Laos, a different genotype for virtually every valley, but the procedure for eating it is everywhere the same: You reach into the common mound of cooked rice and grab a gooey handful, which, true to its name, is adhesive enough to hang wallpaper. You shape your clump of rice as you like, usually in a ball, so that it will not fall apart. You then mash it into whatever paste or sauce is offered, perhaps, if the pot is rich, deftly trapping a flake of fish or chunk of meat with your index finger. Then you bring the whole starchy collage to your mouth. For many people, sticky rice is an acquired taste. I have not acquired it. For me, it is like chewing a rubber ball.

An's house is sturdy and walled with planks, a big step up from the woven mats that enclose traditional shelters. Six or seven feet off the ground, the house is reached by a steep stairway, not a ladder. The far end of the veranda gives way to a bridge linking the house to its kitchen, a mat-walled hut with a thatched roof. On the bridge is a washing station where we freshen up from a bucket, and on the handrail of the bridge a macaque sits tethered before a tiny pile of cold rice. With long, black-nailed fingers, the monkey brings the rice to its mouth, grain by grain, as though counting every morsel.

We spread our sleeping bags at one end of the veranda under mosquito nets. Government posters cover the wall behind us. One depicts a cartoonish saola and urges hunters not to shoot it. Another poster contrasts a well-tended landscape—fertile fields, abundant forest, limpid water—with its exploited twin, a scene of tree stumps, eroded fields, and mothers looking aghast at wan children. Near the door hangs a notable pair of portrait posters: one of a regal-looking Kaysone Phomvihane, the revolutionary hero and Pathet Lao leader regarded as the father of postcolonial Laos, and another of the dashing Souphanouvong, scion of the royal family, who by allying with the Pathet Lao lent stature to the Communist cause and earned himself the nickname the Red Prince. Robichaud says that Touy, as a descendant of the royals, can claim the Red Prince as an uncle of some kind.

Close to the equator, night descends like a curtain in a theater. There is no leisure in the sunset. One minute you bask in yellow light, the next you barely see your hand. When full dark descends, we retire, crawling into our bags beneath a gauze of mosquito netting. The boys stay restive for a while, but Robichaud and Simeuang are almost instantly still, and soon their snores resound, sonorous and rhythmic, like breakers on a shore.

February 25

Ban Tong

hrough sleepless hours I conjecture without satisfaction what daylight will bring, imagining the journey that will take us up the Nam Pheo from Ban Tong to Ban Nameuy, at the limit of settlement. I cannot picture the land or its villages in any detail, yet the effort diverts me from an array of discomforts. The long-held postures of the boat ride have stiffened my back so that I cannot lie supine without my lumbar muscles tightening ferociously. The same occurs if I lie on my stomach. And if I lie on either side, the respective hip complains. So I toss, and my insomnia wanders from the morrow's travel to reflection on the abandonments that accompany every serious trip. Moments before we left Nakai, the last news I got from home was an e-mail routed through Robichaud from my long-time partner, Joanna. She wrote that her mother had died. There was neither time nor opportunity to reply. By now, a day later, she has no doubt plunged into a tangle of difficult tasks — notifying friends, arranging a memorial service, dealing with morticians, and inquiring about transport of the physical body to its distant resting place, and all of this within a fabric of both grief and relief that a long decline has ended. Exactly when I might have been most helpful, I am on the far side of the world.

A second abandonment is also on my mind. Just before departing for Laos, I called on a friend to say good-bye. The visit was more than a little fraught, for Mary had long been fighting cancer, and it was likely she would not be living when I returned. Years earlier, when we met, she was said to be close to death. I had gone to read to her, as a volunteer, but never read a page. We only talked, that day and many more, and became each other's confidants, soul mates of a sort. Mary survived that particular crisis and subsequent others tended only by friends, who, because she had neither money nor insurance, were her only wealth. For four years she miraculously hung on. But then her belly swelled with the enemy inside her, and her dancer's legs, heavy with fluid, grew as thick as tree trunks. The cancer had begun its final advance. It so happened, when I stopped to say good-bye, that I was already carrying one of the waterproof pocket notebooks I had specially bought for the trip. For some reason the blank notebook was on the table between us when my daughter telephoned. I stepped away to take the call. Hours later, at home packing, I discovered that while I had been talking with my daughter, Mary had written the first words in the notebook: "Just call for me if you need a guardian spirit. Love, Mary."

Sometime after midnight, a terrible fit of coughing erupted from within An's house, and a hunched old woman staggered out, hacking and gasping. A younger woman (An's wife?) soon followed and tried to render assistance. In vain. Desperate spasms racked the old lady, and she could not draw a breath. She seemed in the throes of a horrible asthma attack, wheezing and coughing until not a molecule of air could be left within her. Her agony lasted minutes, an eternity at the door of suffocation. My companions awakened. I am sure the neighbors in the nearby houses must have awakened, too. We lay frozen with apprehension, an audience to her agony, until suddenly she drew in a long, deep, whistling breath, which might well have been her last. She held it. And all within earshot held their breath with her. Then she exhaled with the sound of a balloon deflating. And inhaled again like a whale about to dive. And exhaled. Then nothing: a long dangerous pause. And then she inhaled. We all inhaled with her, because we could do nothing else. We grew light-headed with her sobbing efforts as she heaved and gasped her way back into the world of the living. Finally her breathing, and ours, became regular again, and the crisis passed. Then we heard only the two women's murmuring as the old one and the young one huddled together at the end of the veranda, and after a while went into the house.

A fitful hour passed and dawn still lay far away when the house spirits, whom the gift of a T-shirt (it was Touy's) had evidently failed to appease, gave vent to their displeasure. I was drowsing more than sleeping as bells began to toll. The sound swelled from beneath the house. At first one bell, rhythmically. Then two, in different tones. Which were joined by a third, all clanging close beneath us. Then four. Then five, in five different pitches. And soon the last vestige of rhythm was lost, and the ringing and clanging converged in a chaos of sound, as though a band of fiends were banging pots and pans in an infernal kitchen. Amid the clamor, new sounds of bestial moans and grunts, such as would befit a tribe of witches, rose through the floorboards. Robichaud woke cursing. Simeuang scrambled from his sleeping bag, shed the mosquito net, and ran down the stairway to the ground. He shouted imprecations in Lao and flashed his head-lamp into the darkness beneath the house. I heard sounds of what seemed to be pushing and shoving, and the cacophony tapered to silence. Simeuang returned, muttering. A tentative quiet settled on the village.

In the morning, over a breakfast of sticky rice, fish sauce, and fish soup, I learn that the riot of bells and grunting had resulted from a proximate, mortal cause. Robichaud explains that five or six water buffalo, all belled, had converged under the house and started a shoving match, or a bull had tried to mount a female, with every other member of the pod agitating around them. Hence the diaboli-cal clamor. Hence also the urgency of quelling the scrum, not just to restore quiet but to prevent the house posts from being knocked flat and bringing down the entire structure. As far as I could see, these facts remained compatible with my hypothesis of unhappy spirits. Although outsiders know little of the cosmology of the people of Ban Tong (or any other village in NNT), it hardly seemed a stretch to suppose that a cranky house spirit might choose a water buffalo as a vehicle for mischief.

Robichaud is not much charmed by such speculation. His mind is elsewhere. As we breakfast, he lays out the situation with Mr. An, meanwhile tossing fish bones to an emaciated three-legged cat begging for scraps. (Its raw, amputated stump, showing shriveled tissues along a peg of white bone, testifies to an encounter with a snare.) We need to ascend the Nam Pheo to Ban Nameuy, and the boats in use on the Nam Pheo are smaller and lighter than the one that carried us across the lake from Nakai to Ban Makfeuang. Mr. An insists that we need four of them. Robichaud says we can afford only three, and that not easily. So Simeuang, Olay, and he will walk to Ban Nameuy, and Touy and I will accompany the boats and safeguard the gear. That is the plan at seven in the morning, but it cannot be implemented until the boats are readied and we haul our gear a kilometer farther, to Ban Peu, which overlooks the put-in on the river. The boats and boatmen are only now being recruited, so we are told. An's son will round them up and let us know when all is ready. Which is to say, we have time on our hands.

A gauze of clouds lifts from the surrounding hills as Ban Tong begins to bustle. Engines growl; planers whine. Amplified music argues with both. A house is under construction nearby. The belt drive from a hand tractor powers a generator, which in turn runs the planer. The planer smooths timbers that have been chainsawed from trees felled in the forest. Clutches of children scurry like dust devils past the work site and through the gaps between houses. They chatter; they play some kind of keep-away; they stop and stare at the pale strangers. Three tykes push a bicycle lacking handlebars on which three even smaller children improbably perch. Girls in ragged skirts sweep leaves from the hard bare dirt; only incidentally do they broom up the scraps of Styrofoam and plastic wrappers nested among the leaves.

Children, Ban Tong.

Robichaud narrates the scene, chuckling. He offers background: Some time ago, a do-good organization explored prospects for eco-tourism in a protected area in the north of Laos. The researchers began by surveying villagers' attitudes. They asked, "What do you think tourists would least like to see?" and they distributed small cameras so that the villagers could provide their answers in the form of pictures. When the results came in, images of fallen leaves, notwithstanding that they were swept up daily, led the portfolio of anticipated tourist annoyances. It was not what the pollsters expected.

There was a logic to the villagers' answer, says Robichaud. Leaves harbor fleas and other vermin. It is not good to keep them around, so people get rid of them. But consumer trash, notwithstanding its ubiquity, is another matter. It went unmentioned in the survey, despite lying everywhere. It seemed to be invisible, perhaps because until recently it did not exist. Previously, the only wastes thrown down from the houses had been "wrappers" like banana leaves or kitchen waste that pigs and chickens quickly scavenged. When cellophane and Styrofoam joined the waste stream, they somehow did not register. They were a new species of nonentity, subjects without verbs, an illustration of the subjectivity of culture.

"This place is unrecognizable from what it was two years ago," says Robichaud. But now he isn't talking about the trash. The motorbikes and machinery are the important things. "What does it mean for a protected area that the villagers can use timber more easily and consume more of it? And where is all the cash coming from for the bikes and power saws and Beerlao and the gasoline, stereos, and satellite dishes?" It was the same back in Ban Makfeuang. The satellite dishes are part of a familiar cycle: they carry Thai TV, which shows the people of the villages what they do not have. It introduces them to the glitter and thinginess of consumer culture. And who is to say that the people of Ban Tong should not have the same material advantages as the people of Vientiane or Bangkok? The bind is that for them to rise to such a level, the protected area will be commensurately depleted.

Back before he knew Touy, Robichaud knew Touy's father, the deputy director (and later director general) of the Department of Forestry. He told Robichaud, "Look, the residents of Nakai–Nam Theun will have education, health care, and food security, but their standard of living will never be as high as people in town. If they want that, they will have to move to town. We cannot bring it to them in a national protected area." Those bold words have since been forgotten, in part because the government of Laos, under pressure from the international community, has promised to bring every village in the country up to the standards of the Millennium Development Goals established by the UN in 2000. The goals themselves, which are humane and compassionate, are not the problem. It is the roads, machines, electricity, and improved access to markets that come with them. These things have cascading consequences, not the least of which are the consumer appetites they awaken. Pursuit of the standard of living mandated by the millennium goals turns out to be neither humane nor compassionate toward wild nature in NNT.

The current burst of wealth is incongruous, Robichaud explains. The WMPA provides a small amount of employment in the watershed, and most villagers can sell a water buffalo when they badly need cash, but such limited sources of wealth cannot explain the magnitude of what we are seeing. Serious money—for motorbikes, generators, and a range of newly available luxuries—almost certainly has to come from trade in animals and precious wood stolen from the forest.

Nearly all the smuggling runs across the mountains to Vietnam, and the greater part of it continues on to China, the magnet of the East.[1] Some years earlier, prior to the Beijing Olympics, the price in NNT for poached rosewood peaked at $8,500 per cubic meter. Preparations for the games included detailing tens of thousands of elite apartments and hotel rooms and the manufacture of hundreds of thousands of elegant gifts, chairs, trays, tables, chopsticks, and mementos. Rosewood is dense, workable, and hued with warm, bloodlike colors. Craftsmen justly prize it for ornamental and finish work of all kinds, from guitar backs and chess pieces to exquisite turnings, cabinets, and furniture. It comes from trees of the genus *Dalbergia*, including *D. cochinchinensis*, or Siamese rosewood, which is native to Nakai–Nam Theun. Well past the Olympics peak, rosewood in the watershed is still said to fetch five thousand dollars per cubic meter (a price that rises to twelve thousand dollars or more after it arrives in China)—more than enough to send small armies of village boys and men into the forest to hack away at every *Dalbergia* they can find and then to scurry along faint trails with punishing loads on their backs to deliver the wood to the border. It is also enough to draw more armies of men and boys out of Vietnam to do the hacking in Laos themselves. Contrary to the intentions behind the NT2 Hydroelectric Project, the WMPA has so far failed to restrict or even dampen the illicit export of rosewood from the pro-tected area.

The same is true with respect to wildlife. Among animals, turtles are the leading makers of village fortunes. The price for turtles is high and rising, and since the animals are small and easy to smug-gle, traffic in them will likely continue until extirpation terminates supply, with remnants of a few species surviving on turtle farms far beyond the bounds of NNT. Shells and other turtle parts are used in various medicinal "cures," but what really drives demand is a thirst for fresh turtle blood, which is viewed as effective in treating a host of ailments, including many cancers. Turtle blood is the "chemo" of choice in TCM — traditional Chinese medicine. Administered in many ways, including direct injection, it is widely believed to offer the last best chance to defeat the death radiating from a rotting pancreas, colon, or liver. Culturally, the sky-high prices people pay for a dose of turtle blood are logical. For tens of centuries they and their ancestors have revered the turtle as the very embodiment of health and longevity. They want to put that life force in their own bodies.

Economic growth in China and Vietnam means that each year more millions of people possess the means to buy expensive reme-dies. Commanding the highest price is the Chinese three-striped box turtle (*Cuora trifasciata*).[2] In Lao its name is *tao kham*, which translates as "golden turtle" or perhaps "wealth turtle" because it enriches anyone who finds it. When delivered to Guangzhou (for-merly Canton), a live specimen weighing only a kilo or two might sell for several tens of thousands of dollars. By the time it gets to a desperate late-stage cancer patient, perhaps one of China's many new millionaires or a wealthy relative who is watching a spouse or child or mother die, the price has certainly multiplied again. Even at the root of the supply line, in remote places like Nakai–Nam Theun, a villager lucky enough to find such a turtle (usually with the help of a turtle-sniffing dog) might trade it to a Vietnamese peddler for ten thousand dollars a kilo — a sum exponentially greater than the villager's annual income.[3] This is the life-changing equivalent, in the remoteness of the watershed, of winning the Powerball lottery.

Ideally, NT2 was to have provided improved protection for the flora and fauna of NNT, from rosewood and turtles to muntjac and saola. The hydroelectric project was predicated on the idea that by providing the protected area real protection, it would justify the sacrifice of lands on the Nakai Plateau inundated by the reservoir. A document of biblical scope and heft, the Concession Agreement between the government of Laos and the Nam Theun 2 Power Company (NTPC) detailed every aspect of the undertaking and spelled out the terms of the environmental trade that lay at its center. It created various entities to ensure that its promises were kept. One of these was the International Environmental and Social Panel of Experts (POE), which would monitor both the relocation of 6,300 people displaced by the reservoir and the execution of NT2's environmental program. Without sign-off by the POE, which is to say without their determination that the NTPC's social and environmental efforts were on track and that core goals lay within reach, commercial power operations would not be allowed to commence, and the company would face enormous fines.[4] The incentives, positive and negative, were stark.

Additionally, the Independent Monitoring Agency—more experts—would review the WMPA's work annually. If the WMPA's performance failed to pass muster, the IMA could order the NTPC to withhold all or part of the agency's funding, straitjacketing the NTPC until the problems were corrected.

Although the Panel of Experts agonized about unresolved resettlement issues and big gaps in environmental protection, including rampant poaching, they ultimately gave their approval to the project, and commercial power production commenced in 2010.

The gates of the dam had closed the previous year. Robichaud and Olay, then returning from fieldwork, happened to boat down the Nam Theun on its last evening as a free-flowing river. They encountered a party of Buddhist monks on a sandbar. The monks, who incongruously wore life vests over their saffron robes, were there either to bless the new reservoir or to honor the death of the river—it wasn't clear which. They might as well have added a blessing for the wildlife of the protected area, for the poaching impacts Robichaud had seen on that trip were at least as bad as any he'd seen before. That was his most recent trip into NNT's deep backcountry. Now he had returned, and if only we could procure boats to complete our journey to Ban Nameuy, we were within days of getting a fresh look at conditions in the forest.

The better part of the morning has slipped away, but at last An's son, a teenager in a long-sleeved T-shirt bearing the words LAOS BOMB DISPOSAL, arrives on a red motorbike to tell us it is time to ferry our gear to Ban Peu. He straps a rice sack to the rear fender, hefts one of the larger packs onto his back, and straddles the seat of the motorbike. We pass him another bulging sack, which he settles across his knees, barely leaving space to turn the handlebars. Brow furrowed, he mutters something about other motorbikes arriving soon and guns the overmatched engine. We watch him wobble down a steep trail and across a slippery plank spanning the stream where we bathed the night before. The bike growls and fishtails up the muddy slope beyond. In due time two more bikes appear and groan away similarly burdened. We say good-bye to An as well as to a charming, birdlike old woman whose picture we take (was it she who nearly expired the night before?), and then we, too, well laden with gear, set out on the muddy trail.

In Ban Peu, An's son seconds his father's prediction that three boats won't be enough. He says reports have lately come down the river that the water level is dropping. Three boats bearing our gear would be too heavy; we will have to rent four. The extortionate price quoted yesterday is firm. Robichaud grudgingly accepts the deal. Strangely, the new arrangement means that there will now be places in the boats for everyone; no one has to walk, even though, to my untutored eye, three men and their packs—the portion of our group who would have traveled by land—more than equal the capacity of a single boat. We soon find ourselves idle again, lounging against tree stumps in the trash-strewn yard of a home where a few sodas and crackers are offered for sale. The fourth boat is said to be on its way.

"Don't worry," I say to Robichaud. "The saola will wait for you."

"If the Vietnamese don't get to them first," he grumbles, pain in his eyes.

Finally we hear the *putt-putt* of the fourth boat arriving. We shuttle the gear down the river bluff. Simeuang produces a dozen large plastic bags, incongruously pink, which he obtained at the market in Nakai. We use them to waterproof the packs and rice sacks, making our loads look like heaps of dead flamingos. Finally we shove off, one passenger (or, in the boys' case, two) and one boatman in each *chak hang*. I am paired with an unsmiling fourteen-year-old

Loaded boats on the Nam Pheo, Ban Peu.

in fashionably torn jeans, a green Levi's T-shirt, and a wide black belt with a rodeo-size buckle. He wears half-tinted sepia shades — the crowning touch of his interpretation of Bangkok punkdom. His show of coolness is sadly violated, however, by a round canvas hat, which sits on his head like an inverted flowerpot.

We shove off, and our boats become four angry wasps snarling up the surface of the river.

But something is wrong. Although Flowerpot guns the engine to excruciating rpms, the fury of the motor has no effect on our speed. The prop is slipping on the driveshaft. Or the prop has lost its fins. Or something. We glide to a landing only three hundred meters from where we started. Simeuang's boat glides in, too. The other boats disappear around an upriver bend. Our two beached boatmen scramble up the riverbank while we wait in frustration. Twenty minutes later they return with extra cans of gas. A boy half their size tags behind, carrying a garland of propellers strung like fish on a loop of twine. As though he knows he missed the mark, Flowerpot has exchanged his canvas hat for a straw one. It is an improvement, but still not cool. Even less cool is the discovery that one of our motor mounts has broken. Flowerpot tries to loosen the remaining mount — maybe he contemplates switching engines with another boat — but he breaks the wings off the crucial nut, leaving us stuck with what we have. Effective repair is impossible. Undismayed, Flowerpot takes our frayed bowline and, without untying it, runs it to the stern and wraps the last eight feet or so around the nonfunctional engine mount in bulky, redundant loops, which he ties off with a flaccid knot.

And then we are under way again, boring up the wet green cave that the river cuts through the forest. Patches of sunlight cast spangles on the water, and the water, tumbling past boulders, shoots diamonds into the air. Our boat is slender, unstable, and predictably loud. Small birds — wagtails — strut on the rocks, then flee before us. A small, bluish kingfisher, all head and beak, peeps an alarm and darts upstream. Flowerpot guns the boat up fast little rapids, veering sharply to follow the bends of deeper water. Our *chak hang* makes its way in as little as seven inches of water. Even so, we often scrape bottom, this being the end of the dry season. When rains come, the river will swell, and judging by the height of the banks and the absence of wrack (which high flows carry off), the increase must be fearsome.

Back at Ban Peu, while awaiting the fourth boat and mourning the depletion of our funds, Robichaud told the story of a group of Frenchmen at the dawn of the colonial era who were the first Europeans to reach Luang Prabang, then the seat of a kingdom and today a popular tourist destination. Laden with supplies, they set forth from the vicinity of present-day Vientiane and pressed north. In every village they propitiated the headman with gifts of pots, cloth, knives, and other goods, but each headman demanded more than they had expected and threatened to deny them passage if he were not satisfied. The Frenchmen had to comply. By the time they arrived at Luang Prabang, they were exhausted in both stores and spirits. Having nothing left to trade, they departed with less, ultimately limping back to Vientiane bereft of shoes, clothing, and, not least, their health. The prospect of our looming insolvency, said Robichaud, laughing, was not unprecedented.

Now the river grows still shallower, and we lodge on the rocks. Flowerpot jumps out to push us off. We go a little way and lodge again, harder. We both jump out and drag the boat to deeper water. It is tricky getting back in. Flowerpot keeps the engine screaming, and when the boat is free, it takes off. You have to be ready, at the first hint of acceleration, to make a one-footed hop inboard without slipping on the river stones or capsizing the boat. You do this again and again, at least a dozen times in a thousand meters. Time your jump late, and you get left behind. Time it too early, and the boat hangs up again. Lugging the boat across shoals, I glimpse a flash of silver under the water. It is the fin of a broken propeller, a trophy of the river rocks.

After three hours of wet, halting progress, with Simeuang and his boatman just behind us, we round a bend to find the other two boats drawn up on a sandbar. The boatmen, led by An's son, stand in a knot by their crafts. Olay and Touy stand a little way off. And Robichaud paces by himself, looking red.

We land. Simeuang confers with Robichaud, then goes to the boatmen. A great deal of Lao is spoken, several voices at once, very fast. Robichaud, resolved to keep his anger in check, has the look of a cardplayer in the middle of a long run of bad hands. The boatmen say they will go no farther. The river is too shallow. They will leave us here. To me, "here" looks like nowhere: a sandbar in a river in a jungle. But Robichaud explains that the village of Ban Beuk lies up a trail to our left behind a screen of trees. His frustration is directed as much at Simeuang as at the feckless boatmen. Simeuang should have been clearer that we would pay them only when they delivered us to Ban Nameuy. An's son maintains that he agreed to take us only "as far as the boats can take us," which has become, in Robichaud's view, "as far as is convenient."

Now there is a stony silence. The boatmen will not budge. We propose to off-load all passengers and to hump the heaviest packs up the trail while they drive the lightened boats to Nameuy. No deal. Simeuang then says we'll pay them at a reduced rate. After all, we now have to hire porters in Ban Beuk to get our gear the rest of the way. The silence grows stonier. Each side waits for the other to make a move.

I pass the time scribbling notes: "This is part of what makes the saola so elusive . . . so difficult even to reach the place where you start looking for it."

The sandbar occupies a widening of the river, where the forest stands back and the canopy breaks open to reveal a whitened sky and a distant peak. This is Phou Vang. *Phou* means "mountain." *Vang*, in Vietnamese, means "gold": Golden Mountain. Saola live — or at least they used to live — in the forests at its foot. Our destination is the forest on the far side of Phou Vang, the remote watershed of the Nam Nyang, which is too steep for paddies or farming and lies well beyond the fringe of village settlement.[5] Robichaud briefly skirted the upper edge of the watershed a few years ago. Aside from him, probably no Westerner has visited any part of the Nam Nyang. From where we stand, the gauzy outline of Golden Mountain seems impossibly distant, the Nam Nyang a fantasy.

Robichaud is pulling a pack from a boat. Simeuang and the boys do likewise. The standoff is over. We have lost. The boatmen help us lug the gear up the riverbank and quickly depart downstream. Simeuang goes ahead to Ban Beuk to find porters. This will entail another unbudgeted expense. An hour later we are hiking on a well-worn trail. The gradient has eased and is almost flat. To our surprise, we hear a boat making progress upriver. Through the trees I catch sight of flamingo-pink cargoes. Our Ban Beuk "porters" are ferrying, not carrying, our goods upstream. We arrive in Ban Nameuy within minutes of the boat. The river evidently deepened after the sandbar. An's son and his compatriots should have known that it would, and maybe they did. Robichaud is redder than ever.

We proceed to the headman's house, where his wife and daughter welcome us, but the headman himself, Kong Chan, is away. He will return soon. Meanwhile, the women kindly give us sections of sugarcane to enjoy as we wait.

It is a good snack. First you peel back the coarse outer layers of the cane, using a knife if necessary. Then you bite off a chunk, if you can, or just gnaw on the pith. You chew it as you would gum or tobacco, extracting the flavor. When the cellulosic lump in your mouth is tasteless, you spit it over the railing of the veranda, and a grunting pig scarfs it up. Children gather to stare at the masticating foreigners. You smile back, maybe snap a picture. Kong Chan's house is raised particularly high off the ground. Like An's, it is reached by stairs. The treads are only a few inches deep, but treads they are, not rails. The house has plank walls and a metal roof. A pair of solar collectors on stout posts stand before it like the raised eyes of a crab. Kong Chan, by village standards, is wealthy.

And now we hear him coming, a voice approaching amid a hubbub that boils through the village. It verges toward the house. Kong Chan lingers at the foot of the stairs, jabbering good-byes, growling promises for tomorrow. He clumps up the stairs and sprays a fire hose of words at his daughter in the kitchen and at his wife, who stands at the turn of the veranda and shrugs knowingly toward Robichaud. Kong Chan, bent far forward and staggering to keep up with himself, rounds the turn, spots Robichaud, and lunges for him like a love-starved Labrador.

"WIL-YAM! WIL-YAM!" He throws his arms around Robichaud's neck and sags against him. "Wil-yam! You are here!" He strokes Robichaud's face, bringing his own face close, nuzzling him, alternately cooing and exclaiming. Then he rears back, holds Robichaud at arm's length, and looks rapturously into his eyes. In a half roar, in Lao, he declares, "Wil-yam, I am sorry I am drunk, but I thought you were dead!"

Then he pulls him close again, hugs him, and hangs on him. Robichaud is nearly smothered.

Robichaud needs airspace in order to speak. When he has some, he mutters, "It is really nice to see you; I missed you, too." In quick asides, he also translates Kong Chan's exclamations for me. I am standing a meter away and I can smell the fumes Kong Chan is exhaling. Robichaud quips, "No open flames here!" And Kong Chan continues, "Wil-yam, where have you been? I thought you were dead. It has been so long."

Kong Chan is seventy years old. He is lean of build, tall for the village world, and obviously energetic. He has a long, squarish face, thick dark hair, and a sandpaper voice that recalls the rasping American disc jockey Wolfman Jack. During the Indochina war, he soldiered over much of Laos, and he has reigned as headman of Ban Nameuy and the villages surrounding it for many years. "I am the village chief, and the people love me because I am so handsome," he says with a big, bleary grin. In truth, he is an able and conscientious politician, and in the days we linger at his house, we see him constantly attending meetings, receiving visitors, and responding to complaints. No doubt his duties require attendance at many *hiits* and a great deal of alcoholic lubrication. He is clearly up to the task.

Now that Kong Chan is home, we move our gear off the veranda and into the house. The front half of the big room is empty, the floor covered with thin mats of all colors. Two-thirds of the back half is taken up by a pair of cubicles, thinly walled off, which serve as the family's bedchambers. Their entrances, closed by a simple curtain, have sills two feet high, like a door in a ship's bulkhead. The remaining rear portion of the room is piled with old quilts and serves as the visitors' quarters, where we will sleep. Robichaud points out two impressive feathers displayed on the wall. Each is easily a meter and a half long and intricately speckled, like the skin of an enormous trout. They belong to the crested argus, another exotic denizen of the Annamite Mountains and the source of the longest (and some say widest) feathers in the wild avian world. Aside from the feathers, there are no decorations on the walls, only clothes hung on nails and pegs.

Over a lean dinner of sticky rice, chili paste, and several small, bony fish, Kong Chan, speaking Lao, holds forth, not mildly, on the subject of wildlife. "There are still saola here," he says. "And yes, tiger, too. The tigers have not gone. Liars should be arrested. Anybody who says there are no saola here is a liar. Arrest him!"

As for our intention to set up camera traps to photograph saola, he says, "Don't waste your time. I can tell you they are there. Saola are very smart. They avoid the snares, and they move with the seasons." Kong Chan's contention that saola are smart about snares is one we will hear from others.

He moves on to a subject nearer his heart: economic development. "All the other guys sold a lot of rosewood and got rich, but I didn't. I was stupid but good." What he needs now, he says, is a hand tractor. He's got to have one; he can't be headman, can't help his people, without one.

"But I saw one under the house," counters Robichaud.

"That one's no good," says Kong Chan. He wants another, better one. And a road. A hand tractor is no good without a road to run it on. He insists that Robichaud needs to understand the importance of these things, not just to his standing as headman but to the future of Ban Nameuy and its sister villages.

Kong Chan's monologue becomes a medley of complaint and demand. The fact that Robichaud, a Lao-speaking Westerner, has come to Ban Nameuy with the blessing of the WMPA tells him that Robichaud has access to money and influence. Although Robichaud tries to deflect Kong Chan's barrage to Simeuang, who despite his youth is the WMPA's agent, Kong Chan will not be deterred. The warmth of his welcome was real. He has affection for Robichaud, but he is a relentless lobbyist. He wants a hand tractor and a road.

Chan Si, Kong Chan's wife, carries away the low woven table that held our dinner. She is small and cherub-cheeked and wears a sweatshirt with the face of a smiling cartoon cat on the front. She settles in dimness at the end of the room with two young women, one of whom holds a baby. They watch us. A fluorescent tube, linked to a solar-charged battery, burns over our heads. The conversation turns serious. Robichaud and Simeuang discuss with Kong Chan the porters we'll require, the route we'll take, and the soldiers needed to provide security on our trek to the Nam Nyang. Part of Kong Chan's responsibility as headman is to recruit the manpower that official visitors require. I listen idly and steal glances around the home. The women sitting in half darkness shyly hide behind each other when they catch my gaze.

The time comes for us to bed down, but options are few. There are five of us. The visitors' space along the back wall looks sufficient for four. I throw my sleeping bag in the space where we had earlier been talking and begin to anchor my mosquito net to the side wall. The others look at me with alarm. Their pained expressions say that I am a barbarian. Kong Chan, just back from an errand to the kitchen, absorbs the situation with a glance and shakes his head emphatically: No!

Robichaud says, "You can't do that. The house spirits won't like it."

So all five of us lay out our bedrolls in the guest space, where we cram shoulder to shoulder. I lie between Robichaud and Touy. Then Olay and Simeuang. While we squeeze in, Kong Chan offers a final bit of advice: If you go to take a leak, watch out for the dog. She sleeps on the porch. She doesn't like to be disturbed, and she bites.

From the perspective lent by Kong Chan's now silent house, the "discovery" of saola in 1992 is a curious thing. The animals, of course, weren't actually discovered: local villagers in both Vietnam and Laos, people like Kong Chan, had always known about saola. What changed was that knowledge of the existence of saola crossed the boundaries of habitat and came to the attention of a surprised world.

The folkloric account of the discovery goes roughly like this: A group of field biologists are taking a day off from their survey of the Vu Quang Nature Reserve, in Vietnam's Ha Tinh Province. Some are resting; others are processing specimens or writing notes. One of them, seeking diversion, walks to a nearby village in hopes of scoring some rice wine, an alcoholic recreation with which to while away the day. Hours pass. Finally he returns to camp. He is lamentably empty-handed. No wine, no whiskey. The impoverished villagers have exhausted their supply. But he has brought back something better than liquor: a tale of having seen the most extraordinary horns on the wall of a hunter's shack. It is a new kind of wild goat. Or something even stranger.

Symbolically, the story has much appeal. It suggests that good things happen to those who pop the occasional cork and that the quest for liquor can lead to new knowledge. But according to Le Van Cham, who saw the horns first, that's not how things went. In Hanoi in June of 2011, Cham told me that the story about looking for wine was a joke. In truth, he and his colleagues hungered for vegetables more than they thirsted for alcohol. They had been on the trail a long time. A few squashes or a pumpkin would have made a feast. That's what he was seeking when he came to the village where he saw the horns on the wall of the hunter's shack.

The journey that led to the village and to the discovery of saola, however, actually began years earlier.

Beginning in 1986, a set of reforms called the Doi Moi, or national "renovation," liberalized the Vietnamese economy and started a flood of change. Suddenly farmers were allowed to decide for themselves what crops they would plant. Even better, they might sell their harvest openly for cash, not government coupons. Businesses, too, were allowed to experiment with new products. The downstream effects of these changes may have been more Rube Goldberg than flowchart, but agricultural and industrial production gradually increased. The long lines for staple goods and precious consumer items gradually shortened, and markets sprang up, town by town and city by city, where people gathered to sell, buy, and barter, arguing out their prices face-to-face, independent of government minders. One ancillary effect of the "renovation" was the easing of restrictions against foreigners entering the country. The relaxation was like turning a tap: as the valve opened, a stream of Westerners flowed into Vietnam. Some of them were biologists interested in conservation.

Jonathan Charles Eames (lately OBE) was an early one. A son of the English Midlands and a self-taught naturalist from boyhood, he remembers Hanoi in the late 1980s as a lugubrious city, its men dressed in the green pith helmets and olive fatigues of the Vietnamese army, the women also drab, eyes downcast, minding their business. Nearly every home and shop hung a portrait of Ho Chi Minh where it was visible from the street; secret police tailed every Westerner. Mostly bicycles and a few military trucks traveled the roads. There were no motorbikes to speak of, and the only private cars were Soviet ZiLs and Volgas that sported incongruous lace curtains. The city, with few signs and its shop windows empty, was almost purged of color. Every day at sunset, when the electricity shut down, it plunged into darkness, save for the oil lamps on street-side stalls where old women sold green tea and cigarettes, often one by one from crumpled packs. It was "a pretty wretched place," according to Eames, a hard place to work and live. The countryside was harder. On potholed and boggy roads, it took an entire day to get to Vinh, just two hundred kilometers to the south. You'd drive past moldering collective farms with twenty rusting tractors parked in a line, grass and weeds growing from them. On worsening roads, you'd keep driving, seeking the backcountry, where the forests and biota were still mostly intact. That's where discoveries would be made.

Serious fieldwork, which Eames had come to Vietnam to do, required expeditions three months long. You needed a permit to leave the confines of Hanoi, and then more permits for each province you entered. You encountered all kinds of adverse conditions: you might fetch up in a place on the brink of famine, where the wells were dry and the crops wilting, with nothing available to eat but badly milled rice, full of grit and weevils. On one expedition in 1988, not far from Vu Quang, Eames recalls, "We bought the last few tins of condensed milk in this market town, and that was such an event that the police came and visited us and wanted to know what we were doing buying up condensed milk and how come we got the money to do it."

You had to be a little insane to carry on under those conditions, but the adventure and challenge pulled you forward, and the possibility of a major discovery was always out there, maybe in the next valley or village. Vietnam was a mystery, Laos an even greater mystery. Little significant biological work, least of all by Westerners, had been done in the region since World War II. For nearly half a century, war had trumped every endeavor, and even after the shooting stopped, the oligarchs in Hanoi (like their counterparts in Vientiane) had no enthusiasm for Westerners wandering through their forests. They remembered the last ones too well. But now, in the 1980s, the land was opening. It was *terra nova*, a blank spot on the map of the world's biogeography. What was in there? No one knew. The prospects were as exhilarating as the conditions were horrid. If you were lucky, you found a way to lift your spirits with a jolt of inspiration. For the thirty-year-old Eames, inspiration had a name: John MacKinnon.

Traveling between Vietnam and the UK, Eames (who would later settle in Hanoi) liked to stop off in Bangkok to visit the lanky MacKinnon. The grandson of a British prime minister, MacKinnon was a magnetic figure. He had worked with Jane Goodall on the chimps of Gombe while still a teenager. He had gone on to conduct wildlife surveys across Africa and much of Asia, including every country in East Asia to which he could gain entry.

Eames would track MacKinnon to a "derelict" hotel and find him in a room littered with books and papers, with MacKinnon plugging away—"in his spare time"—on mapping software or a new field guide. It was MacKinnon who had led the way into Vietnam by writing a national conservation strategy for the country in 1984, even in advance of the Doi Moi. He soon helped launch programs there for both the International Union for the Conservation of Nature (IUCN) and the World Wildlife Fund (WWF).[6]

It was MacKinnon who secured funding through WWF for the survey of Vu Quang in 1992 that led to the discovery of saola. He had spotted Vu Quang's dense, unspoiled forests in satellite photographs, then confirmed the habitat quality with a flyover in a small plane. Although it lay a mere twenty miles from the start of the Ho Chi Minh Trail, the target of thousands of US aerial strikes, the canopy showed no ill effects from American bombing. The expedition MacKinnon organized, undertaken jointly by Vietnam's Ministry of Forestry and WWF, consisted of eight men, plus four soldiers who doubled as porters. The soldiers, he said, welcomed the break "from a monotonous wait for an unlikely invasion."[7] MacKinnon, then forty-five, was the only Westerner. Officially heading the team was Vu Van Dung, a botanist and member of the ministry's Forest Inventory and Planning Institute (FIPI). Two of Dung's FIPI colleagues, Do Tuoc, a mammalogist, and Le Van Cham, a botanist, also came along. Nguyen Van Sang, borrowed from Hanoi's Institute of Ecology and Biological Resources, would focus on amphibians, and Nguyen Thai Tu, a faculty member at Vinh University, would sample the fishes. Not to be left out, the provincial forestry department sent along a representative, and a staff member of the newly established Vu Quang Nature Reserve also joined the group.[8]

They set out on May 9 and nine days later reached central Vu Quang, where they bivouacked at a lonely guard post, Border Defense Unit 567, whose soldiers monitored the somnolent frontier with Laos. The team intended soon to shift their survey to another portion of the reserve, and provisions were low. Le Van Cham, who was charged with stocking the expedition's larder, elected to walk to the nearby village of Kim Quang to see what he might buy.[9] His friend Do Tuoc went with him.

Vu Quang had been set aside (on paper, at least) mainly for ecological reasons, but it possessed cultural significance as well. In the late nineteenth century it had furnished a base for Phan Dinh Phung, a revolutionary hero who led an insurgency against the French colonial regime. It also harbored considerable cultural diversity. Like Laos, Vietnam is an amalgam of ethnic groups, each with its own dialect and traditions. Today the government of Vietnam officially recognizes fifty-four such entities, some numbering no more than one or two hundred people, but there are doubtless others even smaller, as there are in Laos — remnant bands and clans in unreachable valleys, the human analog to saola.

The village that Le Van Cham and Do Tuoc wandered into, however, did not belong to one of the small minorities. It was a Kinh village, the Kinh being the main Viet group that migrated south from China millennia ago and spread over the Red River delta, the hinterland of Hanoi. Eventually they continued south along the lowlands and into the delta of the Mekong. Today the Kinh comprise 85 percent of Vietnam's population. Over the centuries, some of them, competing with culture groups already in place, pushed their way upslope into the higher reaches of the Annamites, even to the recesses of Vu Quang, where the wet valleys and steep mountainsides afforded little arable land. Obedient to necessity, they became adept at gathering the bounty of the forest and hunting its creatures.

Le Van Cham is now retired and lives on the outskirts of Hanoi, close by the FIPI campus, where he used to work. With the help of an interpreter, I asked him about the day in May almost twenty years earlier when he first glimpsed the horns of a saola. Cham sat cross-legged in a thronelike chair of heavy, polished wood. A television flickered behind him. His voice was solemn, and he spoke deliberately. Both he and Do Tuoc are known to enjoy a drink, but Cham dismissed the story about looking for wine. He was after vegetables, yet the people in the village had little to offer.

He was just walking, looking. The village was like any Kinh village in the mountains: shacks with porches, thatched roofs, dogs and chickens underfoot, a torpor settling in the heat of day. He passed the house of a hunter. It had to have been a hunter's house because animal trophies hung on the outside wall. He saw two pairs of short, rough, and backwards-curving horns—obviously from a serow, a species of mountain goat. And he noticed another set of horns. They looked odd. They were neither the tined antlers of a muntjac nor the simple short curves of the serow. The trophy consisted of a skullcap with horns that were long and smooth, tapered to a sharp point, and nearly straight. Cham was puzzled. Do Tuoc looked at them, and he was puzzled, too. They inquired after the owner of the house. A young man appeared.

"What animal is that?"

"A wild goat," said the man.

"What kind of wild goat?"

The man explained that there were two kinds of goats thereabouts: the *son duong*, which was the serow, and another animal that was bigger, heavier, and darker but just as nimble, with longer horns.

Cham and Tuoc wondered what kind of variant this long-horned goat might be. They didn't immediately conclude that it was a new species. Logically, they reached for less dramatic explanations, trying to imagine how a serow or some other familiar animal, under what kind of circumstance, might have produced such an intriguing set of horns.

Later, back at the guard post, they described what they'd seen to their colleagues. MacKinnon was not present—he was briefly on an errand of his own elsewhere—but there was general agreement that the horns were worth another look. It was two days later, according to Cham, that Do Tuoc led a group back to the village. May 21 was the last day that the expedition would spend at the guard post before pressing on to Man Tran, in the northeast of the reserve. It was also the last available day when they might visit the village. Cham didn't go—this may have been the day a bout of malaria laid him low. So Vu Van Dung, Dr. Sang, and Dr. Tu accompanied Do Tuoc to the house of the young hunter who'd hung the strange trophy on his wall.

They marveled at the frontlet with the unusual horns. They took pictures (with film, of course, which would not be developed for weeks) and finally acquired the trophy from the hunter. They discussed and opined. No one drew strong conclusions, but they remained on the lookout for more evidence of the long-horned goat. Over the next several days, as the expedition progressed to Man Tran, they collected two more sets of horns, one of which was so fresh it had maggots. The additional horns confirmed that the first set was no fluke: the frontlet discovered by Cham and Tuoc had not been taken from an aberrant serow. The scientists were increasingly convinced that they had encountered a new species of large mammal, hitherto unknown. Do Tuoc, the mammalogist, was fairly sure it was a two-toed ungulate, probably a member of the family Bovidae, which includes cattle, goats, sheep, and antelope.

By this point, according to Le Van Cham, MacKinnon had rejoined the group and was party to discussions about the strange new horns, but MacKinnon himself recalls a somewhat different sequence of events in the early days of discovery.

He recollects that he had not been absent long. He initially stayed away from Kim Quang, the village where the first saola horns were found, because he didn't want the villagers to be distracted by a Westerner in their midst. He feared this might inhibit the gathering of information. He recalls specifically urging Do Tuoc to be on the lookout for evidence of a second species of wild goat, for he thought that goral, a type of goat generally found in higher, steeper terrain than serow, might be present in the area. At his request, Do Tuoc went a second time to the village, possibly alone, to "borrow" a set of horns to show him. As soon as MacKinnon laid eyes on them, he says, he knew they belonged to a new species.

Memory being malleable, perhaps it is not surprising that the recollections of survey team members should diverge after twenty years. All agree, however, that by the time the survey team departed Border Defense Unit 567, everyone, including MacKinnon, was delighted with the expedition's progress. Already they had identified a new species of carp and a tortoise previously unrecorded in Vietnam. They'd found tracks of gaur and elephant and made excellent recordings of grey peacock pheasants and crested argus. They'd awakened each morning to the singing of gibbons and trekked through meadows alive with the cries of laughingthrushes. Thanks to a well-aimed load of bird shot, MacKinnon had taken possession of what he thought was a new species of bird (although this proved not to be the case). To crown all these successes, they now had evidence of a new mammal. A big one.

Upon return from the bush, MacKinnon relayed the news to WWF, which on July 17, 1992, issued a press release from its Gland, Switzerland, headquarters announcing the discovery of the new species. The release was short, as there wasn't much to say. Almost nothing was known about the animal, beyond the fact that it was "a large, horned mammal that may be a kind of goat."[10] Accompanying the release was a photograph showing MacKinnon holding one of the sets of horns. (This was the image, in the *Bangkok Post,* that captured the imagination of Bill Robichaud, then thirty-four, and nudged him in a new direction.) Immediately plans were laid for a second expedition to gather more data.

The second survey took to the field the following November, manned by Vu Van Dung and two colleagues. Over the course of two weeks, the scientists roved Vu Quang, visiting villages and interviewing hunters. In little time, they and others amassed a collection of more than twenty pairs of horns, some with whole or partial skulls, including three upper and two lower jaws, complete with teeth. (The analysis of dentition contributes mightily to taxonomic understanding.) Equally important, three whole skins complete with feet were added to the assemblage of specimens, and samples of skin and hair were sent to a Danish geneticist, Peter Arctander, for DNA analysis.

The initial DNA work indicated that the new mammal belonged to the subfamily Bovinae, which includes two great lineages of bovids: cattle, bison, and buffalo on the one hand and spiral-horned antelope, like gazelles, on the other. Because of its facial glands and other features considered primitive, the new animal was suspected to be a survivor of an early bovid line that existed before cattle and antelopes went their separate evolutionary ways. The fundamental branching within the family was already in place by at least the end of the Miocene epoch, roughly 5.3 million years ago. In all likelihood, saola are considerably older than that.[11] By contrast, the species *Homo sapiens,* the evolutionary entity encompassing "anatomically modern" humans, is a late arrival, having come into being only about five hundred thousand years ago.

The DNA analysis confirmed something MacKinnon, Tuoc, Dung, and the others suspected from early on: the new bovid was not just a new species. It also represented a new genus, of which it was the only known member. Perhaps it even represented a new tribe—a yet broader tier of taxonomic classification. Only continued research would tell. In the meantime, what to call it? "Longhorned goat" was discarded—the creature wasn't a goat. "Vu Quang bovid" was a safe bet, although hardly a delight to the ear, and "Vu

Quang ox" was no improvement, but MacKinnon adopted the latter term for want of better. "Saola" would soon replace it, but the name was as yet unknown to scientists.

As to formal, scientific nomenclature, MacKinnon and his colleagues coined the new genus *Pseudoryx*. Given the Vu Quang bovid's dramatic, dangerous-looking horns and boldly marked face, it superficially resembled an Arabian or African oryx, but it wasn't one; it was *pseudo*. To designate the species within the genus, they initially intended to call it *vuquangensis*, memorializing the locality in which it was first identified, but the idea was rejected when, early in 1993, Nguyen Ngoc Chinh of FIPI found evidence of *Pseudoryx* close to the Laos border, at Pu Mat, a reserve ninety kilometers to the north and west. (Chinh also learned that local Tai villagers called the creature *sao la*. When it was later learned that the name saola had currency in Laos, the group at FIPI adopted it in preference to Vu Quang ox, and the rest of the scientific community followed suit.)

If saola would serve in common parlance and *Pseudoryx* as the genus name, there remained the task of completing the scientific binomial: *Pseudoryx*—what? In deference to the second discovery at Pu Mat, the scientists at FIPI, with MacKinnon's acquiescence, resolved to call the creature *nghetinhensis*, after the former Vietnamese province Nghe Tinh, which had included both reserves. (In 1992, virtually simultaneously with the discovery of saola, the province was divided into Nghe An in the north, which includes Pu Mat, and Ha Tinh in the south, which includes Vu Quang.) The word *nghetinhensis* is a mouthful for Western tongues but sounds something akin to *NGAY-ting-en-sis*. So there it was: *Pseudoryx nghetinhensis*. A formal description of the new species was published as a "letter" to the prestigious British journal *Nature* in June of 1993.[12] By that act, the official count of living creatures on Earth, so relentlessly hammered down by extinctions, increased by one.

Scientists around the world were stunned—and jubilant. The reaction of John Robinson, director of international conservation at the Wildlife Conservation Society in New York, was typical. "Most of us feel we know all the large mammals that are out there," he said. "When something like this comes along, we are floored."[13]

Jonathan Eames, MacKinnon's early acolyte, had a different reaction, tinged with remorse. He was in England when MacKinnon came out of the Vu Quang forest. Even before WWF issued its press release announcing the big discovery, MacKinnon called to share the news. The connection was full of static, but Eames could hear the excitement in MacKinnon's voice. "You are never going to believe this, Jonathan, but I've discovered a new species of large mammal, an ungulate, in central Vietnam." As Eames listened, he felt the blood drain from his face, as though he were, in his own words, "terror-struck, cold." Not two years earlier, he'd surveyed Bach Ma National Park, two hundred kilometers south of Vu Quang. In one village, at his request, a hunter dumped out a bag of miscellaneous animal parts. Eames leaned over and picked up a single, slender horn. It was long, smooth, and sharply pointed. A companion happened to snap a photo of him holding it. At the time he figured the horn had probably belonged to a hormone-challenged serow, but as he listened to MacKinnon, he knew he'd been wrong. Now there was no question what the horn was. It was perfectly clear. Although Eames would go on to name five new species of birds and twelve subspecies, the miss in Bach Ma would continue to rankle. It was the species he didn't discover, the grail he didn't grasp. He said nothing to diminish MacKinnon's high spirits, though, and only offered congratulations.

February 26

Ban Nameuy

Competitive roosters start crowing in the wee hours. At first light, competitive boom boxes join them. The racket is constant, the air cool.

Puppies seeking a warm place to nap climb atop a pile of sleeping black pigs. Packs of children swarm through the open spaces of the village. Voices call house to house. A steady *thump, thump* resounds from a rice mill, I can't tell where. Ducks *harharr*. An emaciated dog limps by, one of its legs footless in a gory stump: another snare amputee. A young man with a rifle heads down the trail to the river, a carry basket belted to the small of his back. A troop of girls takes the same trail, burdened with plastic water jugs tied in bundles. Some carry a water bow, an ancient implement consisting of a sturdy curve of bamboo that balances easily on the shoulder. Notches at either end allow heavy burdens, such as full water jugs, to be hung from it.

One such water bow leans against the rail of Kong Chan's porch. The bamboo is hard and dense, burnished with age. Its arc is elegant, as is the taper of the ends. I am admiring it as Robichaud appears.

"How'd you sleep?" I ask.

"Okay, but tonight I'm gonna find the switch for the light Kong Chan left burning," he says. "And you?"

"Fine. I went out to take a leak and didn't get bitten."

Simeuang and the boys are already in the kitchen, where Touy is roasting scraps of meat on a paddle of steel mesh. The fire, smoldering on a bed of clay, consists of three small logs arranged like the spokes of a wheel. The hub is a mound of embers. For a hot fire, you push the logs into contact. For less heat, you pull them apart.

Simeuang has skewered three small fish, mouth to tail. He cut the skewers from a length of bamboo, except that the material in his hands is no longer considered bamboo. Once bamboo is cut and put to use, it becomes *tok,* a material so universally useful it receives a new identity. Now, with a stroke of his machete, Simeuang splits a slender two-foot section of *tok* lengthwise, but not all the way. He lays the skewered fish crosswise between the parted rays of the *tok* and closes the open end with wraps of still narrower *tok,* which he twists into a knot. He scrapes a quantity of embers away from the center of the fire and props the array above them. Meanwhile, Olay pounds chili and greens in a mortar to make paste. Breakfast is almost ready.

Ban Nameuy: *ban* = village; *na* = paddy; *muey* = gaur. Somewhere nearby is the paddy where somebody encountered a gaur, or a herd of gaur, the immense, curved-horn wild cattle native to these forests. I have also seen the name of the village spelled Namoy and Namouy. Given that NNT is a place of oral culture, few but outsiders worry about spelling, and the results vary widely.

Not twenty minutes' walk from Ban Nameuy is Ban Nameo. Again, *na* is paddy; *meo,* perhaps onomatopoetically, means "cat." Cat Paddy. Robichaud was told that someone once saw a tiger there, but since it is bad luck to name a place for a tiger (because a name is a way of summoning the thing that's named, and you don't want tigers paying visits), they named it for a cat. That was long ago. The people of Ban Nameo, according to their astrological calendar, can pinpoint when their ancestors founded the village. It works out to about three centuries ago, within years of 1700.

The people of Ban Nameo, Ban Nameuy, and Ban Beuk are Sek, and the Sek are one of more than a dozen ethnic groups found in and around the watershed of the Nam Theun. Each group has its own language, with Lao being the lingua franca. Sek—also the name of a language—belongs to the Tai-Kadai family of languages, which includes Lao and modern Thai. Not many years ago, linguists who puzzled over the origins of modern Thai hypothesized the existence of a protolanguage from which the dialects in current use evolved. Following well-established principles that predict how vocalizations shift over time and how words and usage change, they postulated the sounds and grammar of this hypothetical proto-Tai, ancestral to modern Thai and its sibling tongues. Then somebody took a look at Sek, and there it was: Sek had the lineaments of the proto–mother tongue, just as predicted.

Some centuries ago, on the Vietnamese side of the mountains, the Sek occupied lowlands beside the sea. They have a folkloric reputation for being good at finding gold, and possibly the Vietnamese or Chinese masters of the area (who battled to and fro) had placed the Sek there as miners and prospectors. Something—probably a persecution—prompted them to decamp and cross the mountains to the Lao side, settling near Golden Mountain, Phou Vang. It is also likely that, a century or so later, as Thai warlords from west of the Mekong did their best to lay waste to the region, the Sek then recrossed the mountains to Vietnam for safety. It seems that during the mid 1800s the Thais concluded that their best defense against a possible Vietnamese or Chinese invasion was to render much of what is presently Laos uninhabited and uninhabitable. Armies could not cross scorched earth, and so they stripped the area of its people and crops. They also enslaved many of the tribesmen whose villages they destroyed and sent them as forced labor to distant mines. Not all the Sek made it out to safety or returned after their captivity: there remain today several Sek communities in northeast Thailand whose occupants, in their oral tradition, remember such places as Ban Nameo and Ban Nameuy.

From the look of Ban Nameuy, the Sek are now on a demographic upswing. Every young woman seems to be nursing an infant, and every girl, down to the youngest child able to walk and carry, lugs around a baby brother or sister. At times the village sounds like a squalling maternity ward.

In the early 2000s, when the baseline data for "sustainable development" of the watershed were being collected, a census counted 5,800 people living within the protected area. There were gaps in the count, and the true number was surely higher. At the time, in some communities the curve of increase was already bending upward, raising questions about the capacity of those communities to support themselves agriculturally over the long term.[1]

The Sek comprise about 15 percent of the population of the watershed, or somewhat in excess of 870 people. Far more numerous are the Brou, who represent 60 percent. Ban Makfeuang is a Brou village, as is Ban Kounè, which lies a kilometer or two upriver from Ban Nameuy and belongs to the cluster of otherwise Sek villages headed by Kong Chan. As much as any permanent village, Ban Kounè lies nearest to true saola habitat. It is not clear when the Brou came to the Nam Theun watershed, although it was probably late in the nineteenth century. As sedentary farmers, they moved in among bands of hunter-gatherers, just as the Sek had done, sometimes cohabiting an area with them and sometimes, no doubt, displacing them.

The descendants of those hunter-gatherers comprise NNT's third major population group, the Vietics, who are marvelously diverse. As the name implies, the various tongues the Vietics speak belong to a family of languages that includes Vietnamese. (This is the Vietic branch of Mon-Khmer languages; Brou, by contrast, belongs to the Katuic branch of Mon-Khmer, a group that includes Cambodian.) Kong Chan's wife, Chan Si, is Vietic. She is a Kri from Ban Maka, one of the remotest of NNT's communities, which nowadays is actually three settlements: Ban Maka Neua (Upstream), Ban Maka Kang (Middle), and Ban Maka Tai (Downstream). Kong Chan met her there in 1968, when he was a soldier. Today the Kri, at more than forty-five households, are the most populous settled group of Vietics in NNT. When Chan Si's generation was young, in the 1950s, they had become part-time swidden cultivators but still moved around a good deal. Other Vietics, like the Phong of Ban Tong, meanwhile, had by then become entirely sedentary, while still others, like the Atel, continued to roam the forest until the late 1970s, when they finally succumbed to government pressure to settle in permanent villages.

Governments like their people to have fixed addresses, not least so that they can be counted and "governed," if not taxed. Nomadism smacks of anarchy. From the government's point of view, the relocation of nomadic people is both necessary and just, because no group of humans can develop economically without staying in a fixed place where they can build and accumulate things. In exchange for settling down, the government promises economic improvement.

The contrary view is metaphysical and fraught with pain for people like the Atel: the spirits of the old places don't agree with the move to settled villages. Nor do the spirits of the people's ancestors, who remain in the places where their mortal forms dwelled and died. When forest people depart their home ground, they become separated from the invisible but animate world that nurtures and defines them. Torn from their home ground, they can no longer "feed" or honor its spirits, and with the spirits no longer available (or willing, because of a lack of offerings) to protect the living from sickness and misfortune, life goes out of balance. Happiness departs. Hearts break. They languish. They get sick. They die.

The situation bears considerable similarity to life on Indian reservations in the western United States in the late nineteenth century. In fact, a lot about Nakai–Nam Theun recalls the Old West: ostensibly "wild" people are settled in fixed places and urged to become farmers; a central government strives to extend its hegemony to new lands; and manufactured goods increasingly penetrate economies that have never seen them before. Industrially produced alcohol is one of those manufactured commodities, and in copious amounts it joins the flow of traditional local brews, resulting in significant negative consequences for health and social relations. The aggressive harnessing of natural resources is another obvious similarity. So is the cultural condescension of the national society toward the "backward" inhabitants of its undeveloped territory. Less obvious but no less emphatic is the war on wildlife. Subsistence hunting—taking deer, wild pigs, or equivalent species for the local pot—is part of any economy in which people live in tight reliance on the land, but the transborder poachers of Nakai–Nam Theun, the resolute and determined men who cross from Vietnam and labor under heavy packs to harvest virtually every vertebrate creature that walks or crawls, have much the same motive and method as the fur trappers and buffalo hunters of that other time and place. The trade in animal parts is marking Laos as heavily as the quest for beaver hats and bison robes did the American West.

Even the names of people and places, in translation, evoke a western ring. Phoukhaokham Luangoudom, for instance, directs the WMPA's ecotourism program. His first name, Phou-khao-kham, would be rendered "Golden Horn Mountain" in English. Many an Apache would be happy with that.

Porters and guides for the big trek to the Nam Nyang won't be ready until tomorrow, at the earliest, so today we'll visit Ban Kounè and call on a certain hunter, Mr. Ka, whom Robichaud regards as a particularly far-ranging and capable woodsman. If there is valuable information about the backcountry to be had, Mr. Ka will likely have it. Olay has put on leech socks, but Simeuang advises that they are unnecessary and will only get wet. So Olay takes them off. Simeuang, meanwhile, wears under his cap a dish towel that hangs in folds over his ears, a sight that amuses Robichaud. The towel cannot be for sun protection—the sky is thick with clouds. Robichaud believes its purpose, notwithstanding Simeuang's advice to Olay, is to fend off leeches, one variety of which drops on its victims from leaves overhead and has been known to crawl into any available orifice. The towel is a new strategy, Robichaud says. Simeuang used to stuff his ears with cotton.

To my mind, leeches are one of nature's least savory features, and I have dreaded our entry into their habitat. In my daypack I have a pair of leech socks Robichaud has loaned me. I also have disinfectant swabs and a sheaf of Band-Aids—leech bites easily become infected. The leech socks consist of minimally tailored tubes of heavy material that reach to your knees and have a drawstring to keep them up. You wear them inside your shoes or sandals, and they ensure that once a leech gets on you, you have a chance to pick it off before it can climb past the sock and sneak into your shorts. Leeches inject a small dose of anesthetic as they puncture your skin, so most people never feel the bite. Leech saliva also includes an anticoagulant to keep you bleeding. By the time you see them—or someone sees them on you—they can be as big as your little finger and bloated with blood. Robichaud tells a story of sleeping on the forest floor and flopping around in the night so that his arm fell outside the protection of his mosquito net. When he woke up, he was aghast to see that his limb looked like the site of a botched transfusion. Blood everywhere. Fat leeches crawling away. It was the stuff of nightmares, but relatively mild ones as far as leeches are concerned. Although the tale strains credulity, I have read of a leech making its way up the urethra of a man's penis, requiring field surgery of the most terrifying delicacy.

Saola habitat is leech habitat, and that is where we are headed. Leeches and saola like moisture. Most of Nakai–Nam Theun has a two-season climate, dry and wet, with the rains usually starting in May and lasting into September. But some of the forest is wet year-round, especially where low passes in the chain of the Annamites allow monsoons and other moisture-laden systems to blow through from the Pacific. The damp forests of the range's middle altitudes may be a remainder, or an approximation, of habitats that spread more extensively over Southeast Asia during earlier epochs. Saola, which depend upon those habitats, now cling to the shrunken islands that remain, which extend like an archipelago down the spine of the Annamites.

The Annamite Mountains themselves are a kind of island, a Madagascar surrounded by terrestrial seas—not of salt water but of low plains that isolate the biota of the mountains just as decisively. It seems that, although the boundaries of habitats have undoubtedly shifted, their core conditions have been stable for a very long time. Like Madagascar, where lemurs have branched into scores of species, the Annamites are home to an extraordinary amount of endemism — plants and animals that evolved there through deep time and that are found nowhere else. A curious feature of the Annamites region is that many of its most singular creatures — Edwards's pheasant, the crested argus, the Sunda colugo, and at least a dozen more — find their closest relatives southward along the Malay Peninsula and on the islands of western Indonesia. These close genetic relations testify to repeated instances over the last two to three million years when glaciers bound up much of Earth's water and caused the level of the oceans to drop. At the last glacial maximum, about eighteen thousand years ago, sea level was as much as 120 meters lower than it is today, eliminating many water barriers that now exist. Not just land bridges but whole territories emerged from the sea. Under such conditions, islands like Borneo, Sumatra, and Java became linked to the mainland, enabling the fauna of the region to spread and mix across a vast landscape, as biology and opportunity permitted.[2]

Ban Kounè lies slightly downslope of a mountain pass where rains from Vietnam blow through. A forest partridge chants its call as we climb a trail that on this day is mercifully dry and free of leeches. Still, we feel the humidity rise, as though we are climbing into a low, thin cloud. We pass a recent swidden. At least a hundred acres have been cleared, and much of the felled timber and slash is piled along the edges of the swidden to fence out wild pigs. A crude hut, where the farmer sleeps when he tends this patch, stands toward the center.

Swidden agriculture excites considerable controversy among the mavens of international development and conservation. Many characterize it as a scourge of natural habitats and a threat to biodiversity. Reality is more complicated. There are hundreds, perhaps thousands, of swidden systems that vary according to the amount of land cleared,

the thoroughness of the clearing, the duration of cultivated and fal-
low periods, and a host of other factors. As a result, these systems
vary enormously in their environmental impacts. The swidden agriculture practiced by the Hmong in Laos is especially damaging. It
typically results in the long-term conversion of forest to grassland and
helps account for the territorial restlessness of the Hmong as they
abandon exhausted lands and seek new opportunities to farm and
hunt. Other swidden systems, like those of the Sek and Brou, permit
the forest to regenerate and appear to be sustainable over long
periods—indeed, it is probable that certain kinds of long-rotation
swiddens, provided they are not asked to support too many people,
are the only sustainable agriculture possible in tropical forests. The
field we have encountered on the trail to Ban Kounè is perhaps three
years old and represents a colossal investment of hand labor. It will
produce steeply declining yields of rice for another few years, until
the riot of regrowth chokes out the possibility of meaningful harvest.
Then the forest will reclaim it, until it is cleared again, years or
decades later.

When at last we reach Ban Kounè, we behold the village from
the bank of a raw, garbage-choked gully, where a plank that once
bridged the mud has been upset and abandoned to the mire. A generation ago, because of some kind of plague or sickness, the village
moved to this location from its former site across the river. Spread
beneath a gloomy sky, Ban Kounè, with its damp, faceless houses
and run-down sheds and pens, has the look today of a hard-luck
mountain hollow dusted by light snow. The snow is an illusion. The
white patches on the ground are masses of discarded silver-white
cans that once held Vietnamese beer. There are hundreds of them,
lying in clusters. Also ubiquitous are innumerable deposits of pig
shit that might have rained on the village as the wrath of a discon-
tented god.

Although Kong Chan's authority as chief of the village cluster
extends to Ban Kounè, the village has its own headman, and so we
go to his house. But no one is home: the ladder is pushed up. We

77

then seek out Mr. Ka, the hunter with whom Robichaud has traveled. He is gone, too, his wife tells us, but should be back before long. So we walk another kilometer up the trail to visit an army post close to the border, in the pass that leads to Vietnam.

In the 1930s the French mined gold from river sands below this pass. According to local memory, they conscripted labor from Ban Kounè and other villages and beat those who would not cooperate.

When we arrive at the army post, the bored soldiers are playing a game of pétanque, which is similar to bocce or boules. A new but roofless wood-plank building stands behind the thatch shack that is their barracks. We meet under the naked rafters with an officer who wears shoulder boards adorned with three stars. He solemnly inspects our papers while his scribe studiously takes notes. Simeuang then gives a formal speech expressing the comradely sentiments that the WMPA desires to extend with heartfelt warmth to its esteemed friends in the provincial army, yadda, yadda. Soon we learn that thirty soldiers are assigned to this detail. Their mission is to prevent Vietnamese traders from penetrating the protected area. Secondarily they patrol for snares. Half of them stay here, half in Nakai, on rotation. While here, they go on patrol four or five days per month. Otherwise, they play pétanque.

Patrolling so little, the soldiers cannot be expected to accomplish much. Vietnam is a walk of only two hours away. The soldiers' primary job may be to regulate the passage of Vietnamese traders crossing the border, but as long as the unit stays mainly in its barracks, the illicit traffic in rosewood, wildlife, and other smuggled goods can flow around it as easily as creek water around a cobble. Secondary goals, like projecting a forceful presence along longer reaches of the border, are entirely neglected, leaving saola, together with the rest of the biota of these extraordinary forests, perilously undefended.

Reentering Ban Kounè, we again hear the chorus "Wil-yam! Wil-yam! Sabaidee!" It is everywhere the same. Since the unlamented departure of the French, the number of white outsiders who have come to this lonely place can probably be counted on one hand. Robichaud is known and remembered, a kind of celebrity.

Kong Chan suddenly appears, calling to us down a village lane. He has chosen today to make one of his regular visits to Ban Kounè, and although Robichaud is already well known, Kong Chan takes boisterous pleasure in introducing us to everyone we encounter. My presence provides him a punch line. Robichaud and I are twins, he says. We do exactly the same things; we even share the same wife. Yes, adds Robichaud, Monday she's his, Tuesday mine, and so forth, until Sunday she rests. The joke is macho, formulaic, and produces a laugh. Kong Chan and Robichaud are a team.

Mr. Ka is now home. He greets Robichaud as an old friend, although his warmth is hardly effusive. He gives us permission to take a bone sample from a saola trophy on his wall, and as we spread our equipment on the floor of his large house, he watches with a cardplayer's eyes — seeing much, revealing little.

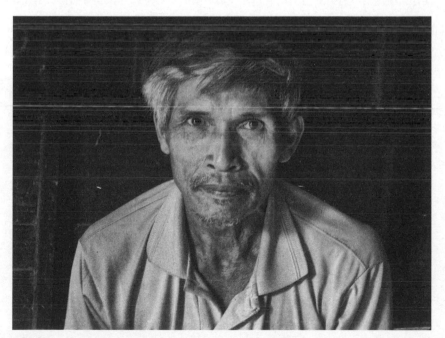

Mr. Ka.

Ka means "crow." He is Mr. Crow. He is sixtyish. He professes not to know the location of a mineral lick, or *poung*, we have heard about, which we would like to evaluate as a possible location for setting camera traps. The matter is slightly awkward. We know—and Ka knows we know—that if anyone can tell us where to find the *poung*, it is he. Mr. Ka has ranged these mountains all his life, and the trophies on his walls attest to his prowess as a hunter. There are multiple antler sets from muntjac and also sambar, which is a larger species of deer comparable to North American elk (or, more particularly, wapiti).[3] There is also a saola frontlet, a patch of skull bearing horns that are half a meter long. Deer and other cervids grow and shed their antlers annually. Goats, antelope, saola, and cattle, on the other hand, produce horns, which remain with the animal for life.

Robichaud removes the saola frontlet from its place of honor on the wall and places it on the floor in a patch of sunlight. Kneeling, he slides off the dark keratin sheath that is the "skin" of the horn. This reveals the bone beneath. He pulls a small cordless drill from his pack and readies a vial into which he will place the flecks of bone to be drilled from the horn. He dips the bit in alcohol. The moment is an anxious one for me. I bought the drill for Robichaud at a building-supply store in New Mexico and in the haste of trip preparations was never satisfied that the battery had fully charged. If it fails, we have no backup, except perhaps to whittle off a sample with a knife. When the tool whines and the bit begins to turn, I feel a flood of relief. Olay and Touy huddle around Robichaud to catch the drill dust on a piece of paper and pour it into the vial. Robichaud will send the sample to a laboratory in Portugal, where advanced work on the evolution of wild cattle and their genetic relatives is under way.

When the sample is secure and the tools stowed, we move out to Ka's broad veranda, where he and Kong Chan have been chatting. A faint aroma of fermentation hangs in the air. Ka apologizes that he has no rice wine to offer us. He hosted a *hiit* yesterday, and his stores of drink are exhausted. Holding the saola frontlet, he poses for pictures. A toddler wobbles from the kitchen waving a machete as long as he is tall. He takes a few whacks at a porch post. Ka's wife scurries out to take the big knife away from him, but the child won't give it up. She pries his fingers off, one by one, as the child wails. Now Ka asks for a photograph of himself with his pretty, buck-toothed wife. He calls for his children to be part of the event, but they hide in the kitchen. So it is just the two of them, sitting two feet apart, not touching. Robichaud, teasing, tries to get them to move closer to each other, but neither budges. They are like matching newels at the foot of a stairway. Neither betrays a hint of emotion until we show them their images on the screens of our digital cameras, and then they point and smile.

Ka has told us that the others in the village who possess saola frontlets—there are several—have gone this day to their swiddens. They won't return until dark or later. If we want more samples, we should come back after our journey to the Nam Nyang. We say we will, then make our good-byes and take the trail for home.

As we walk, Robichaud is pensive. The saola horn we sampled, he explains, was decades old, probably a family heirloom. The last time he visited Ka, a couple of years ago, there were three other saola frontlets in the house. He asked Ka what happened to them, and Ka's answer was evasive: "I just gave them to friends and relatives." The exchange caused Robichaud to suspect that perhaps Ka sold the frontlets to a trader. Maybe a market for them has begun to develop.

One of the few things in the saola's favor—and a strong indication of the animal's historical isolation—is that it is unknown in traditional Chinese medicine. Because TCM commands an otherwise encyclopedic inventory of Asia's natural world, the omission is noteworthy. TCM values hundreds of animals and thousands of plants for the specific medicinal properties they are believed to possess. A central concept of TCM is that the *qi* of an animal—its essential energy, or spirit—inheres in its physical body and can be beneficially

transferred to humans through ingestion of its parts. A turtle's longevity, an elephant's strength, a tiger's vitality and power—these
qualities can prolong or enhance the life of the human who incorpo-
rates the material of the animal into his or her own being.

Accordingly, TCM and its cousin pharmacologies throughout
Asia commodify the animal parts they deem potent and offer them
for sale. And millions upon millions of people buy them. Demand
for TCM's highest-priced items—turtle blood, tiger bones and
penises, bear gall, rhinoceros horn—drives the wild creatures that
provide them ever closer to extinction. Not even taxidermied museum
specimens are safe: in 2011 thieves made off with rhino horns and
skulls from as many as thirty European museums, galleries, and private collections.[4]

No doubt some of the substances used in TCM produce actual
biochemical effects, but many claims are preposterous. Rhino horn,
for instance, is all keratin, essentially the same material as fingernails, horse hooves, and hair. Despite serious laboratory experiments
conducted to identify active biological agents in rhino horn, none
has been found. And yet those grand, unlikely animals are being
driven to extinction.

Demand is equally insatiable for many lesser-known animals,
including some of the world's strangest—the furtive pangolin, for
instance, which resembles an anteater but is clothed in scales considered potent in treating urinary disorders and other ailments. The
antlers of every kind of deer also have uses, as do otter skins, python
fat, monkey hands, and a macabre catalog of digits, genitalia, protu-
berances, and inner organs belonging to a host of other creatures.

Surprisingly, the saola, despite its massive, pungent scent glands
and horns as singular as a narwhal's tusk, somehow escaped the list.
One presumes the cause was the saola's age-old isolation. The far-
ranging traders of antiquity seem never to have learned of it. The
saola lived in a land whose people were too obscure and too poor to
bring their straight-horned mountain goat to the attention of a
remedy-hungry world. Moreover, even in the distant past saola were

probably never plentiful. Like unicorns, they were at most an eva-nescent presence.

As long as no new market for saola develops, the gravest threat facing it is the danger of being taken incidentally as bycatch, like a sea turtle in a shrimper's net. The hardworking snare-setting hunt-ers who cross the mountains from Vietnam want muntjac, wild pigs, sambar if they can find them, and pangolin and porcupine—the money species. The occasional saola is a bystander, felled in the gen-eral mayhem. Or so the kindest reading of the facts would have it.

Another reading lends a different perspective: there are no non-target species, no accidental or incidental victims. Everything that can be taken will be taken and ipso facto becomes a target. If it has flesh and can be gotten, the getters want it, whether it walks, crawls, flies, or slithers. If an animal can be eaten, if it can make a cure or a house ornament, or if it can be passed off as something else with appreciable value, market hunters want it. In any case, their snares do not pick and choose. The trigger snaps, the bent sapling springs up, the noose of wire closes on the leg, and the animal flips upside down, there to struggle until the foot comes off or merely to hang for days or a week until fatal thirst has its way. By this accounting, it might not matter much if Mr. Ka sold his saola frontlets to a Viet-namese trader. Equally, it may not matter if government posters and word of mouth about the saola's endangerment have sparked the notion that saola, rare as they are, may have a special and therefore commercial value. Once the war on nature reaches a level at which nothing is safe, it doesn't matter if the intensity increases. The incre-ment of greater blood thirst will be no more noticeable than the slight acceleration of a jet already streaking through the sky.

Mr. Ka has seen a saola in the wild, not once but several times, although he is vague about specifics, maybe because he shot several of them. The last time he saw one was in 2005 in the watershed of the Nam Nyang, where we are headed. A small but substantial num-ber of other village hunters and forest travelers in NNT have also glimpsed the living animal, as have residents of saola habitat throughout the creature's range. But as far as I have been able to determine, not a single Westerner and only one scientist has ever glimpsed a saola in the wild, and the scientist who did so—not once but three times—was not yet a scientist at the time. Cao Tien Trung, a genial and energetic professor of biology at Vinh University, across the border from NNT in Vietnam, was eighteen and only a second-year undergraduate in biology when he saw his first saola and watched a hunter bring it down. It was 1994.

Trung grew up in the town of Quy Chau, in the north-central portion of Vietnam's Nghe An Province. Being drawn to the mysteries of the forest, he frequently tagged along with hunters who plied the environs of what would later become Pu Huong Nature Reserve. Sometimes the hunters used dogs, and dogs were the key to encountering saola. Saola are strikingly but protectively colored; the bold, irregular splashes of white on the face, for instance, no doubt create a camo effect in the vegetation of the forest. Saola make no loud noises, and they are wary. Even when their numbers were healthy, they probably existed at low density, as suggested by their omission from the lore of TCM. All in all, not even the most experienced hunters, like Mr. Ka, manage to find them unless they use dogs.

When a hunting dog scents quarry, its voice rises in pitch and its yaps become excited—"very sharp," in Trung's words. Hearing such a yelp, the hunter and his companions press forward as fast as they can, scrambling up and down steep slopes, through dense vegetation, to join the chase. Trung remembers many such pursuits. Crossing the rocks of the streams was treacherous, the mud bad, the leeches worse. "I was very young, very strong then," Trung told me when I visited him in Vinh. He had to be. Saola habitat is severe. It is wet, steep, and jungled. Sometimes a saola might escape by bounding up a rock face, where dogs cannot follow. More often, the saola, quite unlike a muntjac or serow, will stop and make a stand. Its behavior is distinctive. Robichaud and others have corroborated from dozens of villager interviews what Trung personally witnessed:

when the saola senses that dogs are in pursuit and it cannot elude them, it races to the nearest stream and takes a position in belly-high water. If possible, it selects a pool with a steep bank or large boulder to back up against. Defended by water and with a wall at its rear, the saola lowers its formidable horns and awaits its adversaries, be they one or many.

This defense probably results from thousands of years of predation by the dhole, a wild dog of Southeast Asia. Dholes hunt in packs and are hard to outrun. By facing them in water a half meter deep, the taller saola deprives its attackers of their agility and can use its horns to deadly effect. Interestingly, the cattlelike bovids—bison, water buffalo, musk oxen, even domestic cattle—will also often stand and face a threat. Most antelopes and goats prefer to run.

Unfortunately, an ingrained habit that worked at least middling well against dholes became a death sentence when dogs and their firearm-toting masters came into saola habitat. An embayed saola is an easy kill for any kind of marksman (or an easy capture, if that's the goal). The three saola that Trung saw shot and taken during the mid-1990s were three animals that the saola population of the greater Pu Huong ecosystem could ill afford to lose. There have been no further confirmed records of saola from that district in more than a decade.

At Ban Nameuy, the dogs bark us in. We gather soap, towels, and fresh underwear and take the trail to the river to bathe. More barking. One slat-ribbed cur has a fresh wound on her muzzle. Nearly all the dogs are the same—about the size of a border collie, yellow, and disagreeable. Many have grime-encrusted sores. The exception is Kong Chan's porch bitch: she is chunky, dark, and healthier than the rest. Also less yappy and more broodingly hostile. She glares from her nest beneath the house.

The etiquette for bathing is simple: one strips to one's under-shorts and washes what one can; then, using a towel or sarong to preserve modesty, one strips the rest of the way and washes what remains. The river is broad and tree-hung. I put my things on the prow of a derelict boat lodged on a sandbar. Robichaud banters with several young women who are washing their hair. They are not used to seeing men with farmer's tans, whose unruddy parts are nearly as white as pig fat. They find us amusing. Touy audits Robichaud's flirtatious back-and-forth admiringly, and Olay, off a little way on a sandbar of his own, is doing rapid push-ups. I stop counting at twenty, for he shows no sign of slowing.

Not speaking Lao, I am always late picking up the general news, but word has reached us that someone in Ban Beuk recently found a small golden turtle, weighing perhaps three hundred grams. He sold it to a Vietnamese trader for the equivalent of four thousand US dollars. There is now jubilation in Ban Beuk. Many *hiits* lie ahead, as well as a motorbike or two and possibly a satellite dish and a great many Thai soap operas. Unfortunately, the promise of festivities makes it harder to recruit porters and guides. We need ten men. We are offering the standard rate, set by the WMPA before the recent inflation, which is forty thousand kip per worker per day—about five US dollars. We want to start tomorrow.

In his best Wolfman Jack growl, Kong Chan says not to worry. He will find the porters. A couple of men from Ban Kounè said they will come. There are others in Ban Nameuy and Ban Nameo. Be patient, he says gruffly. He'll work on it tonight.

It is nearly dark, but Robichaud wants to go to Ban Nameo to visit a friend who has been hurt. I check to be sure I have a headlamp and first aid gear in my pack and follow him up the trail. We hear the village before we see it—the usual over-amped music pulses from several dim homes. In the half-light, Ban Nameo is a pretty place. Whereas Ban Kounè looks slipshod and Ban Nameuy erupts suddenly from behind a screen of trees, Nameo seems premeditated and intentional. It straddles a long, grassy slope, its houses generously spaced like trees in an orchard, with paddies and tidy gardens spread in an apron below them.

We head for the lower end of the village, but in the rapidly falling darkness Robichaud cannot find Sai's house. Sai was with him on a memorable earlier expedition, years back, when Robichaud led an impetuous, unplanned attempt to scale Phou Vang. In the effort, Sai proved a diligent and reliable companion.

Suddenly a young man steps from the shadows and asks who we are looking for. He leads us to Sai's ladder, scrambles up, and asks permission for us to enter. Permission granted, he goes in with us. I am guessing he is Sai's cousin or younger brother.

It is dark within. Sai sits in the weak glow of the cooking fire, his wife beside him tending a pot of rice. A child huddles in shadow against her. Sai and his family have no separate kitchen; their means being modest, they cook in their single room. At the sight of Robichaud, Sai manages a smile. His right thigh is wrapped in rags. His face is drawn with pain, worry in every feature. We learn that three months ago, as he was transporting a load of sheet-metal roofing up the river to the village, a stack of sheets broke free and shot back, slicing into Sai's legs. The lacerations tore deep. They missed the femoral arteries, sparing Sai's life, but the injury to even his left leg, the healed one, forms a gutterlike depression in the flesh paved with a gnarled scar.

Slowly, gingerly, Sai unwraps the rag bandage from his other leg. In the light of our headlamps we again see a divot where the meat of his quadriceps has been lost. The depression is deep enough to hide a golf ball, and it is hard and red with infection, oozing at the bottom. Sai's wife explains that she has been cleaning the wound and washing the rag dressing. Robichaud digs into his pack and produces a tub of salve, which he holds in the firelight. I have noticed that he travels with the sparest of medical kits, so he must rate this stuff very high. He explains to Sai that it comes from Australia and is marvelously effective in drawing out infection. He has used it many times with good results. He thinks it would help the wound to heal. Would Sai like to try it?

Sai nods anxiously.

Robichaud cleans his finger with a swab of Betadine, then delicately applies the salve to the wound and spreads it as evenly as he can while Sai's eyes tighten in a sustained wince. I pass Robichaud a patch of sterile gauze, which he places over the wound, then tapes it down. We make a little pile of the things we are leaving: more gauze patches, the tub of salve, and a roll of tape. Robichaud instructs Sai's wife and the young man who showed us in about the importance of changing the dressing and reapplying the salve. Do it every day, he says. Robichaud also hands out packets of Ovaltine and candies (his pockets never seem to empty of treats, which he dispenses wherever he goes). Nevertheless, the atmosphere inside the shack remains morose as we gather our things. If Sai's infection worsens, it may kill him. Or he may end his days a cripple, unable to work, impoverishing himself and his family.

There is little question of his leaving the village and seeking medical attention. Thakhek, the closest source of medical care and antibiotics, lies several difficult days away, and the journey would cost a small fortune. Moreover, according to ancient rules, if he were to die outside the village, his body would not be allowed to return for burial. Worse, if his body were not buried within the domain of the village, his kinfolk could not or would not "feed" his spirit at their family altars, and they would not remember him in their prayers. He would be forgotten. In the villages of Nakai–Nam Theun the advantages of modern medicine must be weighed against the risk of eternal oblivion.

But Robichaud is optimistic. The infection appears low-grade and local; anything worse would have already finished him. The salve will work, he says. "With luck, Sai, you will soon be back on your feet—hobbling, perhaps, but gaining strength all the time." Such is Robichaud's departing message. And then we are on the porch again, finding our sandals, negotiating the ladder, and walking in the dark. Orion burns overhead. It is time to get back to Kong Chan's and eat a late dinner, I think, but no, there is someone else Robichaud wants to visit—he was on the same expedition as Sai, years ago, when a few of them reached the top of Phou Vang in near darkness and then, with their water gone, dangerously descended the cliffs by flashlight.

Bounthai's house is up the slope, at the other end of the village. It is brightly lit, the source of the loudest music. A *hiit* is under way. As we approach, we hear a new bass line under the dervish melodies. It is the chug of a generator.

On the porch a clot of men surrounds a large ceramic urn similar to an amphora of ancient Greece. This one, too, contains wine, rice wine. The circle opens, and the men shoo me into a place beside the urn. I am given a long bamboo straw. Music thunders from the house. Between fits of laughter and fast quips to the assembled throng, Robichaud instructs me. There are four drinkers. The idea is to suck wine through your straw, as the other fellows are doing. As the urn is drained, a referee replenishes it using a water buffalo horn that serves as a dipper. You keep drinking until four hornfuls have been poured into the urn. In the present instance, the traditional buffalo horn having gone missing, a plastic jar is in use. In theory, each man drinks one hornful, but there is strategy to consider. Some drinkers hold back so that others will suffer the effects of the alcohol. Still others, hungry for those effects, might willingly drink more than their share. My motivation is different: I drink fast in order to bring the rite to its close and to escape the sodden communal straw that is now in my mouth.

Unfortunately, the master of the ceremony—the referee holding the horn-equivalent plastic jar—seems not to count the scoops of wine he pours into the urn. He ladles and ladles, with a dazed grin, while I suck down the vapid, slightly astringent liquor. It tastes more like flat beer than any wine I have met. With the drinking in its late innings, everyone is too potted to keep track of the rules. One sucks on, no end in sight. Hope dwindles. At last, I see out of the corner of my eye that Robichaud has broken free of a conversation and is heading into the house. I relinquish my straw and rise. I make a smiling *nop*—a little bow with hands together, as though in prayer— mumbling excuses in a mishmash of English and mangled Lao:

"Khop chay, khop chay"; thank you, thank you. My fellow imbibers look at me askance. Clearly, in their eyes, I am a barbarian, acting barbarically, for I have broken the rules of their drinking game. My gaffe, I pray, is to be expected—and forgiven.

The house is packed with people, including many children. Everyone faces the same direction, expressions rapt. On a crude ledge jutting from the wall stands a hissing television, the screen unwatchable, a blizzard of electronic snow. A second TV beside it shows no sign of life. Bounthai is fiddling with wires and controls, trying to conjure magic from the boxes.

Robichaud and I are directed to seats on the floor near the hissing television, beneath one of four muntjac trophies (all of the large-antlered species) that adorn the walls. We join a circle where Bounthai's vivacious and attractive wife holds court. She is hosting a round of beer in the Lao manner. As hostess, she pours a small glass, toasts the group, and drinks, draining the glass. Then she fills the glass again and passes it to the man on her left. He toasts, drinks, and drains, then returns the empty glass to the hostess, who refills it and passes it to the next in the circle. And so it goes, a single glass making a circuit of the group, of which we are now members. The large bottle runs dry. A second one is fetched. The glass comes around again, followed by the getting of a third bottle and a third circuit, with our queenlike hostess dispensing every drop and monitoring our progressive inebriation with ravenous enthusiasm.

A tiny man to my left is talking in a sweet, gentle voice. Robichaud, to my right, leans our way occasionally to translate. The man's name is Mang: Mr. Mang, if you please. The glass has come around for the nth time, and as I drink Mr. Mang tells me that he has spent a lot of time in the forest, as we will be doing. He likes the life of the forest, the life of the camp. He has traveled many kilometers on hard trails, some of them not far from the Nam Nyang, where we will head tomorrow. But regrettably, he says, his days of roaming the forest are over. He can no longer take to the trail.

Mr. Mang pauses to take a drink, and I look at him closely. His rueful admission makes sense to me, for he appears to be the oldest person in the room, unless I am. But then Mr. Mang, having finished his beer and passed the empty glass back to our hostess, rolls up his left sleeve.

He holds before my eyes an arm that seems to have two elbows. There is the expected elbow joining the upper and lower arms, but there is also a second, almost right-angle bend in the middle of his forearm. When Mr. Mang holds the upper part of his forearm level, as he now shows me, his hand points nearly south. The radius and the ulna have been broken and never reset. The broken radius, in fact, bulges against the skin, like a false elbow set on a disturbingly different plane from the true one. A small cage of bamboo, with cuffs at his biceps and his wrist, splints his forearm in its grotesque position and prevents the broken wing from flopping about. The splint is exactingly made and fiercely strong, with slender, rigid bamboo rods; it is the finest piece of workmanship I have yet seen in the villages. His arm has been this way a long time, he explains. Once, he even made the journey to the hospital in Thakhek, but the hospital lacked an orthopedic surgeon and so could do nothing for him. He came home, still married to his exquisite bamboo cage.

Robichaud inquires how the injury occurred. I was in the forest, says Mr. Mang. On a journey, and traveling up a river. The rocks were wet and slippery. I fell.

As Robichaud translates, I have an unhappy sense of recognition. Back in Vientiane, prepping for the expedition, Robichaud reviewed with me the dangers that might beset our journey: "I don't worry about bad water, dengue, malaria, or animal interactions. If anything bad happens, it's gonna be on those streams." He was speaking of the cascading side streams that drain into the Nam Nyang and of the main channel of the Nam Nyang itself. The streams run on beds of boulders, and if rain is falling or the air is dense with mist, the rocks become astonishingly slick. You step on them, he said, and *whoosh*—you are on your back. If a boulder is behind you and you hit your head, well, that could be that. A colleague of his at the

Wildlife Conservation Society hunted up a pair of rubber shoes that Japanese fishermen wear to keep their footing on wet, rolling decks. They have cleats that resemble shallow tacks, and they work well on the forest waterways. The villagers just wear flip-flops or cheap Vietnamese sandals with soles of soft rubber or plastic. The spongy materials let them grip the rocks as though they were barefoot, and their feet are strong and flexible. The worst thing is the hard Vibram found on the soles of many expensive hiking boots.

I was not happy to hear this. Although the soles of my boots and sandals are not as hard as Vibram, they are only slightly softer.

"Sometimes the guides push the pace from behind," he said, "and you hurry to keep ahead of them, so you can see things. That's when you fall. The key thing is, don't hurry."

Besides having the wrong footwear, I have foot problems and fall problems, too. Age takes a toll on one's balance. I am less steady now than I was at Robichaud's age and a far cry from the rock hopper I was in my twenties. Last spring in the Grand Canyon, descending a ravine in the dark, I had a fall that sliced my knee to the depth of the bone. The patella was only bruised and the tendon uncut, but the injury was tricky to close without stitches and also tricky to keep closed. A surgeon who happened to be on the trip, along with the trip leader, a wilderness medic, gave excellent care. There was no lasting difficulty, but the event remained a humbling confirmation of the erosion of my abilities. Unfortunately, no such medical expertise (let alone the capacious medical kits we had in the canyon) will accompany us on our trip in NNT.

Robichaud and I had planned to bring along a satellite phone in case anything serious occurred. In theory, the phone would enable us to call in a helicopter if a situation proved life-threatening. But something went wrong with Robichaud's Internet order, and no phone was delivered in time for me to bring it from the States. We went to plan B, which was to borrow a sat phone from the local office of the Wildlife Conservation Society. We stopped at a telecom store on the morning of our departure from Vientiane, expecting to open an account, buy an adequate store of minutes, and receive final instructions on the phone's operation. Instead we learned that the phone was broken and useless, and that no, the store could neither sell nor rent us a replacement. That was that. Apart from a fistful of painkillers, our resources for meeting calamity as we plunged into the forest were approximately the same as those that had comforted Mr. Mang.

Mr. Mang has rolled down his sleeve, and the beer has come around again. Is this the fifth time or the sixth? Our conscientious hostess now sets before us a low woven table replete with the fixings of dinner: little baskets of cold sticky rice and bowls of various pastes and sauces. In a flurry of rapid-fire speech she excuses herself again and soon returns with the pièce de résistance, which she places at the center of the table: a dish of fresh pig's blood, fortified with chunks of raw liver. Or maybe heart. The concoction is redder than lipstick. "Kin khao," she says. "Eat, eat!"

Robichaud, beaming with helpfulness, joins in. "Kin khao, Bill! Don't you want some of that strawberry shortcake?"

We are not the first outsiders to be offered so inviting a dish. Some months later, I will discuss saola with George Schaller, the famed naturalist who over the course of almost sixty years has studied nearly every charismatic animal on the planet: mountain gorillas in central Africa, lions in the Serengeti, snow leopards in the Himalayas, jaguars in Brazil, antelopes in Tibet, and more. He has also searched for saola in the Annamites. He will say, "The first thing the villagers do is bring you pig's blood, because they know Westerners don't like it. I always just go ahead and have some. Then they leave you alone."

Schaller's strategy is undoubtedly a good one, and I might have tried it but for the rumor we'd heard earlier in the day that the pigs of Ban Nameo and Ban Nameuy were dying for no apparent reason. People were concerned. Now I was concerned, too. If a mysterious distemper was killing local pigs, it hardly seemed advisable to consume the blood, let alone the liver, of an animal snatched from the portals of organ failure.

I notice that Robichaud has also declined the ruby-red delight. With both of us publicly in default of proper guest behavior, our hostess presses forward, with obvious relish for the headlock of etiquette she has us in. "Kin khao, kin khao," she badgers. "We Lao eat pig like this all we can. It makes us strong. Day after day, we go up the mountain to clear the fields and work hard. We work hard all our lives. When we get old, the government doesn't help us; we just keep working, we keep eating like this, and still we don't die, so you won't die, either. Have some! Kin khao!"

Her speech is much longer than my rendering here. It is also vehement, seamless, and impervious to objection. As Robichaud translates, I feel a wave of sympathy for her husband, Bounthai.

Suddenly a disturbance erupts elsewhere in the room. Attention mercifully shifts from the pig's blood (which no one else in our circle has sampled). Or maybe we have simply run out of beer. The details of the evening are getting hazy. In any event, our hostess soon reclaims command of the situation, having returned from the kitchen with a jug of rice whiskey.

We follow the same procedure and use the same glass as before. Our hostess pours herself the merest taste and downs it in one swallow, then fills the glass about an inch deep for each guest in succession. The rice whiskey has the fruity bite of tequila and far surpasses the kerosene I drank in Ban Makfeuang. An inch of it delivers a solid jolt, and when a second round of equal quantity reaches Robichaud, he shows reluctance.

"Drink up!" says our hostess. "It's New Year's!"

"But our New Year began two months ago," Robichaud protests. (When he translates this for me, he says "two years ago"—a sign that he, too, is losing ground.)

"That doesn't matter. It's the New Year of your host that matters. It's New Year's here. Drink up!"

"But Tet was three weeks ago."

"We're still celebrating!" she says gleefully, and fixes him with a stare.

Robichaud now resorts to a new stratagem. With a smile for our hostess, he pivots slightly to face the wall, kneels, and, in an attitude of prayer, pours a small amount of whiskey through a gap between the floorboards, mumbling inaudibly. Then he turns back to the group, gestures a toast to all, and downs the rest of his whiskey. Our hostess is frowning as she accepts the empty glass from him. Robichaud has made an offering to the house spirits and the souls of departed ancestors, sharing a little whiskey with the spirit world. Our hostess cannot protest.

The next glass is mine, and what the hell, I throw down the firewater once more. Another destabilizing jolt. The pig's blood, meanwhile, appears to be coagulating. No one has touched it or much of anything else. The members of the circle, including the petite Mr. Mang, have scarcely eaten. We are drinking straight whiskey on empty stomachs. At last the glass completes its circuit.

Expressing thanks, good cheer, and best wishes for the New Year, Robichaud starts to rise. "So good to be with you, but we must be going..."

"Oh, no!" exclaims Lady Torquemada. "We must have one last round."

"Thank you, but we have to..."

"We have to drink to good luck for your journey!" She knows she has him now.

"Just a little one, then."

"A very little one."

"Okay." Robichaud sits down.

She pours less than a centimeter of whiskey in the glass and drinks it, then pours another centimeter and passes it to the man on her left. The drinks are indeed small, and the glass moves quickly around the circle until it is Robichaud's turn. All eyes are on our enabler. She shoots a glance at Robichaud, bats her lashes coquettishly, and fills the glass two inches deep. Deaf to Robichaud's objections, she extends the glass.

Robichaud knows he's licked. No offerings this time. The spirits of the dead will have to go sober. He slowly drinks his medicine. He looks pale. The glass goes back.

Now it is my turn. I am already uncertain of my ability to stand up. She pours another two inches. I cannot possibly. To my horror I see that, where I am sitting, mats cover the floor all the way to the wall. There are no floorboards exposed. No cracks. I am given the glass. "Tell them my mother-in-law just died," I say to Robichaud. It is a small lie. I am not married, not quite. But I think of the message from Joanna, back in Nakai, minutes before we took to the boats to cross the lake, telling me that her invalid mother, Nancy, had passed away.

Robichaud is explaining this as I half rise and lurch across the room to a patch of exposed flooring that looks to me like the promised land. Lady Torquemada shrieks her objection as I make a generous offering to Nancy's newly liberated spirit, and I really do say a prayer, or at least I *feel* prayerful, now that words are not coming easily. When I return to the circle, the eyes of my hostess are bright with anger, but everyone else appears sympathetic, and they mutter what can only be condolences.

Lady T's enthusiasm has suddenly waned. Mr. Mang, who may have wanted more, now gets a niggardly drink, and the circle is quickly completed. Robichaud and I begin our escape. He is snared by conversation multiple times on his journey across the room and out the door, but my idiot grin of incomprehension opens a path through the throng. Soon I am down the ladder and into the welcoming darkness, with bright Orion spinning overhead. I lie down on the dewy grass. Orion stabilizes and shines still brighter. The Pleiades gleam, and the moist night settles like a caress.

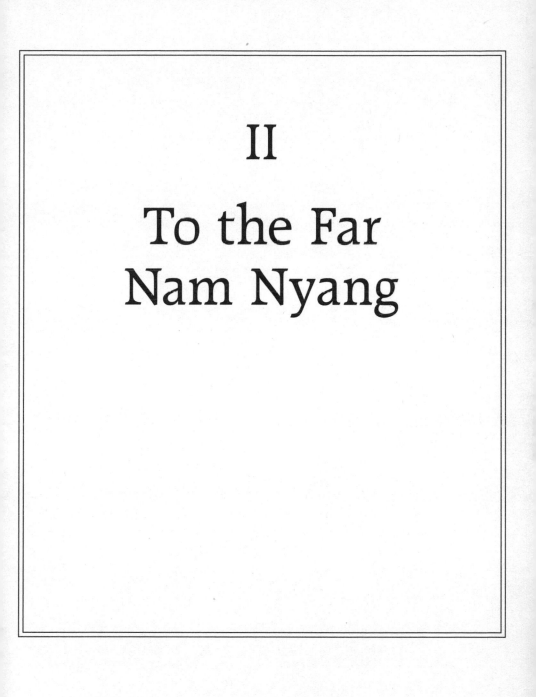

II

To the Far
Nam Nyang

February 27

Ban Nameuy

Pots, bowls, a teakettle, tarps, bungee cords, batteries, a water-proof duffel holding nine cameras and other camera-trap gear, several twenty-kilo sacks of sticky rice, one sack of ordinary rice, Robichaud's pack, my pack, bags of miscellaneous camp equipment and incidental food—Simeuang has divided the gear into ten roughly equal loads and weighed each. The guides will add their hammocks, blankets, and personal items to the loads they carry. The Lao standard is twenty kilos (forty-four pounds) of burden per man, although Vietnamese in the same mountains carry loads half again as large. Everybody knows this. The Lao typically say, "We don't like the Vietnamese, but they're not lazy."

Eight o'clock has come and gone, and only three guides have shown up. We had planned to start at seven, but *plan* is not often a useful verb in NNT. The first guide to arrive was the fellow who followed Robichaud out of Bounthai's house when we left the *hiit* the previous night. Robichaud had joined me on the grass beyond the reach of Bounthai's porch light. We both needed to sober up for the walk back to Ban Nameuy. Suddenly a young man plopped down before us. By the babble that came out of him, it was clear he was lit, too. Right away, he started begging for a job. He said he knew the trails and the wildlife; he loved traveling in the forest, he knew what Westerners expected, he really liked working with them, and on and on. Robichaud translated but said he was leaving out the obnoxious flattery. The young man—he seemed in his late twenties—talked fast and kept talking. He yammered about how good he was and how much he wanted to go with us, but his obsequious manner caused Robichaud to have doubts. Still, we needed more men, and Robichaud finally agreed to take him. Whereupon the young man jumped to his feet, effused his thanks, and headed back to the party. As soon as he was gone, Robichaud muttered, "I think I might regret that."

His name turns out to be Viengxai. He is taller than most of the other village men, slender and handsome. But his good looks have a preened quality that shows he knows he looks good, which makes you want to look somewhere else. Alone among the guides, however, Viengxai has come on time. He sizes up the loads Simeuang has allotted, hefting each pack, gauging its weight. In the end he chooses mine, which seems a vindication. I'd been afraid of bringing too much, traveling too heavy. Viengxai's choice seems to confirm that my pack is lighter than the others, or else an easier carry.

As it is, only Robichaud and I will have our main packs — containing our tents, sleeping bags, clothes, and other items — carried by guides. On the trail we'll wear smaller packs that contain day-use items such as rain gear, water, camera, and binoculars. Although this arrangement smacks of the white sahib (and it used to make him uneasy), Robichaud has traveled this way for years. It allows him to survey for wildlife with greater alertness, to be more agile when pursuing good sightings, and to retain sufficient energy after dark to complete his notes. I am hoping the same will be true for me. Of one thing I am sure: if I carried my whole kit, fatigue would render me *non compos mentis* by the end of the day and maybe by lunch.

Viengxai gets restless waiting for the other guides. He again hefts each of the loads and complains that all of them are too heavy. Simeuang banters back that he must have grown suddenly weaker, because only minutes ago he thought the loads were fine. Last night Viengxai groveled for approval; now he has turned petulant. He slings my pack over his shoulder and announces that he will meet us in Ban Nameo. In seconds he is down the stairs, striding off through the village. Ban Nameo is on the route we will travel, and so, truculence aside, Viengxai is not out of line in starting out on his own. Nevertheless, watching my worldly goods vanish from sight on the back of a moody stranger leaves me fighting down a gorge of objections.

The morning is half gone by the time a couple of teenagers from Ban Beuk show up, but there is still no sign of the men from Ban Kounè. Simeuang sends the teenagers back to Ban Beuk to recruit others. Kong Chan says it's a bad time of year: people are planting their gardens. And we don't pay enough. What's more — and there is always something more — it would be one thing if we were going to be on good trails, but nobody wants to go wandering around the forest just to wander. Kong Chan is grumpy. He laid into Simeuang at dawn, even before the tea water was hot, reprising earlier themes about his need for a tractor and a road and, by extension, about the cockeyed priorities of the government and the WMPA. As soon as Robichaud came yawning onto the veranda, Kong Chan redirected his harangue: "Wil-yam, the village needs a road; the government neglects the people of these villages; they are poor; how can they hope to advance?" Kong Chan harps on relentlessly: he wants a road, he wants a road, he wants a road.

Robichaud has heard enough of Kong Chan's ranting. He quickly reviews last-minute details with Simeuang and asks him and the boys to come along as soon as the teens from Ban Beuk get back. Robichaud and I depart for Ban Nameo.

We take to the trail with our daypacks and soon pass the dirt-floor schoolhouse that serves the village cluster. No one is there. It seems no one has been there in some time. Only one of the three rooms appears available for use. The other two shelter jumbles of desks and chairs, mounded as though for burning. Out front, the banner of Lao PDR droops from a flagpole.

We stop at the edge of Ban Nameo, at the foot of the village gardens, to wait for Simeuang and the others. Although I am anxious to locate Viengxai and my gear, we refrain from entering the village lest some alcoholic hospitality await us. A black-crested bulbul sings a long, sweet song beside the creek. Phou Vang towers, misty, to the south. I try to photograph it but fail. As the scribe of the expedition, I am here to record Phou Vang and the things that happen in its view, but no matter what exposure I set my camera to, the mountain dissolves in haze. We doze. When we awaken, the others still have not come.

In August of 2009, at the weeklong meeting of the Saola Working Group in Vientiane, where I met Robichaud, I was the only writer present, and as the days crept by, I increasingly doubted the wisdom of having come to Laos. The biologists, who hailed from at least five nations — Lao PDR, Vietnam, the UK, France, and the United States — discussed survey protocols, government relations, research funding, and related matters. Spreading the word about saola protection seemed a distant priority.

When the meeting dispersed, I asked Robichaud for an interview. Notwithstanding that he'd been working full bore as host and effective chairman of the group since long before the meeting convened, he agreed. Shortly after I turned on the recorder, he delivered a monologue that included this:

> So saola is this underdog. It doesn't hurt anybody. Nobody gains anything by killing it. It doesn't go eat crops, and it doesn't kill any domestic animals. It doesn't kill people, and people don't lose anything by not killing it. So it's kind of just this quiet, beautiful animal just wanting to be left alone and doing its little role of providing an element of beauty to the world. The only thing to achieve is to just leave it alone. But humans find it very difficult to leave things alone....
>
> The thing is, you go into these villages and out of the seventeen provinces in Laos, there's only probably three, maybe four or five at the outside, where this animal is found. And even in those provinces they're only found in a strip that

touches the Vietnam border. The same thing on the Vietnam side. So you go into a village in Laos and the local villagers — some of them have never been to the provincial town — they don't know that saola aren't everywhere. To them, saola is the same as one of the barking deer that are found in all the countries of Southeast Asia, the common muntjac. Once you start talking with them and you start talking about saola and you say, "You know saola is only found in the Annamite Mountains, the Sayphou Louang?" Or you're talking about saola and they say, "Do you have a lot of saola in America?" "No, it's not found in America." "Do they have a lot of them in Africa?" "No, there's no saola in Africa." You see the light going on in their heads. They say, "Thailand, they must have a lot of saola." "No, not found in Thailand, either. You know, it's not even found in Luang Prabang Province in Laos. It's not even found in Xainyabouli Province in Laos. The only place in the world saola is found is around your village." You can see the shift going on in their brains. . . .

We return to Ban Nameuy from our unrewarded wait in Ban Nameo to find Kong Chan's veranda crowded with people. All is ready, except we have only nine guides, not the ten we need. (Though the word *guides* is a euphemism. Only two or three will know the land well enough to help with trail finding; the rest are simply porters.) We have to leave behind one load — one sack of rice. This is a serious disappointment. It means we can't cover as much ground and will have less time in the forest to accomplish our tasks. Robichaud wears a long face as he contemplates the situation, but no improvement is in sight. Our tide is on the ebb. We have to make use of the men now assembled and get on the trail.

It is 11:30 a.m. by the time we are back at Ban Nameo with the entire group assembled, including Viengxai, whose mood has not improved with waiting. No longer petulant, he is now insolent. He says he has to have cigarettes and that Simeuang should buy them—they are essential provisions, part of the guides' compensation. Simeuang relents and dispatches a small boy with a fistful of kip to buy a carton from the one family in Ban Nameo who keep a supply. The genial Mr. Mang observes these matters from the edge of the group, cradling his broken wing. Next to him is his brother, Mok Keo, who will go with us as the most senior of the guides and therefore a team leader. Mok Keo has a mild demeanor and a round, solemn face. He wears a military hat and tunic, and I wonder if he is police of some sort.

Three others among the group carry Soviet AK-47 assault rifles in addition to their packs. One is dressed in camouflage fatigues. They are members of the local militia, assigned to us as security. We will have to rely on them if we encounter armed poachers.

Cigarettes having been procured, Viengxai now objects that his pack—my pack—is too heavy. "You chose first," Robichaud reminds him.

And the destination is a problem, Viengxai complains: "You want to go to a place that is no good for anything." Robichaud ignores him.

Viengxai isn't finished. "Look," he says. "The morning is already gone; it is too late to leave today. We should stay here tonight and leave tomorrow."

Neither Mok Keo, as senior guide, nor Simeuang, as expedition foreman, has intervened in this performance, although it is their responsibility more than Robichaud's to maintain order. Robichaud shrugs. "Let's go," he says, and every member of the group, including an abruptly silent Viengxai, falls in line behind Robichaud and follows along a trail that winds past the top of Ban Nameo and plunges into the trees.

We cross a low ridge and descend to a creek that Robichaud identifies as the Nam Sapong. From there our path weaves up a valley crowded with paddies and ponds. The ponds teem with tadpoles, just as the paddies will once they are flooded. "This is where you can find king cobra," Robichaud cheerfully points out. The tadpoles produce frogs. A multitude of snakes prey on the frogs. The king cobra then comes to prey on the other snakes. "It's a very snaky place," he says approvingly. A crested serpent eagle soars overhead.

We climb pole ladders, set as stiles, over the fences that separate one paddy cluster from another. We pass meadows of former paddies, now given to grass, where white-winged magpies flurry above the thickets. Bent double, we hustle down tunnels hacked through bamboo and second-growth scrub. The creek grows progressively smaller as we cross it again and again. Patches of trail are cratered with small excavations, toward which Robichaud gestures. "Bamboo rats," he explains. "People dig them out. They're like beavers with a possum coat. You can see them in the market in Luang Prabang. Vendors break off their incisors with pliers so they can't chew out of their bamboo cages."

The tall trees close in as we gain altitude, the forest canopy rising. We cross a divide and descend a new watershed. A dozen small logs, not much thicker than poles, are stacked beside the trail. "Rosewood," says Robichaud. A little farther along is another such pile, and then another. Soon we come to a recently abandoned camp. The fire ashes have not been rained on. Frames of thin poles, lightly planted in the ground, stand ready for the slinging of hammocks and the spreading of tarps. The structures are thrifty but sturdy, each pole neatly reinforced by others.

"No villagers would camp this close to home," says Robichaud. "They'd just go back to the village at night. This camp must be Vietnamese, but I've never seen them so close to the villages before." He shakes his head. "This is not a good sign. They must be cutting deals with the locals." We press on, passing more empty camps, more stacks of rosewood.

Days earlier, back in Vientiane, Robichaud outlined the history of Vietnamese entry into these forests. We were in a hole-in-the-wall café, a favored haunt near the riverfront, where we ordered steaming glasses of thick Lao coffee. Robichaud explained that villagers in Nakai–Nam Theun pinpoint Vietnamese penetration of their area specifically to 1984 or 1985, depending on where in the watershed you ask. Why it took place precisely then is a bit of a mystery. It may have been related to increased trade with China resulting from a partial opening of the border, which had been closed since at least 1979, when the two countries fought a brief war. (Relations were not normalized until 1991.) Perhaps more plausibly, the activity in NNT may have arisen from economic liberalization within Vietnam, possibly anticipating the economic "renovation" of the Doi Moi, in 1986. In any event, the Vietnamese, a coastal people with a long tradition of commerce, saw the doors opening for enterprise of many kinds, and one door led to expanded trade in eaglewood.

Eaglewood, or agarwood, derives from a mold that invades the heartwood of trees in the genus *Aquilaria*. Its effect is like that of the irritant that causes an oyster to make a pearl. The tree fights the infection by flooding the site with resin, forming a dense, exceptionally aromatic wood. An incense made from the wood is coveted in the Middle East and pushes the price for eaglewood as high as two thousand dollars per kilo.

The Vietnamese who wandered the heights of NNT in 1984 and '85 scoured the country for eaglewood. They hired villagers to cut down and saw up *Aquilaria* trees in search of the internal burls that held the precious resin. Pay was in the range of one hundred kip per hour—it sounds like mere pennies, and, strictly speaking, it was, but in those days kip ran about five hundred to the dollar, and the pennies added up to some of the first cash the laboring villagers had ever earned.

When the eaglewood ran out, the Vietnamese in the borderlands turned to other goods, including golden turtles, which in the early days might sell for no more than one hundred dollars per animal. Said one villager, "I traded a golden turtle to a Vietnamese for a T-shirt." Said another, "We used to eat thirty a year in our village." With golden turtles now as scarce as eaglewood, such statements evoke a lost world.

Those who sought turtles and eaglewood had to feed themselves, and so as they traveled they shot and snared wildlife as opportunity allowed. If they snared a tiger, their fortune was made, and if they saw an elephant, they shot it for the ivory. Villagers say elephants used to range high into the mountains, but in the 1980s, after the Vietnamese came, the survivors fled to the plateau, never to return.

Ironically, some of the Vietnamese involved in these extractions probably entered the country legally. They came across the mountains on a trail that was guarded by a border post so isolated it had to be supplied by helicopter. From there, the trail led to the Kri village of Ban Maka (original home of Kong Chan's wife, Chan Si). Because Ban Maka and similar villages were so remote, the Lao authorities considered it merciful to permit Vietnamese traders to visit them. Without the traders, the only way the villagers would have been able to obtain such essentials as batteries and clothing was to undertake a long, arduous journey. The Vietnamese traders hauled their stores on their backs like the old-time drummers of Europe and America, carrying nested washbasins, flashlights, needles, sandals, and other goods. No doubt they took payment in precious wood or in turtles or other wildlife, and no doubt they sometimes bribed the authorities at the lonely border post to allow them homeward passage without too close a look at what they carried.

At some point—probably within a few years of 1990—Vietnamese traders introduced a new device to the village world: wire snares. They were far stronger than traditional snares twined from vines and other native materials. They were also faster to set and more reliable. Traders showed the villagers how to use them and promised to return periodically to buy the marketable portions of their catch.

By the early 2000s, rosewood began to dominate transborder trade, and it continues to do so today. With eaglewood and turtles scarce, rosewood smuggling is the get-rich-quick scheme of the day. Its attractions are unlikely to fade until the last rosewood tree in NNT is felled, sawed up, and borne away on sweating human backs.

Most of the Vietnamese who traffic in Nakai–Nam Theun fit one of three profiles: the traders who come legally, the rosewood and wildlife buyers who also supply bicycle cable for building snares, and the rosewood and wildlife poachers who camp in the forest and take what they want directly. The picture is clouded by the fact that sometimes one individual fits all three descriptions. Even without the Vietnamese, protecting the "protected" area would remain a daunting challenge. The needs of the resident villagers, which are compounded by population growth, guarantee constant pressure on the resources of the forest and constitute a sustained threat to the survival of rare species like saola. With the pervasive additional impacts brought by the Vietnamese, however, the pressure becomes overwhelming. Until the transborder wildlife trade is suppressed, no one can argue that the saola of Nakai–Nam Theun, or its other wildlife, have been protected.

In midafternoon we stop to rest along the edges of a broad but nearly dry streambed. The three militiamen, who carry their rifles as casually as walking sticks, sit slightly apart. As a plastic bag of cooked sticky rice makes the rounds, Robichaud tells us that in 1999 he placed a camera trap at this very place. When he later examined its images, he saw a photograph of poachers going up the trail at the end of a day and a second image, taken the following morning, of a tiger coming down. It was the first image ever taken of a free-ranging tiger in Lao PDR. The good news was that the tiger had evaded the hunters and lived to roam another day. Sadly, though, despite its being a first, the photo was also probably the last of a tiger in NNT.[1]

Our immediate destination is Thong Kouang, *thong* meaning "grassland" and *kouang* meaning "large" or "grand": the Grand Grassland. We have kilometers yet to go and a mountain ridge to cross. Our journey takes us through a forest of giant dipterocarps, of which we can see only the massive, buttressed bases, which are extravagantly flanged, like swamp cypress but on a greater scale: some of the flanges are so large they could form the wall of a house. The boles of the trees rise arrow-straight and nearly branchless, disappearing a hundred feet overhead in the massed green of the canopy.

The trees surround and contain us, and the unavailable sky exists only as an idea, far out of sight. We are earthbound, small creatures in a forest of soaring giants, and I want to stop and linger here, to explore the feel of shade and space, to attend the silence that pools among these immense wooden columns, but there is no pausing. We have a destination to reach, still far away. We have an animal to find. We continue our march at an unvarying pace, Robichaud in front, then me, then Viengxai, almost walking on my heels, and the rest in single file behind.

Our arrival, thirsty and footsore, at Thong Kouang is abrupt. We exit the forest like flotsam pitched onto a beach. Suddenly the limitless heavens soar above us once more, and we are back in ordinary, sun-filled air, in the bright element where we started. Phou Vang, still hazy with distance, towers in the south. The grassland spreads before us more than a kilometer long and half as wide. We sprawl at its edge, beneath an egg-white sky. But we do not rest for long. The *thong* offers no water; we cannot camp here. Soon we are up and

Traversing Thong Kouang.

109

marching the length of the expanse. Clumps of brush and a few scrubby trees interrupt the monotony of grass, which is low and brittle and seems recently to have burned. Then we plunge again into forest, until we come to a hard-used campsite beside a sluggish creek.

After a supper of the usual sticky rice and chili paste, Robichaud and Simeuang gather the guides and present the rules of the camp. Rule 1: always keep water boiling (to purify it for drinking). Rule 2: make the breakfast fire and start the rice cooking before dawn every morning (sticky rice must boil for an hour, and cooking it is the primary obstacle to an early start on the trail). Rule 3: no talking on the trail (we are always on the lookout for birds and other animals, to say nothing of Vietnamese). Robichaud and Simeuang explain that our purpose is to evaluate potential saola habitat along the Nam Nyang and to assess the intensity and impact of wildlife poaching wherever we go. They promise a bounty to be shared among all the guides: one thousand Lao kip (about thirteen cents) for every snare collected. The guides discuss this. They say the bounty is too low. How about fifteen hundred kip per snare? Robichaud says, "It's a deal. And fifty thousand kip if you catch a Vietnamese poacher!"

Amid laughter, someone asks if *phi kong koy* is here. (The first syllable is pronounced "pee.") *Phi kong koy* is the Sasquatch or yeti of Lao forests. He has cousins throughout the wilds of Southeast Asia: in Vietnam, a similar creature is called *nguoi rung. Phi kong koy* is a reddish little man whose name is said to replicate the sound of the cry that he wails at night as he stalks the forest, occasionally taking a human victim. According to some accounts, his feet point backwards, which makes him difficult to track, not that anyone would want to.

It is unclear to me whether *phi kong koy* eats his victims, takes them captive, or simply scares them to death, but the hairy little man is greatly feared and loathed—and widely discussed, in keeping with the universal tendency among those who camp in wildlands to discuss things that go bump in the night.[2] None of the guides claims to have seen *phi kong koy* or even to know firsthand anyone who has. The discussion ends in a comfortable consensus that "probably there aren't any around here."

The guides sling their hammocks by the stream. Robichaud, Simeuang, the boys, and I retrace our steps a quarter mile to Thong Kouang, where we pitch our tents in the open. The air is pleasantly cool, and neither mosquitoes nor other insects trouble us. Robichaud and I sit on our camp stools and talk. Phou Vang is an outline of blackness against a moonless, starlit sky. From different directions, indicating several animals, comes an occasional, explosive *huff*— the "bark" of barking deer, the various muntjacs. When surprised or claiming territory or perhaps when impressing a mate, the deer produces a loud cough, almost a grunt. The bark contains the slightest touch of something that sounds metallic, like sheet metal shaken at a great distance, which helps to carry the call.

An Asian barred owlet begins its eerie quavering trill, and then a collared owlet begins piping from back toward camp. Yet another owl calls, more *ha* than *hoot,* and Robichaud identifies it, but I am too tired to write down the name. Later in my tent, I lie in my bag and stare out the door at the Big Dipper, low in the north, pointing toward Polaris. I have left the rainfly off the tent, and Orion, Leo, and the Pleiades beam down through the netting of the roof.

I hear the murmur of Simeuang talking with the boys, some distance away. Night settles, and a mountain scops owl pulses the high, sweet notes of its two-syllable call. The bird book gives the call as *toot-too,* but I hear it as *khop chay*—"thank you"—followed by a pause, then thank you, and another pause, and again, gratefully into the night.

February 28

Thong Kouang

In dim first light, the trees hemming the *thong* detach from the sky. The forest becomes a misty encirclement, like an army ranged around us. Behind the lines, where darkness hangs in the trees, voices begin, breathy and haunting: *Whoo-AH, whoo-AH.* The calls on the left echo those on the right; there are others to the rear. *Whoo-AH, whoo-AH.* It is the singing of gibbons.

The slender apes summon the day, females calling to their mates, the males answering, the pairs advertising their presence to other pairs, asserting their occupancy of discrete patches of forest. Their song lies beyond metaphor, beyond the ordinary meanings of words. There is *hoot* in it, but it is not a hoot. There is *whoop* in it, but it is not a whoop. It is too joyful for a scream, too relaxed for a shout, yet the song carries great distances, even through a million leafy boughs. It is conversational, the emotion mild. The animals are not trying to find each other; they are just talking, yet their talk is not chatty. It is declarative and serious, and each utterance ends in muted shrillness, a final sharp tail of emphasis. It is a song between partners, and one is tempted to hear in it an expression of affection, a breathy cousin-primate coo of attachment. The gibbons' song stirs my own longings, and I think of Joanna and wonder how she is faring with the death of her mother and whether she also feels the loneliness of moments like this. The feeling ebbs as the apes sing on, infusing the day with a quiet exaltation.

They have cheered Robichaud. He smiles as he emerges from his tent. "It's my favorite sound in nature," he says. Even better, the presence of gibbons at Thong Kouang means that "a big part of the forest here is still intact."

Before the sun has topped the trees, the gibbons turn quiet, and we set off into the now unenchanted forest. We smell something dead by the tree line and resolve to investigate later. A grey peacock pheasant yammers its Dopplerish cry at the strangler fig tree where we set camera traps the night before. The fig is fruiting, and we had hoped it might attract a civet in the night, but the results are disappointing: none of the cameras captured images of animals, and two failed to operate even when we walked in front of them. We take them back to the tents, and Robichaud immerses himself in the operating manuals. Several guides, including Viengxai, arrive and watch us as though we are a show in a theater.

Viengxai observes closely as I roll my sleeping pad. When I set the pad aside, he picks it up and fingers the strap that holds it. He peers into ditty bags and opens other containers. When I shoo him off, he retreats with a sarcastic smile. He lifts the empty and unstaked tent and shakes it as though it were a trophy. When I take it from him, he hefts my nearly empty pack and pantomimes a great burden. Anything I set to the side he fondles as he might a toy. When I stuff my last things in the pack, Viengxai leans in closely to watch the placement of each item. I cinch the top flap tightly, sealing its contents the only way I can, and go to help Robichaud decipher the cameras.

We are testing three models of varying cost and complexity—a total of nine cameras. The cheapest ones have proved nearly worthless. Toward the end of our time in NNT, we will set the cameras in locations yet to be determined that seem promising for saola, and we will leave them in place through the coming rainy season. Somewhere near Ban Kounè seems a likely prospect, but Robichaud's plans are constantly changing. Many factors merit consideration, the potential for theft being one of them. When Robichaud opens the back of one camera, Viengxai, who has come to hover at his shoulder, exclaims, "Look at all those batteries!" He points and counts out loud. "One, two, three, four..." Robichaud looks up from the camera. In English he says to me, "My bad feeling about this guy isn't getting better. If these cameras disappear, I will have a prime suspect."

As a test, Robichaud has decided to install an array of cameras at a mineral lick near Thong Kouang and leave them there until we return from the Nam Nyang. On our way to the lick, we encounter the remains of a muntjac. Robichaud determines that it is a large-antlered muntjac, a rare species about which little is known. The remains consist of little more than a black puddle of hide and bone. One of the hind hocks is skinned to the tibia, where the noose of a wire snare had closed around it. There is no hoof. The deer fought free, at mortal cost, and didn't make it far. We follow a faint trail into the forest and find two snares; one of them, the agent of death, is sprung and broken. We disarm the other one and collect the wire, which is instantly recognizable as bicycle brake cable, a commodity universally available.

The land here is nearly flat, and the sloughs that drain it are deeply incised. One such slough now bars our passage. Its clay walls are nearly vertical, and they come undone under the least pressure. We cannot climb them. At last we find a tree fallen across the slough and continue by this bridge to the *poung,* which occupies a boggy wetland. Presumably its clays contain salts that the wildlife favor. It looks to be a promising location, for a set of fresh sambar tracks traverses it.

Robichaud takes his time selecting positions for the cameras. He adjusts the angle of view by sliding wedges of wood between the cameras and the tree trunks to which they are strapped. He adjusts the bungee cords that hold them in place. Olay, hopping past the camera like an oversize rabbit, does his best to imitate a quadruped, but the camera doesn't fire. Consternation. Robichaud guesses that Olay's ever-present rain parka shields his body heat from the camera's infrared sensors. Olay slithers out of the jacket as though it were a dress (the zipper is broken) and tries again. Success.

Robichaud checks and rechecks the settings, pressing menu buttons with his thumbs: sensitivity level, field of view, still photograph versus video, interval between photographs, flash on or off, and more. Finally he is satisfied. One camera done, two more to go.

We don't want to disturb the area with an excess of trampled plants or scent, so I stand on hard ground at the edge of the bog with the guides who have accompanied us. Viengxai is at my shoulder. He looks almost dashing today. While most of the guides wear nylon trunks or cutoff sweatpants, he sports a pair of tight-fitting blue jeans with fashionable embroidery on the back pockets. Alone among the guides he also wears leech socks — a khaki pair, freshly laundered — which give him a high-booted, uniformed look, further accentuated by his trim-fitting camo-green jacket. His small machete — a bamboo knife, really — hangs from a loop of plastic twine at the small of his back, and this morning he has borrowed (or commandeered) a rifle from one of the militia. Fully fitted out, he's the NNT equivalent of a cowboy duded up for Saturday night, and he stands with hips cocked, weight on one foot, the rifle slung barrel-down over his shoulder, as though it always lived there.

As I write in my notebook, Viengxai edges closer to peer over my shoulder, staring hard at my runic scrawl even as I jot his description. His face is inches from mine. I am breathing his exhalations, thankful that his breath is fresh. On the ground before us a sambar track is pressed into the mud. Viengxai vigorously points to it. "Yes," I say. "I see it." Then he points even more emphatically, as though I am blind. "Yes," I repeat, but he is not satisfied, for I have not yet done what he is bidding me to do. Probably he wants me to photograph the track, as he earlier saw me photograph the decomposed muntjac, but in a photograph the hoofprint would show only as a black hole in the ground; moreover, the last thing I want to do is start following his meddlesome prompts. Our not-quite conversation, however, provides a kind of satisfaction. Standing almost cheek to cheek with Viengxai, I've deciphered the tortured script on the rhinestoned visor of his ball cap. It says LOVE YOU FOREVER, which

strikes me as fitting: Viengxai, who once promised slavish cooperation, is as sincere as his hat.

In an hour the camera traps are set, and we head back. When we
pass the carcass of the muntjac at the edge of the grassland, Robichaud stays behind. He draws his machete and begins hacking at
something. He is amputating the remaining back foot.

"Collecting a sample?" I ask him.

"No," he replies tersely. "Something for me." End of conversation.
Head down, he continues hacking at the dead leg.

Although I have stayed at his home in Vientiane and he has
stayed at mine in New Mexico, and although we have spent cumulative days in conversation and have traveled this past week together, I
realize that I have far to go in learning who he is.

Once, at a meeting of conservation biologists, I watched one of
Robichaud's colleagues draw a visual guide to the antlers of the several species of muntjacs found in the Annamites. He sketched the
different sets of antlers freehand and quickly, with no wasted
strokes. Then he labeled them. The result was a handsome key to
identifying male animals within the confusing taxonomy of the
genus *Muntiacus* in Indochina, which few people understand past a
rudimentary level — none better than the author of the guide, whose
name is Rob Timmins.

Timmins's coworkers acknowledge him as the best field man in the
region. Said one, "Timbo can learn more about a protected area's wildlife in a week than most others can in a year." On another occasion
Robichaud said to me, "If you got paid for wildlife survey the way you
get paid in international soccer, Timmins would be up where David
Beckham used to be, taking down twenty million pounds a year." Timmins is a Cambridge graduate with a heavy Midlands accent. In his
telling, the sites where animals are found become "soites," which he
"disgusses" with his colleagues. Timmins confides that as he studies or
travels through a habitat, he builds a mental map, which is ever in his
mind's eye. The map, like a GIS database, is layered with information—

or informed intuitions—about climate, topography, vegetation, species sightings, and so forth. The richer he can make the map, the more predictive it becomes, sometimes leading to conspicuous success in deducing where a certain animal will be.[1]

The grail of a survey biologist is the identification of new species, and Timmins has logged an impressive list that includes the Annamite striped rabbit (*Nesolagus timminsi*);[2] the bare-faced bulbul (*Pycnonotus hualon*), Asia's only bald songbird; and the *kha-nyou* (*Laonastes aenigmamus*), a rodent that dwells in holes in karst limestone and that is even more distant from its surviving evolutionary relatives than the saola.[3] Amid competition for first identifications, however, the meticulous Timmins is sometimes slow to publish and does not always get the credit he is due. This was the case in the discovery of both the large-antlered and Annamite muntjacs (*Muntiacus vuquangensis* and *M. truongsonensis*), which came to the attention of Western science soon after the discovery of saola.

In those days, an obligatory stop for any biologist working in central Laos was the wildlife market at Lak Xao, close by the northern border of the Nakai–Nam Theun protected area. (*Lak Xao* translates literally as "kilometer twenty," and some Lao maps show it as B. LAK 20, or "Ban Lak 20.") In the 1990s Lak Xao was merely a widened gash along one of the few highways to Vietnam, twenty kilometers from where the French used to maintain a border post guarding the route. It was a frontier town, rough-hewn and dusty. Illicit, big-money timber deals were rumored to take place there, as was heroin manufacture. Wildlife trafficking may have been the least of its evils. At the town market, trade in large animals was mostly under the table, but on a typical morning one might see twenty-five species of songbird and plenty of small mammals laid out among the chilies and vegetables. The Lak Xao market produced the first record for Laos of the strange, arboreal colugo (*Cynocephalus variegatus*), a relative of tree shrews that is sometimes incorrectly called a flying lemur (it is not a lemur, and it glides rather than flies). It was also there that Timmins first spotted the Annamite striped rabbit.

The potentate of Lak Xao at the time was General Cheng Saya-vong, whose helicopter Robichaud had once looked on with envy. Cheng headed Bolisat Phathana Khet Phoudoi, the Mountainous Areas Development Corporation, better known by its initials, BPKP, which was a military-run, government-owned enterprise. BPKP dominated all nonsubsistence economic activity for a hundred kilometers in every direction. It cut timber for export and brokered other commodities. It built roads, relocated villages, and did whatever else General Cheng cared to do.

The general's interests included wildlife, and he caused a small zoo, really a menagerie, to be built in Lak Xao. It was at Cheng's modest collection of pens and cages that Robichaud spent two weeks observing a captive saola in 1996. It was also there that Timmins and Robichaud together examined a small, dark muntjac that they realized was neither the widely distributed red muntjac (*M. muntjak*) nor the large-antlered muntjac (*M. vuquangensis*), which was named from the Vu Quang reserve in Vietnam two years after the discovery of saola. Timmins and Robichaud backed up their discovery with a skull of the anomalous animal, which they obtained from a nearby Hmong village. Although others, under strange circumstances, were first to publish a description of an animal that was probably of the same species, now identified as the Annamite muntjac, or *M. truongsonensis,* most people interested in the barking deer of Laos and Vietnam defer to Timmins on matters of taxonomy. The puzzles are many and ongoing. For example, while the species status of large-antlered muntjac is generally agreed, one might ask whether others — the proposed Annamite and Phuhoat muntjacs (*M. truongsonensis* and *M. phuhoatensis*) — are truly separate species or instead races of the same line.[4]

At the meeting in Vientiane, after the antler sketches of various species were shared, parsed, and thoroughly discussed, Timmins popped a quiz. He showed a series of camera-trap photographs of various muntjacs and asked his colleagues to identify them as to species. The gambit was not for sport. As Timmins's friend and collaborator Will Duckworth explained, the large-antlered muntjac was likely next in line for extinction, after the saola. Therefore, correct identification and preservation of camera-trap photographs was vital in documenting the animal's status and distribution before it vanished. Tellingly, as a measure of the difficulty of the subject, and of survey work in the Annamites generally, performance on the quiz was abysmal. Duckworth led with four right answers out of five, but several experienced field-workers scored none.

Later that day, I asked Timmins about a population estimate he had made for saola years earlier. In 1996, based on a patch-by-patch analysis of saola habitat and informed guesses as to species density and threat factors, he calculated an estimate of between seventy and seven hundred saola remaining in Laos. He said if the higher number was right, saola might still exist. If the lower number was correct, by now they are gone. "There might be a few here or there, but as a population they may already be past the point of recovery. We don't know."

"The attrition is that aggressive?"

"Yeah, and it applies to all large mammals, anything bigger than a dog or a porcupine."

"It's like they're falling off a cliff?"

"Off a cliff—even the pigs, and pigs will always be the last to go."

The day has warmed. Simeuang and I go to find the source of the death smell on the path to the strangler fig. The intense buzzing of carrion flies, to say nothing of the stench, draws us quickly to the source. It is another large-antlered muntjac in a wire snare, tangled in brush, its hindquarters dangling from the wire, the head and shoulders dissolving into a pool of grease on the ground. The death grimace reveals the teeth of the upper jaw, where one of the long, distinctive canines of the muntjac has fallen out. Nearly a fang or a tusk—an incongruous feature in a family that includes Bambi— the ivory tooth lies in the rot seeping from the carcass. Like an elk tooth in North America, such a relic is a kind of prize, a symbol of longevity, the last part of the animal to decompose. I consider taking it, cleaning it, and keeping it as a souvenir or talisman. Earlier this morning I similarly pondered the shed skin of a king cobra, which lay beside a path between the *thong* and camp. Five or six feet long, it was translucent and bore the lacelike imprint of the scales. I debated rolling it up and stowing it in one of the rigid containers in my pack or simply cutting out a sample. In the end I did neither, and I also now leave the muntjac tooth where it lies. I have no business taking anything from this forest. To be honest, I am a little intimidated by the juju of these things, or, more to the point, by not knowing what kind of juju they have or don't have. I imagine my friend Mary, frail and wan, whispering in my ear, "Leave them alone."

Mary should know. Long ago, at the ruin of an ancient Indian village in New Mexico, Mary took something she ought not have taken. Or one of her young sons may have taken it. Or maybe her memory deceived her and nothing happened, and there was no connection to what happened later. But she recalled that as soon as she arrived at the ruin, led there by a man she should not have trusted, she knew she should leave. And as soon as she picked up the shiny object—a fetish, a jewel, a sacred stone?—a wave of foreboding swept through her. She dropped what she was holding. She turned to the children and said, "Don't touch anything. Don't take anything. Go back to the car. Go now!"

Days later, at home in the cottage behind her grandmother's house, her dreams appalled her. Strange dancing figures demanded the return of something she could not find. The spirits were violent and adamant, unappeasable. She woke in a fever of anxiety: Had she taken something from the ruins? Had she put something in her pocket? Had William, the younger boy, possibly picked up what she put down?

She wanted to believe that all of it was a dream, but her older son told her it wasn't: "Mama, I remember going to the ruin." She thought of these things again, replaying them in her mind, in the terrible autumn when her father died, William was murdered, and she was diagnosed with cancer.

• • •

The morning is nearly spent when at last we shoulder our packs, and our line of fourteen burdened travelers begins to snake along the trail toward Thong Sek, another big gap in the forest, fourteen kilometers away. From there we will climb a tall mountain, nameless on the map, and after descending the far side, we will drink the water of the Nam Nyang.

We walk almost double time, at a pace too quick to allow true observation. It is as though we are late for something, rushing to catch up, the way one might exit the subway after a delay, still hoping to make a meeting on time. But here the hurry does not last for a block or two. Robichaud wants to make up for our late start, and so we scurry onward, even though we have no particular destination. We'll just see how far we get. The trail is rough, broken by roots and rotting logs; sometimes it is not even a trail, only a crease through the vegetation. I keep my eyes on my footing lest I trip, and so the miracle forest streams by unnoted and scarcely sensed, a continuous collage of leaves, green and brown, and angled stems scrolling at the edges of my vision. A Tarzan sound track of lunatic birdsong and insect screech resounds in our ears as we hustle, hustle, hustle forward.

We do not slow for gullies, which as often as not are bridged by two or three thin poles laid close together. The guides dance across them. Robichaud teeters forward like a tightrope walker. I cross, my heart pounding like a trip-hammer, less afraid of injury than of the shame of falling in front of everyone. Where poles cannot bridge the gullies, our predecessors on the trail, quite likely poachers, have hacked shallow steps into the clay banks. Where there are no steps, or where the earth is too loose to hold a shape, we scramble up, pawing at the bank, feet churning.

At last Robichaud calls a pause for water and rest. I sit against a tree of massive girth, the bark of which peels off in giant flakes, as though it were clothed in potato chips.[5] Several guides crowd around to watch me write in my notebook. They seem never to have seen writing before, but, recalling the school on the trail to Ban Nameo, I say to myself that this cannot be true. Perhaps it is only that they have never seen Roman script. Then again, the school was nearly a ruin. The guides watch with broad smiles, their eyes focused on the point of the pen as it marks the page. Not far away, a lineated barbet chants *ti-tonk, ti-tonk*.

A short distance down the trail Robichaud investigates yet another abandoned poachers' camp. He comes back with the skull of a large-antlered muntjac, our third in two days. A female. Perhaps only antler-bearing male skulls are worth lugging back to Vietnam. Simeuang frowns as he examines the skull. Despite the heat, he is wearing a thick brown turtleneck, torn at the shoulder, and he looks as fresh as he did at breakfast. Touy and Olay, both in their raincoats on this rainless day, are cool and relaxed, too, without a single bead of moisture on their foreheads. My thin shirt, meanwhile, is soaked, and I have sweated through the disintegrating sweatband of my hat.

Moving again, we hurry but soon stop to identify a bird, then hurry and stop again. The sights of the forest are trumping Robichaud's haste. Now he points out a black giant squirrel — not merely a black squirrel of large size, he says, but a member of the genus *Ratufa,* known as Asiatic giant squirrels; the black giant squirrel is *R. bicolor.* He mentions that the population of the squirrel is declining, as it is heavily hunted. We stop also to examine a pitted clearing of bare red earth, littered with chunks of yellowing sapwood, the site of rosewood diggings. Poachers carted off the aboveground portions of the area's rosewood trees months or years ago; now they dig for heartwood in the roots. One shard of stump is signed in Vietnamese, as though it were a work deserving authorship: THE ONE WHO DUG AND CUT THIS — TAM. Farther along, at a similar excavation, the message and signature end in a cryptic series of numbers. We ponder the mystery until Mok Keo, the only one among us who reads Vietnamese, laughing, bursts out, "I know what it is!"

"What?" asks a surprised Robichaud.

"A phone number!"

"Jesus," says Robichaud. "They're advertising. These sonsabitches have the balls to advertise!" He withdraws from his pack a plastic bag, from which he extracts a small sign printed in Lao and Vietnamese. He proceeds to tie it to a tree with red plastic twine.

When I ask what it says, Robichaud replies, "It's a WMPA notice that says it's illegal for outsiders to cut timber or hunt here, and anyone caught faces arrest."

"That sounds pretty futile, under the circumstances."

"Times like this, I just want to leave a message. We at least need to let them know that we know what's going on. To not be silent. Of course, nobody has bothered to reprint these things. This is the last one I've got."

A kilometer farther along we come to a stand of stately trees, of which six or eight of the largest have been felled, another violation of the limp safeguards of the protected area. Close to the villages, there are zones where residents have rights to harvest trees for houses, boats, coffins, and other noncommercial uses, but we are miles from any such area now. Robichaud and Simeuang look for clues, walking the logs from the hacked stumps to the former canopies. They gesture much and discuss the scene in Lao. "Rattan," Robichaud finally announces. "They cut down the trees to get the rattan."

The term *rattan* embraces hundreds of species of palm, but not the signature trees of island beaches and desert oases. Most rattan palms are climbing vines, and here the rattan has laced itself through the tops of old-growth trees. This particular variety has fierce, hooked thorns, like a rose on steroids, and its palmate foliage is intensely green, still fresh. Some of the guides busy themselves snipping sections of it. Most people know rattan as a source for woven furniture and baskets. Here it is also a food. The growing tips of the vine are tasty and nutritious. The trees lying jackstrawed before us were sacrificed, says Robichaud, "for a couple of meals."

123

. . .

We are making good time toward Thong Sek when hubbub erupts among the guides. The three militiamen drop their packs and race into the forest, rifles in hand, closely followed by Viengxai and one other. The vegetation swallows them, and then the sound of their movement fades away as well. One of them spotted a trail, freshly used, where a trail should not have been. Perhaps it leads to a Vietnamese camp. We wait. In ten minutes they come back. Nothing.

It is getting late, and we have still not reached Thong Sek, which can only be a kilometer or two ahead. Robichaud confers with the senior guides. There is no reliable water on the mountain divide that lies beyond Thong Sek, and if we attempt to cross the mountain, we won't reach the Nam Nyang until hours after dark. The guides agree: it is probably better to camp at Thong Sek. I cannot say I am disappointed. I will be glad for a long drink of water and a quiet place to pitch my tent.

Thong Sek is brittle with heat. It is less grassland than scrub savanna, a scattering of scraggy, angular trees with narrow crowns walled in by forest. Like Thong Kouang, it has recently burned. The char on the trees suggests flame heights of six feet or more, and the fresh grass sprouting underfoot cannot be older than one or two weeks. Now we conference anew. Robichaud is laughing. The guides say they are willing to push on up the mountain—we ought to be able to find water somewhere along the way—but we won't make it if Robichaud "keeps stopping every three hundred meters to look at birds."

It's true. Perhaps because we agreed to make camp early at Thong Sek, Robichaud, always at the head of the line, has been stopping more frequently. We halt just now at the edge of the *thong* as a flock of robin-size birds dives and darts through the scrub. They cackle loudly and merrily. "Laughingthrushes," declares Robichaud. "My second-favorite sound in nature." Oddly, laughingthrushes are not closely related to thrushes but are a genus of their own: *Garrulax,* as in garrulous.

Robichaud agrees to keep moving, and so we cross a lazy, warm-water slough on bamboo poles, then climb a slope that recedes in successive benches: a steep pitch followed by a flat, then another pitch, and a flat, and so on up the mountain. On one bench we encounter a poachers' camp of at least five recent fire circles, each with several pole frameworks for tarps and hammocks. At eight men per fire (a manageable number for meals and cooking), the camp when fully occupied held a sizable platoon. I pick up a discarded cigarette package, one of several scattered about. The writing on it is Vietnamese. It still smells of tobacco.

As we depart the big camp, a new chorus of murmuring arises from the guides. They have concluded that the Vietnamese carried their water to this place, and confidence that we will find water any-where on the mountain is now lost. They want to turn back to Thong Sek. It will be dry, they say, until we descend the far side of the mountain to the Nam Nyang.

Robichaud asks, "Why didn't you say this before?" He grimaces and stares at the ground. Then he hunches up his pack and starts walking down the slope the way we came.

A couple of guides call after him, "Okay, we can go to Nam Nyang. We'll only be an hour and a half in the dark, but all our water will be used up."

"No: we go back," says Robichaud, and he motions for everyone to follow.

Thong Sek is not one grassland but several, divided by corridors of trees and small declivities. We camp beside the largest of the open areas, where a warm-water slough laps at the edge of the forest. As soon as we have chosen our site and thrown down our packs, Mok Keo begins cutting spinachlike leaves from a plant at the slough's muddy edges. He brews the leaves, along with the rattan gathered earlier, into a delicious, briny soup. Robichaud breaks out a flavored paste he especially covets. His girlfriend, Akchousanh Rasphone, brought it from Luang Prabang just before we left Vientiane. It tastes of ginger, citrus, and garlic, and it makes the sticky rice worth having in your mouth. As we eat, sitting on the ground at a tarp folded long and narrow to serve as a legless table, yellow butterflies cluster on the straps and other sweat-damp places of my daypack. I assume they are drawn to the salt.

When the bowls are put away, Robichaud calls everyone together and formally enrolls the guides, entering their names in his record of the expedition. Most senior is Mok Keo, brother of Mr. Mang, a small, wiry man in a hat and shirt that appear borrowed from a uniform. I had thought he was a district or provincial policeman, but no, he says. Although he was long a soldier, he is now retired, a civilian pure and simple.

The two older militiamen are Meet and Sone. Both appear to be in their early thirties. Meet, like Mok Keo, hails from Ban Nameo. He is the more assertive of the two, his manner serious, almost dour. He is dressed in tattered camo shorts and an olive-drab jacket.

Supper on the trail. Touy is closest on right.

He knows well the lay of the land, at least the portion we have traversed thus far. It is Meet to whom Robichaud turns when the trail grows faint or splits into multiple routes. Sone (pronounced "sawn") is Brou, from Ban Kounè, and married to a Sek woman from Ban Nameuy. He lives with her there, close to Kong Chan. He sports a wisp of a mustache and a blue watch cap. His automatic rifle is particularly old and battered, and he lovingly wipes it clean of dust at our rest stops. A fever has dogged him from the beginning of the trip, and this evening it is worse. His gaze is wan and bleary, but all day he carried the most ungainly of our packs without complaint. It was a rice sack with only a doubling of plastic twine to serve as shoulder straps. The twine was tied to the neck of the sack and also to the pigtailed bottom corners. It must have cut his shoulders fiercely. Sone retires to his hammock as soon as Robichaud puts his name in the book.

Phaivanh, from Ban Beuk, is the third militiaman—courteous, in his midtwenties, with a broad and open smile. I do not believe I've seen him frown during the course of the trip, unless it was a time when everyone else was frowning, and so he did, too. His pink T-shirt shows an outline of the Statue of Liberty with the words *New York* duplicated hundreds of times around it.

Bone, Kham Laek, Phiang, and Thong Dam, all teenagers, also hail from Ban Beuk. Bone ("bawn") exudes a bright, joyous charm and an alertness suggesting quick intelligence. The others are withdrawn, shy with a foreigner such as I, and apt to sit behind each other, hiding a little. Sometimes when I look up from my rice bowl or notepad, I find solemn eyes in a blank expression focused on me. How strange I must look to them: blue eyes, white whiskers, eyeglasses, a skull built from European genes, the top of it furred in gray. How much I wish I could converse with them. We could entertain each other a long while.

Last of the nine guides is Viengxai, so unlike both the gentle and industrious boys and the experienced and focused men. He is scornful when I broach a word or two of Lao, and he is always fiddling with things, usually my things. He has the sharp eyes of a thief on the watch for unattended treasure, no matter how small, and he is always working his angle, complaints at the ready, a jailhouse lawyer.

While the enrollment progresses, I ask the boys to write their full names in my notebook. They seem surprised and a little flattered, and each writes slowly in round, clear letters, not omitting the honorific:

Mr. Soukphavanh Sawathvong (Touy)
Mr. Chamthasome Phommachanh (Olay)

Simeuang is busy recording a parallel enrollment to Robichaud's, but I will soon get his full name: Mr. Simeuang Phitsanoukan.

Formalities concluded, Robichaud chats further with the guides in Lao. After a little while, with several of them looking at me, I get the sense that I am the subject of their conversation. I shoot Robichaud a glance. He explains, "I am telling them that in the United States you live in a protected area like this one, where there are bear and deer and animals like sambar, dhole, and even a big wild cat like a leopard."

He's right, although I'd never thought of things that way. I live in a village in the southern Rocky Mountains surrounded by national forest. Our elk, or wapiti, are like sambar; our coyotes analogous to dholes. And the mountain lion, I suppose, is a very distant cousin to the leopard. The comparison goes deeper. In its early days, the protected areas of northern New Mexico had many holes in their "protection." The first decades of government stewardship saw local extirpation of such big mammals as grizzly bear, wolf, white-tailed deer (but not mule deer), bighorn sheep, and elk. Both the predators and many of the game species they fed on were hunted and trapped until none was left. Game managers eventually reintroduced elk and bighorn sheep from distant populations, but the local genes were lost forever. Nakai–Nam Theun now tumbles through a similar decline, but with its greater diversity, it has much farther to fall.

. . .

When we pitched camp at Thong Sek, the birds were in full concert. A barbet sang, "Half a lump, half a lump," its liquid notes a steady cadence, the timbre hollow, like the sound of blowing in a bottle. Against that rhythm a second chimed in, chanting the same notes in identical cadence but a split second out of phase. And a third barbet joined the others, and then a fourth, each bird singing the same song and rhythm but never in unison, so that the repetition of their competitive notes sounded like an airy, modernist composition by Philip Glass. Overlaid on the chorus of barbets came the chattering mimicry of a drongo, lively as a mockingbird on amphetamines. The drongo's melodies danced in and out of the chorus. The result was not better than Glass's work, but neither is the most masterly of Glass's compositions better than what we heard at Thong Sek.

After supper, as the light wanes, so do the barbets, and the *thong* is quiet when Robichaud and I make a last recon. Robichaud leads, stepping carefully and softly across the brittle ground. At the least movement in the trees, he freezes in place and raises his binoculars. He insists that I stop as quickly and as silently as he, so that what ensues is a clumsy version of Simon says, with me on tiptoe stalking behind Robichaud, stepping where he stepped and struggling to maintain balance at each unadvertised stop. We see some of the birds we'd been listening to, hear a bar-backed partridge, and glimpse what might have been a pigeon of significance, but the light is poor and the bird streaks by too fast to confirm its identification. In the distance the *pop* of several isolated gunshots reminds us that we do not have the forest to ourselves.

March 1

Thong Sek

R obichaud says there was commotion in the night. Neither he
nor I heard the ruckus, because it started on the far side of
camp.

Since this was a one-night bivouac, the guides did not string their
tarps. By 4:00 a.m. falling dew had chilled them, making sleep
impossible, and so they gathered around the fire. When headlamps
came down the trail from the mountain, the three militiamen
scrambled for their rifles and with a few others gave chase. But the
interlopers—undoubtedly poachers—sprinted back up the mountain and vanished like deer. No one glimpsed more of them than
those first small lights in the darkness.

Now it is dawn, and the gibbons are just starting to find their
voices. To be as exact as possible, the gibbons we are hearing are
southern white-cheeked crested gibbons (*Nomascus siki*), but exact-
ness does not come easily in the taxonomy of gibbons. The boundaries between species and subspecies are dimly understood, and the
field-checking of assumptions about which species live where has
been sporadic.

Yesterday Robichaud recounted to me an obscene and misogy-
nistic Lao folktale explaining how the gibbon got its call:

A husband and wife are living by their rice field. A thief comes
and enters the hut. He fights with the husband. In their struggle, the husband pins the thief on his back, and the thief's
loincloth gapes open, revealing his privates. The wife likes

what she sees. And so when the husband shouts to her, "Give me the knife!" she hands it to him backwards. In the fury of the fight the husband can only hammer the thief with the handle, but the thief gains advantage of the knife and presses the blade into the husband's chest, piercing his heart. The wife now says to the victorious thief, "Take me with you," but the thief tells her, "Wretched woman, you just killed your husband; I want nothing to do with you!" Whereupon the wife realizes the horror of her actions and is overcome with remorse. She goes mad, and for the rest of her life she roams the forest, grieving for her husband, her *phua*. When she dies, her great sin causes her to be reincarnated as a lower life-form, a gibbon, and today all gibbons repeat her cry: *phua, phua, phua*.

Now, knowing the story, I hear more *phua* in the gibbons' call (pronounced with a hard *p*: *púa* to English speakers), but the song nevertheless retains a tinge of European police siren, a delicious taste of lunacy.

I walk again with Robichaud to survey birds and whatever else we might encounter. We perform another teetering (on my part) reenactment of Simon says. We log more drongos and barbets, an owl, a warbler, and some sly frogs that call to each other in the pitch range of birds. Robichaud says Thong Sek looks like northern Cambodia. Its scrawny, narrow-topped trees violate the arboreal rule that a tree will spread as wide as crowding will allow. These trees have lots of room and plenty of strength, yet they stay skinny. I am more than ever convinced that both Thong Sek and Thong Kouang are maintained in their open state by burning and that, for want of lightning, humans must be the source of ignition. Robichaud agrees, yet he says the guides and every villager he has asked disavow knowledge of people starting fires, notwithstanding that the effect of the fires is benign and adds much to the diversity of habitats. I wonder if they fear interference from the authorities if they own up to fire-starting.

The yellow sun of dawn is now high and white. Robichaud said he wanted to take this walk at 6:00 a.m.; we started at 6:45. He said he wanted the whole group ready to hit the trail at 7:00 a.m.; it is now 7:10, and we are out watching birds. Robichaud is unafflicted by the hobgoblin of foolish consistency that Emerson decried. Our unpunctuality even brings a prize: on our way back to camp a mob of white-crested laughingthrushes envelops us in their raucous party.

Everyone has eaten. The group waits only for Robichaud and me, and they have been good enough to leave us a breakfast of a few morsels of grilled meat—which I fear may be the last we will see— and a skewered rice cake apiece, heavily salted and roasted to crisp-ness. We take to the trail, munching.

Our order of march has changed. Robichaud goes first, as ever, but because an encounter with Vietnamese seems likely, Meet and Sone (who says his fever has abated) follow next with their weapons. Then me, and then the rest. We climb again as we did yesterday, up to and now past the sprawling poachers' camp, and along a trail strewn with decaying plastic bags and other litter. Obviously the Vietnamese crews feel no need to conceal their presence. They act as though the land belongs to them.

Bit by bit, Robichaud has been telling me the story of his two-week sojourn at Lak Xao with a living saola. After his trek across the Nakai Plateau, he joined a cadre of expat biologists bent on making an inventory of the country. One of the nonprofits supporting their efforts was the Wildlife Conservation Society (WCS), the renamed New York Zoological Society, based in the Bronx. Gradually, WCS folded Robichaud into its operations, and late in 1995 he was asked to coordinate its fledgling Lao country program. His boss was Alan Rabinowitz, an adventuring field biologist whom George Schaller had mentored and brought to WCS.

Soon after saola were discovered in Vietnam, biologists con-firmed the animals' existence in Laos. Again the evidence was a set of horns, which was spotted by biologist Bob Dobias, a former Peace Corps volunteer, early in 1993 in the village of Nakadok, just outside the northern boundary of what would soon be gazetted as the Nakai–Nam Theun National Biodiversity Conservation Area. (Designation as a national protected area came later.) Under the auspices of WCS and the Lao PDR Department of Forestry, Schaller and Rabinowitz surveyed NNT for saola in January of 1994, walking more than four hundred kilometers, examining along the way ten sets of horns, and collecting testimony from villagers about the habits of the animal. Their joint paper is one of the early scientific accounts of the species.[1]

Rabinowitz returned to Laos two years later to help Robichaud organize the WCS office and to prioritize areas for future survey.

Soon, however, events dictated a new set of plans.

Late on the evening of January 10, 1996, only a few days after Rabinowitz's arrival, two WCS contractors, Nancy Ruggeri and Matt Etter, pulled into Vientiane dirty and tired from yet another survey in Nakai–Nam Theun. Telephone service in Laos then ranged from bad to nonexistent, and they'd driven seven or eight hours from Lak Xao to tell a breathless tale: "You won't believe it," they said "There's an adult saola in the Lak Xao zoo." It had been delivered that day. They'd seen it. They had pictures.

By chance, Robichaud and Rabinowitz had reserved a helicopter for the next day in order to make an aerial survey of forest cover in the vicinity of NNT. They even planned to land and refuel in Lak Xao.

They flew out the next morning, paralleling the Mekong, down to the lush, rugged forests of NNT. They scanned a green sea of foliage from above, noting areas of primary forest, concentrations of swidden patches, and open wounds where pirate logging let the red earth show through. At last they set down in Lak Xao.

They would have called on General Cheng, but he was away on business in Hong Kong or Taiwan. As Ruggeri and Etter had said, the saola was there, looking somewhat battered from her capture. It was a female and an adult, a sight no Westerner had previously beheld. Cheng's people had installed the saola in a small pen about the size of a hotel room. Its previous occupant had been a serow. In the back was a shallow stone grotto that afforded modest shelter.

Robichaud and Rabinowitz began by collecting basic information. They learned that several days earlier, on January 8, a Hmong villager from Ban Nachalai, upslope from Lak Xao in Bolikhamxay Province, had captured the saola in anticipation of a reward from General Cheng. Not long before, the general, who had a passion for wildlife, put out word that he would pay the equivalent of one thousand US dollars for a live saola caught for his zoo. The villager had been hunting. His dogs scented the saola and gave chase. The saola ran to a stream, splashed into a pool, and turned at bay with a boulder at its back. The villager lassoed it. A runner was quickly dispatched to Lak Xao to notify General Cheng, and the next day the general sent his helicopter to retrieve the animal.

The saola had suffered multiple cuts, some of them possibly dog bites, on her barrel, rump, and legs, and she favored a rear foot, which might have been strained in the capture or bound too tightly during transport. One eye was also weepy, evidently injured. Otherwise she appeared healthy.

Robichaud knew what he needed to do. He told Rabinowitz that despite the administrative work that awaited him as head of a new program, "I think I should stay here and watch this thing around the clock and take notes on it."

Rabinowitz agreed: "You get off the helicopter and stay here. Keep me posted."

While Rabinowitz flew back to Vientiane, Robichaud took a room at the incongruous Phudoi ("mountainous area") Guest House, which was a Communist-modernist jumble of structural triangles, a Soviet echo of Le Corbusier plopped down in Lak Xao. It lent a touch of the surreal to an already otherworldly place. Besides the menagerie, Lak Xao supported a sort of boarding school for the children of tribal ethnics, also courtesy of General Cheng. It was supposed to showcase the cultural diversity of the general's domain, but the program was, to be polite, anthropologically incoherent, dressing up children from one ethnic group in the garb of another and demonstrating "rituals" that were cobbled together from any number of sources. One never knew how "voluntary" a child's enrollment might be, and given that no clear boundary existed between the children's dormitory and the pens and cages of the animals, the boarding school and the menagerie seemed uncomfortably similar. Beyond these few creations of the general, the rest of Lak Xao was as raw as a frontier town in a spaghetti western.

Robichaud set to the task of watching. His observation post was a chair about twenty feet from the saola's pen. He sat in it day after day, observing and writing. His primary emotion was awe: awe at the rareness, the beauty, the utter uniqueness of the animal and awe that he was there to see it, not to mention study it, for as long as fate would let him.

The Lak Xao saola was the first adult but not the first of its species to be observed outside its habitat. In 1994, in Vietnam, the Forest Inventory and Planning Institute acquired two saola calves, one of them not even weaned, and attempted to care for them at its campus outside Hanoi. After a few months, both died, having given up few secrets about their species. The full-grown female at Lak Xao presented a different kind of opportunity.

On occasion, taking pains not to upset her, Robichaud went into the cage to examine the saola more closely. He recorded her dimensions. Tallest height along the back: 38.4 inches; horns 17 inches long; length, head to rump, along the black dorsal stripe of the back, 60 inches. To his astonishment, the saola calmly let him stretch his tape around her neck, under her belly, along her back. She required no restraint.

Her color was medium chocolate brown, which paled at the neck and around the curve of the belly. Robichaud noted the chocolate-brown flesh of the nose. He peered into the round pupils of the eyes, and the dark brown irises shone orange in the beam of a flashlight.

He marveled at the extraordinary tongue, which was long enough for the saola to lick flies from her eyes and which was armed along its upper surface with fine, rearward-pointing barbs. Her form was thick and compact, good for pushing through dense vegetation. She had four mammae, like a cow, and white bands, like bracelets, just above her hooves. Her tricolored tail—brown, white, and black—was ten inches long. When relaxed against her body, it blended exactly into matching bands of color on her rump. She had a black chin strap and bold slashes of white across her face. Robichaud knew from the two FIPI juveniles and published descriptions of saola skins that not all these markings were fixed within the species but varied by individual.

No physical feature of the saola was more remarkable than a pair of large glands on either side of the muzzle, below the eyes. A thick muscular flap covered them, and the animal could raise and lower the flap, as though flaring a second large pair of nostrils. The glands produced a foul-smelling gray-green paste recalling the musk of weasels. Robichaud observed the saola scent-marking the walls of her grotto with this substance, and he also saw the glands flare open on the sole occasion when the saola became alarmed.

General Cheng's chauffeur had a lapdog, a rare sort of pet for anyone to bring to rough-and-tumble Lak Xao. Robichaud remembers it as "about as big as a decent-size Wisconsin farm cat." It was an old-lady dog, and Robichaud was in the pen beside the saola when the dog approached. The saola caught its scent and "freaked."

Says Robichaud, "Her back arched up like a cat's. She dropped her head to point her horns at the dog. Her eyes rolled up in the back of her head. Her tongue hung out. She drooled. She flared her premaxillary glands and started snorting and facing her horns wherever this dog went." The air reeked of musk from her facial glands. It was her species' inured reaction to canids—dholes and all their relatives—which hunters had reported. Oddly, although the saola was primed for battle, she paid no heed to the human standing next to her.

Robichaud cites this incident when people gainsay his most significant observation about the saola, which was her otherworldly disposition. Skeptics say that her behavior was mild because she was in shock from capture, injuries, and confinement. They argue that her abnormal state skewed her reaction to human contact. The scientific term for this is *post-capture myopathy*. Robichaud believes such a characterization fails to explain her surprising calmness, a trait said to be shared by other solitary tropical-forest mammals, including okapi. He argues that an animal deep in shock would have been incapable of instantly leaping to a heightened state of arousal, as the saola did when the lapdog happened by, and that it would have been comparatively numb to the perception of danger.

Yes, she had undergone the trauma of capture. Yes, she was in unfamiliar surroundings. She was certainly under stress, and Robichaud and others consequently tried to keep human contact to a minimum. But she was also eating, drinking, and monitoring her surroundings, behaving normally insofar as "normal" might be inferred for a creature about which so little was known, and, as the episode with the lapdog illustrates, she was capable of powerful responses.

Around humans she was serene. Robichaud was amazed that within a day of arriving at the menagerie (three days after capture) she showed no apprehension when he or others entered her cage, and she calmly accepted food from the hand. When he first touched her, she would jerk up her head, like a horse rejecting the bridle, but within a day or two, such resistance was gone. He could not only touch her but stroke her, and she did not flinch.

In nearby cages, a serow and a muntjac, both residents of the menagerie for more than a year, skittered away at the first sign of human approach. The saola seemed to belong to a different universe. She was already tamer than any domestic goat, sheep, or cow Robichaud had known.

A Buddhist monk from a nearby temple came to see her, and he and Robichaud fell to talking. The monk said local people had a nickname for saola. It was not a term that Sek or Brou or Hmong would use, but certain Lao speakers in the area called the creature *sat souphap*, which translates roughly as "the polite animal." Saola, according to the monk, move slowly and quietly through the forest. They are never *khi-deu*, which is how you might describe a mischievous child. They even eat politely, cleanly nipping off the leaves they select, never tearing the foliage with a yank of the head, as other browsing animals do. Various hunters have confirmed this trait. They say, in fact, that where a certain plant that saola favor is found with its leaves cleanly and uniformly nipped off, saola are sure to have been present. The monk said that Hmong villagers had captured two other saola the previous August or September and without difficulty had kept them virtually as pets for two weeks before undertaking to walk the animals sixty kilometers to Lak Xao. Unfortunately, the saola died along the way.

Days passed. Robichaud kept his vigil. On the rare occasion when he entered the pen, the saola let him pick ticks from her ears. She conveyed a sense of stoicism, seeming to Robichaud almost Buddhist in the way she reconciled herself to her situation. Because of her calm, he decided to name her Martha, after Martha Schwartz, head of finance at WCS in New York. The human Martha oversaw the flow of money for fifty programs scattered around the globe, some of which were led by acknowledged "silverbacks"—alpha males who never doubted that their priorities should top everyone's list. Amid storms of clamorous urgency, Martha Schwartz remained imperturbable, cool, and patient. In Robichaud's view, Martha the saola, except for her agitation when the dog came near, seemed equally serene.

But serenity did not guarantee health, and no one anywhere in the world, let alone in Lak Xao, had more than a rudimentary understanding of the animal's needs. WCS could have dispatched a highly qualified veterinarian from Thailand, but the global significance of the situation prompted the organization to send out its best from New York. After several days of hard travel, Billy Karesh, the head of the WCS field veterinary program, arrived in Lak Xao and examined

"Martha," Lak Xao, 1996. (Courtesy William Robichaud / WCS)

Martha on January 22, exactly two weeks after her capture. He noted "two 3-mm corneal ulcers and corneal edema on right eye" and applied antibiotic ointment. Her cuts and abrasions "on head, neck, thorax, flanks, rump, and legs" were healing well. It looked as though the Hmong, or someone, had treated Martha's wounds with a topical powder, possibly gunpowder. Martha also occasionally coughed, and through the stethoscope Karesh heard "increased respiratory sounds throughout both lung fields"—she was wheezing, a result of a mild pneumonia. He discontinued the antibacterial injections of Rocephin that a local self-styled vet had started her on and shifted to a combination of different antibiotics, administered orally.[2] In one case he smeared medicine on her muzzle and allowed her to lick it off. Other drugs he dissolved in water and syringed into her mouth. In his notes, he wrote, "Animal accepts readily." He also wrote, "Animal is poorly muscled, thin."

General Cheng had wisely ordered local Hmong near Lak Xao to bring in a steady supply of food appropriate for saola. All subsistence people know their environments intimately, but even by the standards of the subsistence world, Hmong are acknowledged masters of nature observation. The Hmong regularly delivered browse for Martha. Robichaud noted at least three plant species among the bundles. It seemed to be the right stuff. Martha ate it, and Karesh wrote, "Animal bright and alert. Feces and urine normal, good appetite for browse."

Karesh observed Martha for three days, during which her lungs cleared up and the corneal swelling in her right eye subsided. Unfortunately, some damage to her eye appeared to remain, and she may have suffered partial loss of vision. Before Karesh left, he and Robichaud met with General Cheng. Keep doing what you are doing, Karesh advised, keep feeding native vegetation, but try to increase both the volume and the diversity of the food. Martha appeared healthy, but Karesh was worried. Carried on foot from saola habitat to Lak Xao, the foliage delivered to Martha was hardly fresh. And the feeding protocol followed by General Cheng's staff consisted merely of tossing a mass of greenery into her cage, where it lay on the ground, wilting more. Martha ate, but retrospectively everyone agreed that she did not eat enough, either in quantity or, probably, in quality.

Years later Robichaud spoke with a zoologist who supervised a captive-breeding program for okapi, another forest-dwelling browser. Steve Shurter of the White Oak conservation center in Yulee, Florida, told him that okapi eat at least 130 different species of plants in their native Ituri Forest, in the Congo basin, and in the absence of advanced dietary supplements they require at least thirty of these on a monthly basis to maintain health. If the saola's requirements were remotely similar, Martha would never have prospered on a diet of three species of plants. In addition to wasting away from too little food, she probably suffered nutritional deficiencies.

Two days after Karesh departed Lak Xao, on the evening of January 26, Martha suddenly experienced an episode of diarrhea. Previously, her stools had been normal. Robichaud remembers the evening as dark and cold. Martha looked glassy-eyed. He had seen her lie down many times, but always with her legs tucked beneath her, like a camel. She would put her muzzle on the ground straight ahead, her posture precise and composed. Now, however, she lay down and flopped to the side, head on the ground.

General Cheng brought in a local vet, who may have given Martha fluids. They got her back on her feet, although she looked unsteady. Cheng returned to his house, and the vet and everyone else departed, while Robichaud alone remained. It was late afternoon. He watched as she again lay down and rolled to her side. He watched the rise and fall of her belly. He continued to watch as the movement gradually slowed, and then, at dusk, it stopped. Robichaud went into the cage to confirm that she was dead. Then he walked to General Cheng's house, thirty meters away, to deliver the news. It was a Friday in January, and Eastertide was, of course, months away. Nevertheless, Robichaud remembers it as Good Friday, the end of a passion.

In the morning he returned as members of the staff were taking Martha out of her cage.

"What are you going to do with her?"

"We are going to cut her up. Cook her. Eat her." They also said they would preserve the skin and head, as General Cheng intended to have a standing mount of Martha prepared for display.

Robichaud continued to observe. The Hmong had said she was pregnant, and Karesh had agreed it was possible but was not certain. The Hmong proved to be right. Robichaud watched as Martha's butchers removed a male fetus from her abdomen. It was white and hairless and beautifully formed, even to the bony cranial buds, where horns would have grown.

Rumor soon compounded the misfortune of Martha's death. The Hmong had warned that injections would harm a pregnant saola, and word spread among General Cheng's staff that Martha had died because of injections Karesh had given her. But Karesh had given her none, and he stated so in a pair of apologetic faxes to General Cheng. Opinions, however, did not change. Perhaps Karesh had been seen taking a blood sample or squirting antibiotic solution into Martha's mouth with a syringe, and the wrong conclusion was drawn. Observers also might have confused him with the earlier vet who had injected Martha with Rocephin. In any case, the outsider from far away made an inviting target for blame.

About six months later, General Cheng acquired a second saola. He kept it in a larger pen, back at the edge of the forest, away from prying eyes and meddling foreigners, but this one failed to survive even as long as Martha. After the death of the second saola, the general announced he was withdrawing his offer of reward. He wanted no more saola captured and brought to him. It was the right thing to do, lest more animals perish.

Robichaud eventually calculated that, in addition to Martha and the two juveniles in Hanoi, at least ten other saola were captured in Vietnam and Laos in the mid-1990s. All died, except for one that was released back to the wild by its captors. Both Vietnam and Lao PDR soon banned further captures.

In the WCS office in Vientiane, I saw Martha's baby. It was in a large jar atop a bulky cabinet in a back room. Someone had double-sealed the lid with duct tape, but the tape was dry and cracking. No doubt the intent had been to prevent evaporation of the dusky preservative in which the fetus swam. Based on photos of the fetus, Karesh and others estimated that Martha was in her second trimester when she died. The baby was about the size of a rabbit, pale and compact. Its nose was inexpressibly delicate, the hooves sharp and perfect, the soft eyes eternally closed. Notwithstanding dust and casual storage, the contents of that jar represent the most complete specimen of *Pseudoryx* that humanity possesses. All the organs and soft tissue are there. Every other saola specimen—and there are only a few—is literally skin and bones. Given the endangerment of saola throughout its range, Martha's baby may turn out to be the most complete evidence that humanity will ever possess of the species' presence on Earth. It abides behind a barrier of peeling duct tape in a dusty jar, unborn and forever floating.

It is impossible not to admire the Vietnamese. They work hard for what they take. Our journey up the dry mountain out of Thong Sek follows the best trail we've yet encountered. It is marked with blazes and even directional signs, which are written in Vietnamese. It is also well worn, and, on high alert for poachers, we speed along.

When we stop near the top of the mountain to rest, I discover that Viengxai has monkeyed with my backup water bottle. He may have opened the bottle to investigate its filter, which rattles slightly, and failed to screw the top back on securely. Nearly half a liter has sloshed out. I transfer the bottle to my daypack, as I should have done from the start.

After the trail crosses the spine of the mountain and dips down toward the Nam Nyang, it takes us through a south-facing dipterocarp forest with trees as stately as any we have seen. But again, we do not tarry to appreciate them.

I may be distracted by the open grace of the forest or by the call of a silver pheasant, when I embarrass myself. We are clipping along at our usual running-late-to-a-meeting pace, and I have just congratulated myself that I am holding up, feeling good, doing my part. Then *boom*. I trip on a root and go down like a redwood. Fortunately the ground is soft. I land in a push-up position, with no injury except to my pride. I hear Viengxai crack some kind of joke in Lao or Sek, which looses a ripple of tittering down the line. Robichaud whips around and casts him a glare, then sees that I am nearly back on my feet, and keeps marching.

Finally we hear the sound of water, and the trail breaks into sun-light. We crowd onto a low bluff overlooking the Nam Nyang, which dashes before us down a channel of gunmetal boulders. "Look at the fishing!" cries Meet, and there is a happy murmur of agreement. Robichaud is smiling but regretful. "It is only a quarter to ten," he says. "We could have made it here yesterday, easy. As it is, we are now almost a day behind where we need to be, and it all goes back to that late start from Ban Nameuy."

Robichaud's words hang in the air as we take in the walls of intense green, bright in the sunlight, that line the limpid river on either side. The water-smooth rocks gleam. Stream babble and the chirr of insects fill our ears. Robichaud juts his chin toward the river and its verdant canyon. "Apart from a downed US pilot or a totally lost Soviet timber cruiser," he says, "ours are probably the first blue eyes ever to look at this place."

I want to drink it in and also have a drink, maybe fill my filtered water bottle. But there will be no pausing here; we must make up lost time. Meet gestures toward a felled tree that bridges the river, and Robichaud leads off, muttering over his shoulder, "Not many vil-lagers come here. Wish I could say that about the Vietnamese." He points to the stump of the tree, which has been axed down to make the bridge. "Out here, only Vietnamese work that hard."

The span is forty feet long and the tree trunk roughly sixteen inches in diameter. Two thick lines of ants swarm along it, one going, one coming. They almost cover the walking surface, and we cannot help but trample them, making the narrow span slippery with their remains. The bridge is sited high above the river—to avoid flood stage in the rainy season—and a fall to the boulders and water below would have ugly consequences. An image of Mr. Mang's arm flashes through my mind. One ant-crushing step at a time, I wobble across, sensing that I am not alone in trepidation. Should I fall, everyone will be affected, for the care of a serious injury would require group effort. Happily, everyone crosses without incident.

On the far side, the trail bends east, destination Vietnam, and begins to climb the canyon wall. Before the day is out, we will call it the Rosewood Highway. For now, we hope that it might drift north-ward, to our left, contouring the slope and maintaining contact with the river, but with every twist it disappoints us. It keeps climbing, climbing, veering well south of the river's line.

The day has warmed considerably. My pocket thermometer reads just shy of ninety degrees Fahrenheit. Everyone else seems unaf-fected by the muggy heat, but my shirt is as wet as though I had dived into a pool. Olay, as usual, is enclosed in his rain jacket. Simeuang wears his brown turtleneck with the torn shoulder, look-ing as refreshed as when we broke camp. I am like an Arctic sled dog among coyotes. At home in the arid lands of New Mexico and Arizona, I count on being at least as water-thrifty as anyone I travel with, but here my thermostat is confusingly out of kilter. I am over-heating and streaming water from every pore, and I begrudge Viengxai the water he has wasted.

It would be easier to pace myself if I knew when we might again reach water or take a rest. Not speaking Lao, I understand nothing of Robichaud's periodic discussions with Simeuang and Meet and so never learn of such expectations or, for that matter, of where and when we will camp. But today I am not alone. Today no one else has the least idea, either. We will find water when we find it; we will rest when we must; we will camp when we camp.

A fly buzzing at my left ear joins the expedition. I prefer its com-pany to that of Viengxai, who follows me only inches behind. The fly, always on the left, hovers close by me for a kilometer, maybe farther. The trail keeps bearing away from the river. Every forty min-utes or so, Robichaud calls a halt to check our position. He has a problem. We have two sets of maps, at two separate scales, and the data from his GPS places us in substantially different locations on each one. There is evidently some problem of calibration. One loca-tion is right; the other is wrong, but we don't know which, and the difference matters. The trail we are on, the Rosewood Highway, is preferable to any kind of bushwhacking, but unless it soon bends northward, it will take us ever farther from our destination, which is the upper Nam Nyang. At some point we will have to forgo the convenience of the trail and plunge into the tangle of forest on our left, through which, down precipitous slopes, the river lies. Picking the right point of departure requires knowing where we are.

We travel. We stop. We travel. We stop. At each stop the maps fail to agree. Meet says, "I never went to school. I can't help you with your maps." He draws his own map on the ground, scratching the Nam Nyang and the arc of the trail with a stick, placing a rock to represent Phou Vang. "But from where we are—here," Robichaud asks, "does the trail get closer to the river or farther away?" Meet doesn't know.

Robichaud has been hatching and rehatching plans all the way up the ridge. One scheme involves an early break down to the river, with time for the guides to fish before sundown, setting a comfortable camp, and, after a day of recon, taking a smaller group to establish a fly camp and reconnoiter farther upstream for another few days. It happens that Touy needs to return to Nakai and Vientiane before the rest of us to say good-bye to his girlfriend, who is leaving for law school in Indonesia. Even this contingency fit the plans. Robichaud would send Touy back early to Ban Nameuy with Viengxai guiding him, thereby sparing the rest of us Viengxai's increasingly disruptive company.

But the attractions of the Rosewood Highway have pulled us too far from the river for that scheme to work. We'll do well to get to the river today, and it appears we must do so, for we have found no water on the mountain. This is a matter of concern for me, for my water bottles, save for a pair of swallows that I refuse to touch, are now both dry.

Robichaud ventures another idea: we'll send scouts, without their loads, in two directions—up the trail and down to the river—and base a decision on their reports.

Meet doesn't like that idea. He says we shouldn't split up. We should all go forward, on the trail.

146

Everyone edges closer to hear the discussion.

Robichaud counters, "We made it to the Nam Nyang easy this morning in only a couple of hours. Last night you said we wouldn't get to the river until eight o'clock."

"We wouldn't as long as we stop and look for birds all the time."

"Viengxai says I go too fast. You say I go too slow!"

Laughter erupts. Simeuang points out that the Vietnamese built the Rosewood Highway to get rosewood to Vietnam. The trail is not going to sacrifice altitude or direction to curve down to the river. Nevertheless, the decision is made: we'll go Meet's way, forward, keeping to the trail.

We travel, but the distance and conditions begin to blur. Have we gone fifteen kilometers since we crossed the Nam Nyang or twenty? Thirst has dulled my mind and tunneled my vision. All I can do is move my feet, which I do robotically, as half hours and hours accumulate. Then suddenly I almost collide with the man in front of me. Robichaud has stopped at an unremarkable twist of the trail. He does not consult the arguing maps. After exchanging a few syllables with Meet and Simeuang, he steps off the trail into the deep bush, and we follow.

All through the trip I have been trying to purge the word *jungle* from my mind. Robichaud never uses it. He speaks only of the *forest*, although when I asked him about it, he conceded that *jungle* might refer to a patch of forest particularly dense and entwined. He also said *jungle* sounded to him a trifle melodramatic, as though it made the woods more hostile than they had to be. Certainly, in the literature I've read from the Vietnam War, I cannot remember anyone writing about a forest—everything that was not paddy or village was described as jungle.

The same seems true of most Western accounts of central Africa, Amazonia, and any other wooded, tropical place. During many a dull hour plodding up the Rosewood Highway, I have wondered if a jungle, beyond Robichaud's definition of a bad tangle, might simply be "a forest not your own." Maybe it is analogous to an unappreciated swamp or bog, which through a different lens becomes a wetland. In a jungle the observer feels alien; his apprehension draws the trees closer, enlaces the vines more tightly, blots out the guidance of the sun, and shortens the field of view. On this trek I want to travel in forest, not jungle, and to resist apprehension. I want to make the forest if not my own then at least a sibling of other lands where I have felt comfortable.

For days we have been journeying through stands of trees that are sometimes inspiring and grand, other times dense and overgrown, a patchwork much like bottomlands I have tramped along brown-water rivers in the Carolinas. Plagued by mosquitoes and water moccasins, nemeses we are mercifully spared here, those woods nevertheless became forests for me. But not these, not yet.

Robichaud arrows across the slope and down. The group spreads out, each man clambering as best he can. The mountainside, like others we have traversed, is a series of sloping benches with steep pitches between. The benches are well soiled and give good footing, but where the land breaks, the scarp proves no more than a mound of rubble masked by a carpet of leaves. Dehydrated and fatigued, I stumble drunkenly. The trick on a slope like this, as in chess, is to see as many moves ahead as possible, but in this mass of lianas and saplings and fallen debris, I foresee nothing. When I choose my own path, the trip logs and garrotes of thorned vines stagger me. And so blindly I follow now Meet, now Sone, whoever is closest, and try to mimic that person's slalom down the slope. But where he strides, I slide; where he ducks, I lurch. Reaching out to steady myself and check my momentum, I realize, too late, that the slender trunk I am about to grab bristles with thorns. At the point of falling, I lunge for a different sapling, a different shade of bark, surely a safe one — and sink my hand into a living skin of ants.

Our band develops a zigzag rhythm: head east along a bench, then north down the break, then east again, and north. The hard going gets the better of me, and I fall again, and the slick of sweat on my arms reddens along the saw marks of briars, but now there is no tittering from the guides. Although the young ones bounded down like deer at the start of our descent, now, a kilometer later, every member of our group strains with the work, panting and footsore, eager to hear the sound of the river, which will announce our reprieve. But the river does not speak.

It may be Simeuang who notices that the group has split. He calls to Robichaud, who halts. Half the guides are missing. We whoop and whistle. Silence. We sit a while, guiltily thankful to rest but worried about the others. This is no place, late in the day, to lose contact with any part of the team, to say nothing of the supplies they carry. We are short of water, daylight, and energy, and we lack the means to conduct a search safely or well. The leaders whoop again. And again. Finally we hear a faint answer from above and behind. I see the orange wink of a T-shirt through a snarl of green. It resolves into a person — Bone, I think, atop the last bench. Gradually he and the others straggle in.

With everyone accounted for, we start anew, more slowly. In forty minutes we hear the river. Soon we see its sparkle through masses of foliage, but the descent to water is nearly vertical. We reach into the tops of trees and shinny down the trunks or descend ladders of flood-torn branches and roots to reach the water's edge. I fill my water bottle and drink a liter straight off. I am nearly through a second liter when Olay walks by. He looks a little peaked. "How are you doing?" I ask.

"Okay. And you?"

"Good," I say, and Simeuang, two paces away and rummaging in his pack, overhears this and laughs.

"Good!" he mocks, gasping and throwing back his head. "Good!" and he throws his forearm to his brow in a gesture of exhaustion. "Good!" Olay and Simeuang laugh, and I laugh with them, not least because I do feel good, sitting blessedly still, whipped but intact, feeling the water infuse into my body and come out through my skin in a clean new rush of cooling sweat. Today by the map, at first on a smugglers' highway and then in rough terrain, we have covered twenty-seven kilometers, including quite a lot of altitude gained and lost. For the guides, Simeuang, and the boys, and perhaps for Robichaud, it may have been just another day's work, albeit a hard one, but for me, an oldish fellow from the cool, dry Rockies, it was a very long haul through a steamy and inhospitable — I'll say it now — *jungle*.

The inner canyon of the Nam Nyang presses its walls against the river channel, offering little flat ground. We squeeze in at an abandoned poachers' camp on an overgrown ledge twenty feet above the river. Robichaud is in good spirits. Our indecision on the Rosewood Highway, which delayed our descent to the river, caused us to strike the Nam Nyang far up in its watershed. At the cost of a grueling trek, we have returned to our original schedule, in the place and on the day he intended. The sloppy departure from the villages has been negated. We have won back a day.

Dinner — no surprise — consists of sticky rice and a few small, bony fish that Bone and the other Ban Beuk teenagers netted from the river. We eat in falling darkness. I am edging stiffly toward my tent, thinking longingly of my sleeping bag, when Robichaud steps out of the gloom. "How about a night survey?" he asks. "No moon, fair weather — conditions are too good to pass up."

I swallow, hesitate. "Sure," I say, having no notion of what I have agreed to.

Our survey consists of boulder hopping in the dark, moving upriver in silence, playing the beams of our headlamps on shorelines and treetops, hoping to see red or yellow eyes staring back into the light. "Two people make twice the noise of one," he cautions, so Robichaud goes twenty yards ahead of me, promising to blink his light if he sees anything interesting. We hope to encounter a slow loris, a colugo, or some other placid denizen of the treetops. We clamber and leap on dark rocks; we walk calf deep in the shallows, trying to make no splash. I hardly look at the trees; all my energy goes to staying upright and silent, until we pause to pan the treetops with our headlamps. Sadly, no luck. In an hour and a half of wading pools and bounding from rock to rock, no eyes shine back at us.

At last comes the crawl into bed. I have pitched my tent on a postage stamp of ground sandwiched by skinny trees. Overhead a tight circle of sky pours starlight through the canopy. A clan of frogs chants from the river. Half of them croak "Heh." Then others, as though in contradiction, croak "Hah." It is a slow and passionless debate: "Heh," and "Hah," repeat, repeat, repeat. The soporific descant has the rhythm of a tired heart.

March 2

Nam Nyang, Camp 1

Gibbons call far downstream at the edge of hearing, their songs drifting ghostly in the half-light. Delicious minutes pass as the singing continues, then dawn brightens, and their cries fade like dreams. Close to camp, barbets and a grey peacock pheasant start up. Full day begins.

We have at last reached saola habitat, or what we hope is saola habitat. The plan is for separate teams to survey two upstream tributaries that feed the Nam Nyang. We'll look for tracks in the streamside sands and also for plants that have been nipped in the saola's telltale manner.

But trouble in camp thwarts an early start.

Mok Keo reports to Simeuang that our stores of rice are badly depleted. Evidently some of the guides, led by Viengxai, cook an additional meal after the rest of us have gone to bed. They've done this every night. On hearing the news, Robichaud does his best to swallow his anger; still, his eyes look pained and his jaw muscles are tight. "It is so often like this. They say they want to go into the forest, and you tell them how many days it will be, but as soon as they can, they start eating up the supplies so they can go home sooner." It seems we are now short by several days' rations.

The camp manager, in this case Simeuang, and the senior guide, Mok Keo, are supposed to monitor both supplies and the guides' behavior, but laxity has been the rule. Once, years ago, a camp manager on a survey with Timmins and Robichaud actually engineered the sabotage of provisions. It turned out that he was much besotted with a young woman back at home. He could not bear to be away from her, or perhaps he could not bear the thought of other men around her. Whenever Timmins and Robichaud left camp to look for wildlife, he and the unoccupied guides feasted like rats in a granary. Olay's father, Bounthavy, then worked for WCS as a driver. Bounthavy was a fixer; he got things done. He saw through all pretense, and no one could deceive him. Robichaud promoted him to camp boss, and from that day forward there was no more provision-raiding or malingering in the field. Lamentably, Bounthavy has not come with us to the Nam Nyang.

Robichaud calls the guides together to say that supplies are not to be touched except at established mealtimes. Viengxai stands off at a distance, idly hacking a tree with his machete. I watch him with resentment. He stands near enough to hear but far enough away to demonstrate contempt for the group. Essentially he has turned his back on any question of responsibility or blame. The meeting ends with a general feeling of discomfort.

Robichaud assigns Touy to stay in camp and guard against mischief. He also instructs Simeuang henceforward to sleep with the rice sacks in his tent if necessary.

Even with Touy remaining in camp, we are anxious about our gear. The previous day, in an exchange of banter, Viengxai asked Robichaud for more cigarettes. Robichaud answered, "I don't smoke."

"But I know you have them. I saw them in your pack."

It was true. Robichaud kept a small stash for use as gifts, deep in his pack, buried among twenty kilos of miscellany. Viengxai must have searched the pack. Robichaud was flabbergasted. "I have never had one of these guys go through my stuff before." The realization brought considerable dismay. Over many years, he said, the scores of Lao guides he had traveled with had been good companions, many superb. But now a bad apple seemed to be corrupting the spirit of our team.

Meanwhile, I knew Viengxai had picked through my stuff because, apart from the mishap of the water bottle, I'd repeatedly found the placement of ditty bags and other gear rearranged and reordered. Nothing had been taken from either of us, but perhaps the time for taking had not arrived. We worried that while we hunted saola in the forest, Viengxai might hunt for other things among our goods. So we stowed everything in our tents and "locked" them. Using scraps of orange twine that Robichaud claimed was the only orange twine in camp, we tied our tent zippers closed in such a way that they could not be opened without the twine being cut. To the zippers of the two tents Robichaud affixed notes that said in Lao DO NOT ENTER.

On mine I added, in English, MAY A TICK CRAWL UP YOUR PENIS.

Simeuang, Sone, and Olay head out to investigate a side stream roughly opposite camp. Robichaud, Meet, and I will ascend the river past the farthest limit of our night survey and search for sign of saola along a second tributary draining from the back of Phou Vang.

The riverbed, in the present dry season, is a population of limestone boulders laced with pools and twisting channels. The dry rocks range from gray to white and are black when wet, fluted and sleekly carved, like melons scooped with a spoon. The riverbed rises in stages, a pattern known as pool and drop. We clamber up a rockfall, then stroll a bedrock plain. Another rockfall, another plain. The water level has been falling, and where the flats have recently dried, the egg cases of regiments of insects, now hatched and flown, remain cemented to the rock. The bedrock in many places is potholed with concavities of perfect roundness, like boreholes for wells. These must be the locations of recurrent eddies, where flood-stage whirlpools, with an abrasive slurry of gravel at their bottoms, drill down into the rock. Some of the holes are dry, but many hold water and are connected to each other by lateral fissures and subsurface channels. I look in one and see a fish swim by. Farther along, we come to a slab of Swiss-cheese rock that floodwaters have broken loose and tilted vertically, so that its pothole is a porthole, a chest-high window on the river.

We stop to consult the map. Swiftlets swarm overhead, as thick as mosquitoes above a pond. In the forest on river left an Indian cuckoo chants, "One more bottle. One more bottle." From river right we hear the shouts of a red-vented barbet: "Wow! Wow!" The canyon is loud and bright, but Robichaud is concerned that he's seen no otter scat on the rocks near the big pools, where the water is deep. We see plenty of fish in the shadowy depths. The habitat should be ideal for the acrobatic weasels, but none seems present. There is only one conclusion: "The Vietnamese have trapped them out."

The side stream we seek is only a kilometer ahead. As we climb, the shelves of potholed rock become less ordered, more broken. Tossed by floods, their seeming portholes give them the look of scuttled ships. On them grows a thin layer of moss, which is invisible when dry, but with the least moisture, even the dampness of a sandal sole, it becomes as slippery as grease. We jump from one canted slab to another, judging carefully the distance, the slope, and the probable purchase of the landing. Sometimes we carom from the face of a rock too steep to land on in order to reach a boulder where we can. Where the riverbed resembles the contorted pavement of an earthquaked highway, we teeter like tightrope walkers along uptilted spines of rock. We climb laddered cascades where every toehold and handhold threatens to give way. At one treacherous passage, Robichaud calls out, "Black ice here!" although of course it is not black ice but rather the tropical equivalent in frictionless algae. Anyone who tried to cross it and failed would slide down a slant of rock into a crevice whose bottom we cannot see. We skirt the edge of the algae patch, feet slipping uncontrollably, by pulling ourselves along on roots and limbs that hang from the riverbank.

Robichaud has reached the mouth of the side stream. He whistles for Meet and me to come on. Almost immediately we encounter the remains of yet another Vietnamese camp. Then, a little farther, a glint of metal catches our eye. Implausibly, three scraps of aluminum lie half buried in flood wrack from the tributary. We dig them out. They are twisted and mud-stained. It seems likely they once rimmed some kind of circular opening. Rivet holes are spaced along the outside edges. A rounded fold completes the inner edge.

Nakai–Nam Theun held no strategic importance during America's Vietnam War, but Mu Gia Pass, where the Ho Chi Minh Trail veered from North Vietnam into Laos, lies immediately south of the protected area, not far as a jet flies. Virtually every square foot of Mu Gia was bombed to a fare-thee-well. No other place saw worse. If you look at the map for unexploded ordnance in Vietnam and Laos, Mu Gia is a solid mass of red. It had so much UXO that after the war, bomb-removal teams declined to bid on clearing it. It was simply too dangerous. The engineers who finally restored transportation through that part of the mountains ultimately cut a new pass, which was cheaper and safer than restoring the old one.

Although NNT wasn't a target and didn't lie on a regular flight path, pilots might have flown over it if they were lost, disabled, or scouting. Even B-52s, having dropped their loads on Hanoi or Haiphong, might have headed home this way to bases in Thailand. There was also the CIA's disgraceful Secret War, centered farther north, in Laos, for which air support came from units that officially did not exist and that operated from places that could not be found on anyone's map. In our weeks in NNT, we have seen not a single aircraft overhead, nor have we heard any. But in the late 1960s and early 1970s, the skies above the Nam Nyang were unlikely to have been so empty.

Possibly the scraps of aluminum we found had washed down from the wreckage of a plane on a shoulder of Phou Vang, or they came from an ejected external fuel tank or other discarded equipment.

In more populous areas, such artifacts would have been scavenged. Odd scraps of metal might be refashioned as digging or cutting tools, kitchenware, or patches over holes in a floor, or they might be traded to a scrapper for a few kip. Robichaud recalls that on a survey near Mu Gia he occasionally heard something like distant thunder, although the day was clear and the sound seemed to come from the plain below, not the sky. His guide explained that teams of villagers were at work hunting for unexploded bombs. When they found one, they dug a hole beneath it, made a fire in the hole, stoked it, and retired to a place of safety. If the fire was hot enough and burned long enough, the bomb exploded. Then the villagers gathered the shrapnel, which they sold to itinerant metal buyers. Of course, exploding bombs was risky—sometimes the digging jostled a trigger or the fire required more fuel at the wrong moment. There were accidents.

There were even more accidents with the tennis-ball-size cluster bombs that the Lao, borrowing a word from English, call bombies. A few hundred bombies filled a pod, and a pod looked like an ordinary bomb. A plane might carry an array of pods. When dropped, the pods split open in midair, scattering bombies over a large area, the idea being to constrain the movement of enemy troops and supplies. Some were designed to lie dormant until stepped on. Others were supposed to explode on contact with the ground but had a dismal detonation rate, leaving many more dormant. The United States dropped a colossal number of bombies on Laos, approximately 270 million— roughly one for every American back in the States and a hundred for every Lao then living. Nearly a third of them failed to go off. After the war ended, eighty million bombies lay unexploded in Lao soils. Over the ensuing decades many of them greeted the ill-placed foot, the probing of a farmer's shovel, or the curiosity of a child with flesh-shredding vehemence. They made the landscape evil. Civilian post-war casualties in Laos run well into the tens of thousands, and each of those victims has been wholly innocent, many of them children. The gift of bombies, and all the agony, amputation, and fatality that comes with them, is one that few Americans know they have made, but more than forty years later it is a gift that keeps on giving.

We leave behind the metal scraps and start up the creek, where the footing soon deteriorates. It is always my left foot that goes truant, sliding out from me on moss, dead leaves, wet stone, or, as it does now, on stone that wears the invisible coat of algae that imparts slickness to everything at this altitude. The streambed is no more than twenty yards wide, and the humidity of the forest lubricates what stream flow does not.

Robichaud scans the streamsides for certain plants and for shoals where sand or mud might accumulate and reveal tracks. Unfortunately we encounter none of the first and little of the second. One small spit of mud betrays signs of a hog badger rooting for worms, but in general the creek is too steep and flood-washed to hold the material that would record a track. The stream banks, too, tell us nothing, for they are a solid mass of roots. We are disappointed, but the morning is pleasant and no leeches have appeared. The chirping of frogs brackets us fore and aft as we make our way upstream.

I count three Vietnamese camps in the last kilometer. The creek has steepened, and now the height of the waterfalls is greater than the length of the shelves between them. Climbing their wet scarps is like scaling a slick-bark tree in the rain. On one, I carefully copy Robichaud's handholds and footholds: a grip on a knob of rock here, toes in a damp hollow there, then stretch up to grab the edge of a bowl of gravel, but the edge of the bowl breaks off, and I slide harmlessly down a dozen messy feet. I elect to take a more laborious route up the wall of vine and scrub that encloses the creek and join the others on the ledge above. Previously I'd told Robichaud that if it looked like I might slow him down, I would stop and wait while he and Meet continued upward. Now, I say, this looks like the place to do so. I'll let the saola come to me.

All right, he replies, but first we'll eat our lunch together.

Our plastic bags contain sticky rice in roasted cakes, and for each of us a grilled fish not much larger than a man's thumb, mostly head and skeleton. While we pick bones from our teeth, Robichaud says he had a powerful dream the night before. He dreamt that at a banding site he caught a bald eagle, a magnificent, proud, fierce bird, the first he'd ever captured, amid circumstances that were bizarre and full of portent. The dream left him feeling optimistic. He adds that the Lao believe that dreams about dangerous animals, especially snakes, bring good luck. "Maybe I should have dreamt about a cobra."

Meet lets me look at his rifle. It is Soviet-made, with Cyrillic letters marking the on-off setting for automatic fire. He says it is the
third AK-47 he's been issued in a little more than a decade. Con-
tinuing the show-and-tell, Robichaud pulls his field book from a
cargo pocket. He keeps several ten-thousand-kip notes and a picture

*Meet (right) and author climbing a Nam Nyang tributary. (Courtesy
William Robichaud)*

of Martha in it. He shows the picture to Meet and asks if he's ever seen a saola. No, Meet answers. He's only heard about them. What about dhole? Robichaud asks.

Meet says the area used to have dhole, but they are gone now—they all died, perhaps of some disease. Packs of dhole used to take a few buffalo—no one had cattle in those days, and tigers used to kill an occasional pig or other livestock. That was twenty years ago, when he was a boy. He is thirty-three now.

Then Meet makes the spectacular statement that dhole would urinate on a trail, and fumes from their urine would blind sambar and muntjac, making them easy to kill. He says that when he was ten, he used to see places around the village where dholes had rested and slept. About that time, somebody in the village shot a large cat; he can't remember if it was a tiger or a leopard. Everybody came to see the carcass. That was roughly the same time that a large cat, maybe the same one, came into a house in Ban Nameuy and bit someone on the arm, perhaps trying to drag him off. Now the big cats are pretty much gone, he admits, and in his opinion it is just as well.

Not much later, Robichaud and Meet leave to continue their journey up the creek, and I begin to jot down what Robichaud has lately told me of saola habitat and behavior. But my eyes are heavy. I am too drowsy, or too lazy, to write.

A shaft of sunlight falls on a patch of dry, flat rock. My pack makes a pillow. I stretch out, giving in to gravity, my weight on warm stone. In no time, I am asleep.

Points of interest:

• One way to think of saola is to imagine an ancestral not-quite cow, not-quite antelope back amid the eons of the Miocene, between five and twenty-three million years ago. The Earth is changing. Forests that are far more extensive than those of the present have begun to yield to grasslands and savannas. Ancestors of today's bovids venture into the new habitats, taking advantage of a grass diet, adapting as the millennia pass by, and branching into new species that will lead to the many forms present today. The ancient protosaola, however, remain loyal to their forest home and feed not on grass but on the leaves of trees and herbs, which delight their descendants still.

• Saola are found in broadleaf evergreen forests in the Annamite Mountains that have little or no dry season. Some authorities speculate that the persistence of so ancient a species in so small a geographical range indicates that the Annamites have been ecologically and climatically stable over a remarkable span of time, even as — during the Pleistocene epoch, for instance — other regions experienced major habitat shifts. If this is true, then today's saola may be an indicator of forests that are among the oldest on the planet, their origins going back tens of thousands of years.[1]

• At least in some areas, saola are believed to move with the seasons. In the early 1990s Vu Quang hunters said saola moved downslope from the higher mountains during the winter dry season, when the rains decrease and small streams dry up. The rains in Vu Quang can last as long as eight months and produce more than three meters of precipitation — a drenching of more than half an inch a day. Hunters placed their snares to intercept saola and other animals as they moved from high elevations to low ones and back.

• The hooves of saola, fresh from the wild, alive or dead, show heavy wear at the tips, an indication of rocky habitat. The streambeds along which they find their preferred foods tend to be corridors of boulders, and the mountain slopes where the torrents originate are typically walled with scarps.

• In an act of considerable kindness, George Schaller gave me a track cast made from a dead saola in Laos in the mid-1990s. It consists of a square of black fiberglass into which, when fresh, the hooves of the saola had been pressed. Like all ungulates, saola have cloven hooves. The two toes are strongly curved on their outside edges, making an almost oval print, unlike the triangular patterns of most deer. The front feet of Schaller's sample are roughly two inches long, the rear feet an eighth inch to a quarter inch longer. The track cast hangs on the wall above my desk. Schaller also gave me a second, even more memorable, cast. This one, made of white plaster, shows the light impression of a single hoof. Schaller says that Billy Karesh, the WCS veterinarian, cast it from Martha in Lak Xao while she was alive.

• Once or twice, villagers have reported seeing as many as a half dozen saola at a time. On two or three occasions, they've seen four. Are these exaggerations? Sightings of solitary saola, or of a mother and her calf, are generally the rule, although even these are rare— the kind of thing a village hunter remembers as an epochal event, not to be forgotten.

• It is surprising, twenty years after saola first attracted the world's attention, that so little about the species is known. How big is an individual saola's range, how much land does it need? Are the ranges of male and female the same or different? How do they court? When do they breed? No one has answers to these questions and many others. In the aftermath of saola's discovery, hunter interviews seemed to indicate that the females drop their calves in February and March. But Martha, had she survived, would probably have birthed her baby in May, and the two orphaned saola juveniles briefly maintained in FIPI's botanical garden outside Hanoi in 1994 appear to have been born several months apart.

• Predators of mature saola probably include tiger, leopard, dhole, and humans. Additional predators of young saola may include clouded leopard, sun bear, Asian black bear, and python.

• The diet of the saola is poorly understood, as is the botany of its habitat. Scientific surveys of the saola's remote forests have focused on cataloging animal species. Knowledge of the regional flora in places like the watershed of the Nam Nyang is generally too fragmentary to carry identifications past the level of genus. If species were to be determined, a large number of plants would undoubtedly be new to science. Like the saola, many of them would be endemic to the Annamite Mountains, found nowhere else.

• If saola are similar to other forest browsers, they require nutrition from several dozen types of plants. A staple of saola diet appears to be one or more species of *Schismatoglottis,* a genus of the Araceae family.[2] Village hunters report that no other animals consume *Schismatoglottis* in much quantity. Thus if a patch of the plant bears evidence of browsing, and especially if the leaves appear carefully nipped, saola are almost surely present.

• Like other ruminants, the saola has a four-chambered stomach and chews a cud.

• A bovid horn consists of bone encased in a sheath of keratin. In the case of the saola, the bone within the horn grows nearly to the tip, making the horn strong and indicating that it is a serious weapon, good for defense. Saola horns are typically smooth with wear, and hunters report that saola rub their horns against small trees or thrash dense stands of brush. This behavior may have a social or sexual function. In addition, it hones within the animal a keen spatial awareness and a kinesthetic sense of how to wield its horns with accuracy—to block the attacks of enemies or to gore them.

• The challenges of saola conservation verge on epistemology. How do you save a ghost when you are not sure it exists?

Mr. Ka of Ban Kounè has said, "No one sees saola anymore; they're gone."

Robichaud replied that, although no one was seeing them ten years ago, they weren't gone. One day a neighbor of Kong Chan suddenly encountered one, proving they were present all along. How can anyone be sure they are gone now?

In a moment of candor on another occasion, Ka, contradicting himself, told Robichaud that he caught sight of a live saola on the Nam Nyang in 2005. The next year, he saw saola tracks between Ban Kounè and Phou Vang. Ka knows as well as anyone that a few of the animals might remain deep in the forest, in places like the upper Nam Nyang.

In NNT, as elsewhere in the world, not everybody tells the truth all the time, and, at any given time, not all the truth gets told.

. . .

Small bees wake me. A dozen or more hover close above my face, some nearly in my nostrils, checking out my chemistry. I blow at them, and they retreat a few inches.

Suddenly, branches dance overhead. A face, rimmed in yellow, gazes down at me. I start to reach for my binoculars, and the face vanishes. For a split second, I glimpse a brown body and long, hairy tail as the branches dance again. An indistinct memory tells me the monkey I saw was the second of two. And now the branches are still.

I replay the image in my groggy mind: the haloed face; the flash of body and tail. I want the monkey to be a douc, a rare, colorful creature native to these mountains. To see a douc, especially alone like this, would be quite a gift. But the snatch of color I saw had no gray or red. This monkey was plainer than a douc. All right, I think, not a douc, but still a gift. It was probably a macaque.

A short while later, I hear Robichaud and Meet on the ledge above. They have found nothing. No more metal from war machines, no sand or mud with interesting tracks, no *Schismatoglottis*, no stems that show saola nibbles. We return toward camp, descending the shaded, stair-step tributary, and when we reach the channel where the Nam Nyang holds back the forest on either side, the bright sunlight drives off the forest dankness and lightens our steps.

Heading downriver, we again admire the potholes and kettles that are like chains of aquaria. We note a fresh hatch of river flies with sky-blue wings and, a little farther, a cohort of purplish butterflies carpeting the limestone. The insects rise at our approach in a dust devil of indigo. The river water is cool and inviting. At one of the largest and deepest pools we pause. Robichaud releases Meet to return to camp. Then Robichaud and I rinse our filthy shirts and trousers and spread them to dry on the warm boulders. Stripped, we swim. The water is windowpane clear. Bracing. A modest waterfall feeds the pool, and the falling water feels like a massage. I dive and swim for the bottom. The pool glimmers gray and green, with gravel in the depths. Every pebble is sharp and distinct, but the bottom is astonishingly deep and out of reach.

Back in camp, Sone reports that he might have found something. The stream he explored with Simeuang and Olay was steep like ours, heavily scoured, and offered no soft margins that would keep a track. The only game they saw was a black giant squirrel, but Sone also spotted a plant that he says saola eat. Its leaves had been carefully nipped off, one by one. Robichaud says the plant is new to him—it's not among the saola foods known to biologists—"but everything about saola is new to almost everybody." He presses the plant into his field book.

We have come a long way to learn two negatives. First, notwithstanding the plant that Sone collected, the upper Nam Nyang seems to lack the vegetation saola prefer. It may be too high or too dry—so much so that, as Robichaud puts it, "the formula is off." He says the drainages we've searched haven't "felt right." Robichaud's mind is not closed on the matter—he thinks further exploration of the upper reaches of the side creeks might show something, but for the present he's inclined to redirect our search to tributaries lower on the river.

The second negative is that we aren't effectively in Lao PDR anymore. The people who make use of this watershed—and there have been plenty of them—come from across the Annamite crest. Questions of sovereignty aside, we seem to be in a resource colony of Vietnam, where hunters and rosewood smugglers do as they please.

We gather over the maps. Robichaud lays out several alternative destinations, and the guides speak in Lao and then Sek, their excitement rising, as they debate possible routes. Robichaud and Simeuang briefly speculate about setting a new camp high up between Phou Vang and Phou Hone Kay (Chicken Comb Mountain), above a succession of waterfalls. No one in our group has been there before. It is new territory (except for Vietnamese hunters of eaglewood), and

there is a chance, on the high cliffs, that we might see exotic creatures like black leaf monkeys, whose speciation is poorly understood
and whose local population is essentially unknown. But the idea
passes quickly. Robichaud wants to continue the hunt for saola on
the lower Nam Nyang. He'd intended tomorrow to be a rest day, but
clouds are gathering, and if it rains, the river rocks will be dangerously slick. The prudent decision is to descend the channel while we
can. Robichaud suggests that he and I start down at first light while
the guides are still cooking. "Once they get going," he says, "they'll
be down those rocks like spiders. If we want to see anything, we
have to get ahead of them."

Bone, the least shy of the youngsters from Ban Beuk, is irrepressibly
cheerful. He has a scar on one cheek, and most days, in addition to
his smile, wears a bright orange T-Mobile World Cup T-shirt. This is
his first long trip into the forest, and he shows an interest in everything. After we've eaten (sticky rice, a salty broth, and too few fish to
satisfy our large group), he accompanies Robichaud and me to the
mouth of the tributary that Simeuang and Sone inspected. In the
dusk light, we quickly bait a camera trap with fish heads. The white
river rocks seem to glow as we cross back to our camp in the dark.

We turn in at 8:00 p.m., and in the dark hours I dream of my
children, who are suddenly young again, much younger than Bone.
Responding to an urgent call, I have arrived at a house of endless
corridors to collect them, but the sirenlike mothers of their play-
mates delay me. The women are beautiful and seductive. They sing
to me in soft Southern voices. I am delightedly melting into their
arms when I remember my children. I break from the sirens and fly
away—yes, fly—arms out, legs straight back, like Superman, through
strange, long rooms. The flying feels like swimming, although at
dangerous speeds. I careen around corners, banking into turns. I
look in every room for my children. And look, and look. The lovely
women are gone and their enchanted singing gone with them, and I
am just flying and searching.

March 3

Nam Nyang, Camp 2

More bad news about the rice. Touy tells Robichaud that we have only half of what is needed for the rest of the trip: four kilos, not eight. And we set out from Ban Nameuy with at least forty.

Mok Keo confirms that our supply is sufficient for only two more nights. And we are at least two nights from the villages, he says, so we will have to start back today.

It is a half hour past dawn. The fire is smoky. Mok Keo has just put on a pot of water for the breakfast rice. Robichaud, however, is already coming to a boil. As Touy's news and Mok Keo's matter-of-fact statement sink in, he reddens visibly. When he replies to Mok Keo, in Lao, I hear tightness in his voice. "We have work to do," he says. "This trip has been planned a long time, and we are going to do our work. We have to stay two nights at the next camp and one more at Thong Kouang on the way back. After the next camp, if some people want to leave, that's okay—there will be more rice for the rest of us."

He is playing his hole card, which is to send the whiners home and stay in the forest without them, supplies be damned. Mok Keo and some of the older guides probably came on the trip less for wages than because Kong Chan badgered them into it. They have to stay on the right side of him, or else. They didn't mind a few days of camping, but now nearly everyone, except maybe some of the young-sters, like Bone, would rather be home. So while Robichaud, Simeuang, the boys, and I get by on three, sometimes two, light meals a day, more than a few of the guides have been chowing down on four, eating their way to an early departure for home. The strategy

only works, however, if Robichaud gives in to the shortage of supplies. If he stays in the forest while they go back, they'll have to
face Kong Chan's anger and his vengeance. Worse, if the militia go
back early, leaving us "undefended," the district governor will hear
about it, and the consequences will include a cup of misery for
everyone.

A silence weighs on the group as everyone calculates the merits
of his own position. In truth, the guides have good reason to want to
start for the villages. It is not that they don't want to work, it's that
they have other work that calls for their attention. They have fields
to tend, crops to plant, families to provide for. The five dollars per
day they receive as guides, a rate set by the WMPA, was once a
strong inducement to take to the woods. In the present rosewood
era, however, it amounts to a poor reward for heavy, difficult labor.
Still, quitting would bring a host of unwanted consequences.

Cool now, feeling a shift in the mood of the group, Robichaud
presses his point: "We'll find our way home by compass, carrying
what we can. We'll be okay. Anybody can go if he thinks he needs to."

Mok Keo mutters, "All right, we'll see how the rice holds out," but
Viengxai rudely talks over him, complaining that nobody can leave
at the next camp because, without Robichaud's compass and GPS,
none of them will know the way.

This is nonsense: Meet, who has remained silent, and possibly
even Viengxai, would be able to navigate home from the Nam
Nyang, but the facts are not Viengxai's point. He wants everyone to
feel aggrieved, the better to wrest control of the situation from Robichaud. In any event, Robichaud doesn't go for the bait. He shrugs.
"You can go home the way you came."

"No, we can't," counters Viengxai. "The mountains are too high
that way." He absurdly overlooks our having crossed those mountains to get here. Besides, the mountains are higher along the return
route we've been intending to take.

But now there is another change of plan. Meet mentions that he
thinks we might find a Vietnamese trail high on the slope across the

river. Viengxai chimes in—not that he would know—insisting that there must be one. He is certain of it. How far from the river? Robichaud asks. "Not far, I think," Meet says.

"Not far! Not far!" Viengxai now drowns out Meet, as he did Mok Keo.

"So be it," says Robichaud. "We'll go that way and hope for the best."

Apparently we won't descend the Nam Nyang by the river rocks after all. I feel relief. Why was this route not mentioned yesterday? No matter. At least the issue of the rice seems decided: we will stretch supplies to last a minimum of three nights, for everybody.

The packs must be rebalanced. Because the rice bags are much lighter, the other loads require adjustment. Viengxai grins as I open my pack and remove the tent and sleeping pad, handing them to others. Viengxai shoves his own small rucksack into the vacant space and closes the pack. We stand around as the new loads are negotiated. If anyone looks his way, Viengxai lifts the pack and pantomimes a backbreaking weight. Other porters, including Bone, come by to test it. They lift the pack and laugh and look at Viengxai with jealousy, incredulous that he should complain.

Robichaud and I cross the river to check the camera trap. Robichaud had hoped for a civet, but the fish scraps are undisturbed. Coming back, we meet Bone and Kham Laek. Bone holds a one-liter aluminum bottle I've carried around for almost forty years. Bone asks, "Whose is this?"

"Mine," I say.

"Can I have it?" A grin wrinkles the scar on his cheek.

Robichaud says, "I will get you two of them when we get back."

I say, "No; I'll give it to him." The bottle is as old as the war scrap we found yesterday. My filtered bottle seems adequate to my needs, which leaves nostalgia the only reason to keep the aluminum bottle, and Bone's enthusiasm trumps nostalgia.

Robichaud translates. Bone beams. Robichaud chides him, "But you have to stay at Thong Kouang and go back with us. This bottle spends the night at Thong Kouang." Bone is very pleased. He extends a hand to shake, Western-style, but it is his left. We shake.

"One more thing," adds Robichaud. "When we want hot tea water, we can borrow it back, okay?"

"I'll bring the water myself!" says Bone over his shoulder, as he and Kham Laek bolt for the river.

As they pack the camp goods, Touy and Simeuang discover that our small reserve of instant noodles has also been raided. The guides must have feasted on them nights ago, before our lockdown on the supplies. Robichaud receives the news silently, not speaking to Simeuang, whose responsibility this is, lest he say something harsh. Simeuang, superb on the trail and as a woodsman, has indeed been lax as a quartermaster; perhaps he thought Mok Keo would keep a closer eye on things. Robichaud now instructs Touy, in English, to take extra precautions with the supplies at our next camp. Touy nods agreement, not looking at Simeuang.

As much as anyone, I regret the loss of the noodles, which were our sole alternative to sticky rice. At the outset of the trip, sticky rice tasted merely bland, but meal by meal, it has become repugnant to me, a kind of carbohydrate gristle that one chews without result and finally swallows as a bolus. I have depended for calories on the occasional energy bar, which, in disregard of the Lao custom that one never eats without sharing, I choke down surreptitiously on the trail or after dark in the tent, hopeful that a quick lift of blood sugar will help me sleep. Even so, the tail end of my belt, dangling from the buckle, gets longer day by day. Worse, my hoard of bars is almost gone. I had counted on noodles for the fuel that would power me over the last mountains toward home.

The mood in camp is sour as Robichaud calls a meeting. He says if anyone is to eat noodles, we all eat them together, and that as supplies grow low, we must share. Viengxai stands apart from the group, taking a leak. Simeuang then talks about how we all must be friends, but no one listens.

It is past 8:30 when we finally head out, glad to be going and to escape the cramped campsite and equally claustrophobic tension over supplies. We cross the river, leaping from boulder to boulder, and begin working our way up a slough on the other side. The first level area we come to holds a Vietnamese camp: a fire pit, vertical poles from which to hang hammocks, and a frame to support a tarp roof. An intact fishing net has been left behind, spread as though to dry. We bundle the net and set fire to it, heaping on tatters of plastic, rags, and other flammable trash. We quickly press up the slope, leaving the oddly untended flames bright behind us.

Viengxai pushes forward and seems almost to be racing Meet, our pathfinder. There is no trail, and the slope is steep, the vegetation dense with trees and myriad pole-size stems, deadfall everywhere. It hardly seems the place for competition. Vines with hooked thorns angle this way and that, lacing trunk to branch and branch to shrub in a concertina web.

Up we go on slippery footing, bending low beneath a branch, straddling a log, stepping sideways to slide between vine and tree, and again bend, straddle, and sideways step, bend, straddle, and sideways step, in endless repetition. I feel like a boxer, ducking and dodging, but a boxer in late rounds, reflexes dangerously slow, one punch away from going down. The slope has the angle of a ladder, but there are no rungs, only loose leaves and smallish rocks that slide underfoot, while vines as sharp as band-saw blades grab my hat, snag my shirt, and angle for my throat. I joke to myself that the vines of NNT, like shop tools, come in three grades: weekend hobbyist, contractor, and industrial. This slope bristles with industrial equipment.

Viengxai has outpaced Meet and is the only one among us who is climbing with either energy or enthusiasm. For all his faults, he is strong and superbly athletic, able to glide among the trees with seeming effortlessness. It dawns on me that he has taken the lead in order to be first to encounter the trail we hope to find and thereby to claim credit for its discovery. I crave the ease that a trail would afford but dread the strutting we will be obliged to witness.

We are saved from an explosion of conceit, however, when the putative trail eludes us. After what seems an eon of hard climbing, Robichaud calls a halt. It turns out I am not alone in fighting the bandsaw vines: a mustache of blood, of which he seems unaware, now blooms on his face. He tries to check our GPS coordinates, but the receiver fails to link to the satellites. Perhaps the canopy is too dense or the slope screens a connection. While we are stopped, Viengxai announces loudly that it was Meet who said there was a trail on this slope. His tone is hardly congratulatory. He is hedging his bet. If we find a trail, he'll take credit; if we don't, it will be Meet's fault.

Robichaud indicates the compass bearing he wants to follow, and we set off again, Viengxai and Meet still in front.

I ask Robichaud, "Who's leading?"

"The blind," he says.

Another kilometer of thorny, tangled jungle, and another stop. Still no GPS. Viengxai criticizes Meet for giving bad information, despite his earlier praise and amplification of Meet's conjecture about a trail. This time, when we resume our march, Viengxai drops back into the pack, leaving Meet, worried and alone, at the point of our ragged column.

Another kilometer, another stop. The day is hot now, and I am leaking moisture like a squeezed sponge. A consensus has emerged that the trail, if it exists, lies too far away. We have been traveling upslope perpendicular to the river, roughly north. Our best alternative is to turn west and bushwhack to the tributary of the Nam Nyang that we'd imagined a trail might lead to. The distance is about eight straight-line kilometers—a long haul when the terrain is utter jungle, where straight lines don't exist. Somewhere behind us, the sleek, dry boulders of the Nam Nyang shine in the sun.

Robichaud turns to me: "I don't know why it is, but a law of surveys seems to be that there is always one day every trip when things turn out much longer and harder than you expected. Looks like today is that day. Let's hope it is the only one."

I don't say it, but in my opinion, our twenty-seven kilometers on the Rosewood Highway two days earlier fit that description rather well. Robichaud gives Meet a new compass bearing, and we set off.

For a while we follow a muntjac trail, heavy with scat. Not long after it peters out, we come upon an old snare line. The hedge of brush that its builders constructed had rotted and collapsed, and the snares, set in gaps in the hedge, had long ago sprung. But the material chopped for the hedge left an alleyway of reduced tangle, which we gladly adopt as our route.

Meet suddenly stops. He sees a band of doucs, and they see him. I am fourth in line, behind Robichaud and Simeuang. By the time I come up, the monkeys have fled, the empty branches waving. The pause affords an opportunity to appreciate the forest, which consists of stair steps of understory trees leading to the umbrella crowns of hundred-foot giants, lattices of vines running up to them like the rigging of a tall ship. Glorious yellow sunlight drizzles down.

I rummage in my daypack and dig out a pair of light leather gloves, forgotten until now. As we resume the march, I am self-conscious wearing them but soon feel like the luckiest guy in the forest. I can freely grab the middling stems that crowd my path, thorns and insects no longer a worry. Uphill, I can pull myself along by my hands. Downhill, I can brake. I concentrate on form more than progress, seeking a rhythm with my hands and feet, as I would cross-country skiing or swimming: I am swimming through the forest terrarium. Suddenly I remember my dream from the night before. Is this what the flying was about?

After two more hours, Robichaud consults the contour maps. We've made good progress, he says. We are a third of the way to our destination. "We are all right, but we'll soon run out of the level stuff."

This is not reassuring. If Robichaud thought the last miles were level, he must have been hallucinating.

We stop by a pool tucked into a pocket in the side of the ridge we've been following. The water is clear. I fill my bottle and jot down some notes as a green ladybug walks over my hand. Bone settles close by, against a tree, and rakishly enjoys a smoke. He makes a show of unscrewing the top of the aluminum bottle I gave him and takes a long drink. He flashes me a grin that suggests we share a secret. Robichaud points out a frog in the water, a big one, as green as a new leaf. Bone rises and quickly wades in, cigarette dangling from his mouth. Squinting through the smoke, he expertly herds the frog to a corner of the pond and scoops it from the water. He turns to show it to us and is about to break its legs—the usual method for keeping a frog handy until it's time to kill and eat it—when Robichaud and I exchange a glance. I can picture the frog, moments from now, its beauty and its leg bones shattered because Bone thought Robichaud and I would enjoy a special treat at dinner. Robichaud sees me wince and gestures to Bone, who lets the frog go with no trace of disappointment.

Meet leads us along a faint trail to a ridge crest, and instantly we confront another snare line, a fresh one. It runs out of sight in either direction. The hedge of brush is thick, impenetrable, a yard high. Only a sambar or a teenager could easily leap it. Everything else that walks or crawls, including me, would have to pass the hedge by one of the gaps, where the snares lie. The gaps are spaced every three meters or so, and hidden in the floor of each lies a loop of wire held by a delicate trigger of buried sticks. The wire runs to the top of a sapling pole, which has been fiercely bent over to make a spring. A human foot is too big to be caught in the loop, but the narrow foot of a quadruped, even the foot of a pheasant, which weighs almost nothing, will dislodge the stick that is the linchpin of the trigger. Until that instant, the trigger has restrained the strength of the bowed sapling. But under the slightest pressure, the trigger releases, the sapling snaps upward, and a noose of wire leaps up the leg of the errant foot. The animal that owns the foot, even an animal as big as a saola, flips into the air, dangles, struggles, and far too slowly dies.

The guides are merry now. It is bonus time. They hustle up and down the line, springing the traps and freeing the wires from the sapling poles. They coil the wires and stow them in their packs. Each length of snare wire will add fifteen hundred kip to the pool of money we pay at the end of the trip. We will follow this snare line for almost a kilometer, and it will yield more than two hundred snares.

Not all the snares need to be sprung. Here a hog badger has already performed that service, its foul and desiccated carcass hanging in midair. Over there a dangling jungle fowl, the wild ancestor of domestic chickens, has dried to a disordered ball of feathers. A little farther lies the partial leg of a muntjac, and the sapling that powered the snare has been pulled to the ground. One doesn't want to think too long about the struggle that took place here. The next snare is missing. The area around it is greatly disturbed, suggesting that perhaps a wild pig dragged the whole affair away and went off, maimed, to die somewhere else. Next we encounter the remains of a ferret badger. And a male silver pheasant, the whole of it shrunken and foul but the individual feathers still glorious. I pluck a feather that is small and unblemished—it is the white of Carrara marble, peppered with black   and fold it into my notebook.

We encounter one macabre trophy after another for hundreds of meters. The snare line commemorates the forest's diversity as well as its mortality. Vlad the Impaler, the fifteenth-century Romanian monarch who skewered his enemies on poles and lined the Danube with their corpses, comes to mind. These hedges of death are a wildlife analog.

The ferret badger may be a significant record for the protected area. Two species, separable only by dentition, are known from the region, and because it will be useful to know which species this one is, Robichaud will keep the head as a specimen. Phaivanh obligingly decapitates the badger with his machete. Its lips have shrunk back, baring a mouthful of sharp teeth in a ghastly grin. Robichaud takes the head and holds it as a ventriloquist might do. In a high-pitched voice he pretends to make it speak: "See me? I'm smiling, just like everybody here. But one thing you should know: smiling doesn't always mean we're happy!"

We follow the snare line down a gently declining ridge, walking easily in the lane cleared of brush for its construction. But we watch our step. Hundreds, no, thousands of sharp, woody stubs—the ministumps of machete-hacked bamboo and saplings—bristle like a lawn of punji sticks. It would be a bad idea to step on one, worse to fall among them. We come to another ferret badger. And another jungle fowl, this one not long dead, which we collect for dinner.

I am lagging, scribbling in my book. The others have gone ahead. But I see they have stopped and gathered in a tight knot. They are staring at something, and as I come up I see what it is—a muntjac, snared and dead but intact. The eyes have turned white, and the belly is distended with gas. Bottle flies walk in and out of its gaping mouth. Robichaud isn't certain but thinks we are looking at a juvenile large-antlered muntjac. The pelage of the rump suggests a palimpsest of spots, markings of a fawn. The large-antlered muntjac is almost as rare and as little understood as the saola. "And this could have been a saola," Robichaud observes, snares like this being probably the single greatest threat to the survival of the species.

Mok Keo squats by the little deer and plucks tufts of hair from its hide. He pronounces it only two days dead, still good to eat. In another day, the hair will come out more easily. Robichaud agrees that we should take it, but first he wants to take measurements, and he asks Mok Keo to promise he will save the head as a specimen and also a piece of liver for DNA analysis.

I write down the measurements as Robichaud calls them out. Head and body length along the contour from the tip of the nose to the base of the tail: 94 centimeters. Same end points measured in a straight line: 88 centimeters. Underside of tail, base to tip: 16.5 centimeters.

Sone parcels out to the other guides the contents of the rice sack that has served as his pack. With Mok Keo's help, he slides the

Thong Dam holds a snared juvenile large-antlered muntjac, soon to go into the stewpot.

muntjac into the bag, folding the stiff legs. One of Earth's rarest and most endangered creatures, endemic to the Annamites, will nourish us tonight.

My friend Mary, also rare and in danger, occupied a small home habitat, but not by choice. Her illness kept her housebound. She lived in a drafty postwar bungalow with a dying heating system and an overgrown planting of sage in front, much beloved by bees. Her last venture out of town may have been with me. We drove for a day to visit a friend, himself an invalid, who was recovering—we hoped—from multiple myeloma after a year of savage treatments. He and his wife had built a home on a hill tucked between mesas. It was a split-level affair, divided by small stairways only a few steps high. Our friend would climb a few steps and then stand gasping, leaning against the wall. All his life he'd been an athlete, but now a walk to the car exhausted him. After dinner, he took Mary aside to ask a favor. "Tell me how to die," he entreated.

It was a funny thing, how she kept her spirits up. To hug her was to feel a spine like a blade and a back paved in bone, as though a carapace lay just beneath the skin. She was a beauty, still, with round, mirthful eyes, a sensuous mouth, and slender, long-fingered hands, but she was frail beyond words. Her friends learned to touch her lightly.

We drove home on an August day through an ocean of desert light. A single cloud snagged on a blue mountain. We rolled down the windows, and the cab of the truck filled with wind and engine roar. "I just told him I didn't have the answer," she said. "I told him, I don't know how to die any better than you, but I plan to do it as late as possible." She had the wind full in her face, and her hair whipped around wildly. Her voice began comically to rise. "I told him, all I know is you've got to be fierce!" She was exhilarated by the speed and the violent air, by the scenery rushing past, and not least by the story she was telling. The window framed her as the landscape streamed behind. I remember the Nefertiti curve of her neck, the whirlwind hair, the eruptive grin. Her eyes said she had a punch line coming. "What the hell," she squealed. "If nothing's gonna work, anything might help!"

She laughed at her joke until her insides hurt, then put her face out the window like a collie and closed her eyes.

Our friend died two weeks later.

If nothing's gonna work, anything might help.

It is an illogical proposition, of course. Face facts: if nothing will work, nothing will work. But after many interviews with Robichaud and his colleagues, it struck me that the same odd welding of attitudes may be found among conservation biologists. The essence of Mary's improbable spirit, even as her time was running out, was to combine fatalism with optimism, two attitudes that do not easily mesh. F. Scott Fitzgerald famously said, "The test of a first-rate intelligence is the ability to hold two opposed ideas in the mind at the same time, and still retain the ability to function." If Fitzgerald was right, the ranks of those who labor on behalf of endangered species are filled with first-rate minds. One cannot acknowledge climate change, habitat loss, the wildlife trade, burgeoning human population, the plundering of the oceans, and all the other contents of Pandora's environmental box and sensibly remain optimistic about prospects for the survival of rare species or even the survival of many species that are not yet rare. The outlook is almost universally grim, and yet the funds are raised, the difficult field conditions endured, the bureaucracies contended with, and a thousand complications overcome to allow the work to continue. This kind of predicament is exactly what Fitzgerald was writing about. He continued, "One should, for example, be able to see that things are hopeless and yet be determined to make them otherwise." Fitzgerald was writing about his own "Crack-Up," which occurred when he lost the ability to bridge these opposites, when he no longer, as he had in his youth, "saw the improbable, the implausible, often the 'impossible,' come true." Robichaud, Timmins, Duckworth, Schaller, and others toiling in similar vineyards know very well how steeply the odds are stacked against them, yet they persevere.

One evening by the tents I asked Robichaud, "How do you maintain optimism?"

He looked at me deadpan. "What makes you sure I do?" he answered.

And yet the next day, as I watched him on the trail, in his element, even under adverse conditions, it seemed to me I was looking at a man who, if not described by the narrow term *happy*, was fundamentally at peace to be doing what he was doing.

At 2:30 p.m., still descending the ridge where we found the muntjac, we calculate that we are several kilometers from the stream we seek. Unfortunately, the terrain ahead is dissected by deep ravines — canyons, really — and we will have to cross them. The easy walking in the hacked alley of the snare line is behind us, and the forest has

grown uncommonly dense. Viengxai leads a rising chorus of grousing about the lack of a trail, the onerous packs, and the guides' low
pay. Notwithstanding that his cheerleading helped get us into this
fix, Viengxai now lays the blame on Robichaud, whose patience is
astonishing. Even now, he parries Viengxai's complaints with wit
and humor. I would have told him to fuck off long ago.

The slope steepens, and I am soon sliding on my heels, two paces
behind Sone, but I don't have to see him to follow him. The juvenile
muntjac, in the rice sack on his back, leaves a plume of stench. It is
just as well I don't look at him. Sone carries his AK-47 slung backward under his arm, the angle of the barrel roughly parallel to the
slope. When I glance his way, the rifle has me right between the
eyes. Fatigue is shutting down my brain, and it is easier to follow
Sone than to pick a path for myself. Nevertheless, a question flickers: Does Sone keep a bullet in the chamber?

The last pitch of the slope, as is common in these mountains, is a
cut bank that floods have chewed to the vertical. We search for
handholds on branches and tree roots as we scrabble to the muddy
bottom of the ravine. The guides sprawl, exhausted, beside a large
puddle of buggy, leaf-stained water. I slump down next to Touy and
Olay, who both look glazed. I am too bushed to take out my notebook. This will be the first time that I have not made notes during a
stop. (And so I take out my book to make note of that fact.)

The grousing continues. The slope ahead looks worse than the
one we just came down. It towers above us, and the vegetation is
especially dense — a wall covering a wall. Meet wants to stop here.
This is enough, he says. He's going no farther. He says we should
camp in the ravine, using water from the puddle. We can push on to
the tributary we seek tomorrow. Grumbles of agreement rise from
the others, Viengxai loudest. Robichaud negotiates. He promises to
stop at the next water and camp, no matter whether it turns out to
be the river we seek or another slimy hole in the woods like this.

Robichaud has checked the map. He's sure the next water will be
the long-sought tributary and that it is not far. But the map means

nothing to Meet and the rest of the guides, for they cannot read it, and none of them has been here before. They cannot know how close we are or how much better the next water is likely to be. Even if they did, they can look at the wall in front of us and know that *close* is not *arrived* and that the last climb will try us hard.

I think I have one more climb in me, not more. Past that, I may "hit the wall," in the parlance of marathoners, which is something I did a year ago, and the experience was humiliating and frightening. Hitting the wall means your muscles are out of fuel. Your body begins to shut down. Everything hurts. You are as weak as a worm. Your internal thermostat goes screwy, and you overheat. You can't move. This happened to me in another case of lost trails—one in which, truth be told, I bit off more than I could chew. Had others not plied me with food and water, I might not have made it over the last summit. Even so, after darkness had fallen, a mile from camp, while making a final descent by headlamp, I stepped on a white, almost glowing boulder that had I been more alert I would have mistrusted. It gave way, dispatching me on a moderately spectacular fall, and I was lucky to limp into camp under my own power.

Robichaud's promises are falling on deaf ears. Most of the guides won't look at him. So he raises the stakes on his challenge. "All right," he says. "We'll swap packs! Your packs are too heavy? Who will take mine? I will take yours. Let's switch. Give me one of those heavy ones." He stalks among the recumbent figures, starting with Meet, pulling at the guides' packs as though to take them, but Meet and the others pull their loads back. To give in would be too humiliating. No one consents to trade. So Robichaud begins removing the odds and ends tied to the outsides of the largest packs—a pot from one, a bag of spare clothing from another, a rolled tarp, a coil of recovered snares—and reties them, calmly and efficiently, to his own. He shoulders his pack, now raggedly festooned, and starts up the ravine. Soon he finds a ladder of tree roots and begins climbing the wall. Simeuang, the boys, and I stagger after him. Behind us, I can hear the guides muttering, lifting, moving.

The guides weren't wrong—the climb proved to be as bad as it looked. At the bottom it was like chinning yourself up the side of an apartment building, except that the apartment building was covered with rotting window boxes filled with things unpleasant to touch. Eventually the slope eased a few degrees, enough to let us stand upright, if unsteadily. It became a mere palisade of trunks interlaced with razor-wire lianas. The athletes among us glided no more— even they had to move with deliberation, dodging, ducking, and bulling through screens of resistant branches, the slope always pushing back, doubling the cost of every uphill step. There was no more grumbling. No one could spare the breath.

At the top, we meet another snare line, the fourth or fifth of the day and the second one with its snares intact and armed. The guides instantly recover their energy and scramble to gather the wires. The harvest of death is as before: the foot of a hog badger, a partridge of unknown species, a possible mongoose, carcass after carcass.

Again we follow the snare line along a ridge, avoiding its punji sticks, and for a time the going is good. My mind wanders with fatigue to the dream of the night before: the beautiful women, the singing, and the flying and searching for my children. Part of me wants to drift away and escape into the dream. Another part is scolding. *Pay attention,* it says. *Don't fall. Watch where you're going.*

At a gap on a ridgetop where the vegetation thins, we glimpse a shoulder of Phou Vang, looming a few kilometers distant. We must be close to the canyon of the tributary. One long descent will put us there. A surge of optimism moves through the group.

Then we hit the bamboo.

Bamboo grows dispersed through the forest of the protected area, usually where the land has been disturbed by fire or flood. Technically it is a grass, albeit a woody one, and it can grow as thickly as grass but with the size, toughness, and immovability of trees. Sometimes its thickets are so dense your foot cannot reach the ground if you try to step inside. Sometimes these thickets are scores of acres in size. Most such thickets are clonal, with every stalk the same age, even the same diameter. There are stands of skinny bamboo and stands of thick bamboo. All the members of the stand sprout together and grow, flower, and die together. The bamboo before us once stood twenty feet tall, each stem an inch thick, an impenetrable palisade. All of it had died, and the stems had toppled. With utter randomness, they fell into interlocking heaps whose individual stalks pointed in every direction. Each stack merged into the next, leaving no gap, no boundary, no grain to follow, no weak point to attack.

We cannot outflank the sprawl of bamboo, because a tangled slope too steep to walk bounds it on one side and an escarpment falls away on the other. The guides draw their machetes and try to cut their way in, but the blades bounce off. I stagger against barricades of the stuff, trying first to climb the bamboo and then, failing that, to bulldoze my way through. At last I get on my hands and knees and crawl into the stack, plumbing tunnels beneath the chaos that lead God knows where. I am an ant in a pile of pick-up sticks, but I am an ant with a backpack, which makes me too big. My pack snags again and again. Robichaud, with his ungainly load, and the guides, with their larger packs, must be having a worse time. Every stalk I push sets a dozen more rattling. And thirteen other people are pushing and thrashing the same as I am. The cumulative roar of so many of us flailing in the bamboo sounds like a contest among outboard motors revving to the verge of breakdown. Surely not a sound a saola would hang around to figure out.

Our progress is desperate. We fight fourteen individual battles, crashing, cursing, and heaving our way through. The contest wears on for a furious half hour that feels much longer. Finally the tangle thins. We stand again and straddle the last heaps. Mutely we go forward, the hellish bamboo behind us.

We now start another steep descent. The guides, disgruntled again—who can blame them?—take their own route. I follow Simeuang, having learned that he reads the forest even better than Meet or Sone. He is the chess master with the deepest vision into the game, giving each move the energy it needs and not a quantum more, although today even he looks tired and drawn.

We stagger down a long final pitch, arriving in another dark ravine. But not just a ravine: around us are the lean-tos and detritus of an elaborate, albeit abandoned, poachers' camp. Phaivanh, the only guide who took our route, rifles through a bag of clothing the poachers left behind. He finds a pair of shorts he likes and stuffs them in his pack. We don't linger. In a hundred meters more the ravine spills into the open space of a broad river channel. And suddenly we are out! The nameless tributary we have sought is nearly as large as the Nam Nyang was at our last campsite. It is a rockscape of water-smooth limestone gridded by sparkling rivulets and long, polished ledges. A constant, gentle water music rises from it. The space feels generous and open. I can see two hundred meters upstream and two hundred meters downstream. I can see the sky, where small birds skim and circle. I can feel the movement of the air, a cooling downstream breeze. The guides sprawl on the river rocks, laughing. Robichaud appears, looking filthy, sweat-stained, and unshaven, wearing a grin from ear to ear.

A voice of permission, never more welcome, speaks within me in the tone of "You may now kiss the bride." It loudly says, "You may now drink your fill of water."

As dusk falls, I squat by a smoky fire with Mok Keo, waiting for tea water to boil. Mok Keo, having plucked the jungle fowl we recovered from the snare line, has clamped it in a bamboo press and set it to roast. With a grin he invites me to share a blackened and unrecognizable piece of skewered muntjac. As far as I know, it is my first taste of an endangered species on the IUCN Red List. The muntjac is gamy, like all venison, but also borderline putrid and so raw and tangy that I wonder if it is the rest of the liver that I just helped Robichaud dice for DNA samples. Robichaud had said, "You can use one hand to hold the specimen capsule and the other to hold your nose."

Mok Keo bids me eat more. I conclude this ragged morsel is the heart. Mok Keo exudes happiness. We banter in mishandled scraps of Lao and English, passing the skewer back and forth. The old Pathet Lao soldier is fluent in four languages, none of them known to me. And what he calls my *fa lang,* which is to say, French, is useless to him—not to mention the scraps I know of other European languages. When I say in English, "I don't understand," he repeats the phrase with perfect intonation. He grins and says, "Sabaidee, hello," mimicking my lame accent, then proudly adds, "Hello, love you," which he learned who knows where. Back and forth we go, trading words and meat.

The muntjac pieces by the fire are only an appetizer. For the main course, Mok Keo makes a stew of the rest of the animal. Lest his compatriots find the dish bland, he flavors it with the contents of the muntjac's small bowel. He serves the concoction after the entire group has gathered around a length of tarp in early starlight on a smooth white ledge of the riverbed. Cautiously Robichaud dips a spoon and samples it. Immediately he spits it out, to general laughter. The taste, he explains, as though describing a wine, "recalls baby shit blended with a rind of grapefruit." He discourages further sampling. I resolve instead to offer the hollow in my gut a ball of unloved sticky rice and a few mouthfuls of desiccated jungle fowl. Both require a great deal of chewing, and the latter tastes like old boot. Nevertheless, I feel each swallow hit my stomach and take up welcome space.

March 4

A Tributary of the Nam Nyang

I n camp last night, our bellies full and the day's ordeal behind us, Robichaud told the boys and me a story he'd heard elsewhere in Nakai–Nam Theun:

A team of a dozen Vietnamese discovered a mother lode of eagle-wood within the protected area. It constituted a fortune in incense, and the prospect of riches made the poachers crazy. The team fractured, six on a side, each group plotting to do away with the other and keep the treasure for themselves. One day, half the team goes hunting; the other half stays in camp. The camp tenders prepare a large meal and lace it heavily with poison mushrooms. They wait for the others to return, the pot simmering. In due time the others appear, but they come into camp with guns out, blazing. They kill all six of the camp tenders before any can fight back. Then the victorious six help themselves to the steaming meal, which is still on the fire. Of course, it proves to be their last. No one survives. Days later, a small party of Lao happen upon the scene and reconstruct this account from the evidence of the corpses. The punch line in Robichaud's telling is the title he gives his story. He calls it *Nam Theun 2 Reservoir Dogs*.

Robichaud laces his speech with movie lore. He has a prodigious gift for recalling plots and whole pages of dialog. On one long walk between villages, I happened to mention that I had never seen Oliver Stone's *Platoon*. Over the next several kilometers, Robichaud narrated the action of the film, scene by scene, speaking the lines of leading characters. With a little editing, his performance could have been a one-man one-act play. I do not doubt he could do the same

186

for any number of other films set in Southeast Asia. He told me that in our battle yesterday with the bamboo and on our final steep descent to the river, he couldn't stop repeating in his mind a line from *Predator,* a B-grade sweaty-biceps commando vehicle for Arnold Schwarzenegger: "I've seen some bad-ass bush before, man, but nothin' like this.... Makes Cambodia look like Kansas."

Even apart from the scraps of films in our heads and the scraps of airplanes, bombs, and fuel tanks on the ground, the war is like an echo that follows us around. One day the trail was wide for a stretch, and Robichaud and I walked together. He said, "Here we are, a couple of Americans prowling around in deep forest close to the border of Vietnam. We are traveling with a bunch of Lao guys who wear camo and carry assault rifles, and we are looking for Vietnamese who are doing things we don't like. The Vietnamese, meanwhile, know that people like us are looking for them, and they don't want to be found. Sound like anything you've heard of before?"

Robichaud was too young to be drafted for the Vietnam War, but I wasn't. The war and the military draft that fed it were the overriding realities of my teens and early twenties. My father had served as a midrank officer in both World War II and the Korean War, although he never saw action in either conflict. He hadn't tried to avoid combat; he just wound up in places where it didn't happen. I think this left him with a sense of unease, a feeling of uncompleted destiny. When Vietnam came along, he expected me to answer the nation's call, as he had done dutifully in his own time. He did not dwell on the merits of the war, and he didn't know that while in high school, as soon as I got a driver's license and had access to a car, I started attending meetings of the antiwar American Friends Service Committee. Later, as I finished college and neared the end of my student draft deferment, he was appalled to learn that I was filing with my draft board as a conscientious objector. It was only a gesture on my part. I knew I would not be granted CO status because my grounds for it were insufficiently religious. Still, it was the only moral thing I could think of to do. I firmly believed that the war was unjust and that the slaughter it engendered was criminal. Nevertheless, I had a low lottery number, and it was certain I would be called up. I didn't know whether I would go to jail, to Canada, or to basic training.

Then fate threw a knuckleball. When I took my draft physical, I was a scrawny twenty-two-year-old with a bad cigarette habit. I flunked the physical exam by reason of hypertension, a term I had never heard until then. Smoking may have saved my life. The strung-out hours of the night before might have had something to do with it, too. After the last of the poking, prodding, and palpating of the exam, a burly sergeant looked at my folder, glared at me, and said, "Mr. *Dee*-boyze, you have been examined and found unfit for service in the armed forces of the United States of America. Do you have any questions?"

I was astonished beyond words.

Two years later, I quit smoking and never touched tobacco again. Because I failed the physical, I never had to fight the big fight with my draft board, the military, my conscience, the Vietnamese, or my father, although he and I had other fights that were nearly as difficult. I was safe on multiple levels but also strangely condemned, as he was, to a sense of unease, an awareness of ambiguous fate, of a major test evaded. It wasn't until I walked the trails of Nakai–Nam Theun that I began to see the lingering questions from those days as one of several strands of attraction that drew me to the banks of the Nam Nyang in middle age. There can be no equivalence between my present experience as an older man looking for wildlife and the road not traveled by my younger self, but I could not have been more interested to inhabit, however briefly, the general arena to which my country, once upon a time, would have provided me an all-expenses-paid yearlong tour. My search for saola, at some level, allows me to touch that alternative past, which I was never obliged to live.

Drained by the previous day's hard march, we pass a leisurely morning in camp. I find a sunny spot on a ledge of river rock and catch up on notes. Soon Bone and the other young Sek boys settle next to me to play a game of cards, and minutes later Mok Keo is looking over my shoulder and pointing out individual letters as I write them. The boys temporarily suspend their game to attend Mok Keo's play-by-play description of the symbols appearing at the point of my pen. Five curious heads cast shadows on the page.

My penmanship is deplorable, but I am printing in capitals, so the letters are legible. The boys, if they are literate at all, would know only Lao script, which is as different from the Roman alphabet as the writing systems of Arabic and Chinese. Mok Keo, however, was educated in Vietnam and is literate in Vietnamese, which uses a modification of the Roman system. He knows his ABCs, and he's telling the boys how they work.

It sounds as though he is offering a kind of narration, but he cannot know the meaning of the words I am writing. Perhaps he is telling the boys generally about writing and its purposes; perhaps he is imagining what kinds of things I might be recording. The boys are rapt initially, but soon their attention slackens. So does Mok Keo's. My printing is small, and he signifies he's having eye trouble. He is probably nearing fifty, and if he were more concerned with reading or other small work he would doubtless need reading glasses. I hand him mine to try. He puts them on and immediately feigns great dizziness. Now Thong Dam tries them on, followed by Bone and the others, each one reeling, to the delight of his friends. Returning the glasses to me, they squat and again watch me write, evincing amusement but not envy. Had I been cleaning a large fish, I expect their attention would have been the same.

Ours is a happy camp this day: plenty of food last night, good fishing in the river, fine weather, and a comfortable campsite beside a beautiful, murmuring river.

Robichaud devotes the morning to organizing his specimens and bringing his field notes up to date. Simeuang has counted our haul of snares—more than five hundred so far. Our plan is to survey a couple of nearby streams this afternoon, but for now, Robichaud decides the time has come to document the expedition with a photograph. He calls everyone together on a midriver ledge. The Ban Beuk boys kneel in a line with the snares piled before them. Robichaud places the head of the juvenile muntjac in front of the snares. Everyone else stands behind the boys. I will take the picture. The light is good, the composition balanced. I kneel to fill the top of the frame with sky. Everyone looks proud and fit. Solemnly I count in Lao, "Neung. Song. Si!" As I press the shutter, riotous laughter breaks out. "Saam! Saam!" they call. "Three! Three!" I have blundered. In the concentration of the moment, I counted, "One. Two. Four!"

It is a good picture. It shows my miscount bringing mirth to the faces, smiles beginning to blossom.

Back row, left to right: Mok Keo, Olay, Touy, Viengxai, Simeuang, Phaivanh, Robichaud, Sone, Meet. Front: Kham Laek, Phiang, Bone, Thong Dam. Snare wires and head of juvenile muntjac in foreground.

. . .

Robichaud, Phaivanh, and I will go up the side creek that runs through camp, looking for sign of saola. Simeuang, Touy, Olay, and Sone will hike one drainage farther upriver and do the same.

We have scarcely started when we come upon the remains of yet another poachers' camp. It lies well hidden, back from the river, and has not been used for a long time. It features a crib of stout poles, intended for live porcupines. "Sometimes they set their snares with insulated wire, so that they cause less injury," Robichaud explains. Stuffed in a bag, porcupines are easy to transport, and they are worth more alive than dead, fetching high prices in the restaurant trade in both Vietnam and China. Robichaud adds that the manifests of ships plying the Vietnamese coast in the seventeenth and eighteenth centuries mention eaglewood, turtles, and rhino horn. "The trade in wildlife and precious wood is nothing new," he says. "It's just that now we are seeing the particular ugliness of the endgame."

While Robichaud and I go up the creek bed, Phaivanh, wearing his Statue of Liberty T-shirt, will flank us, checking the canyon side on the left for snares. I watch him go. His feet clad in flip-flops — I doubt he has worn a shoe in his life — he ascends the sheer slope, each step with equal strength, each foot placed exactly, always in balance, always with the same poised ease, whether moving forward or stepping back to avoid an obstacle. Walking and carrying loads are among the most mundane activities in life, but some people are better at them than others. The Sek and other residents of Nakai–Nam Theun acquired wheeled vehicles only a few years ago, when hand tractors and motorbikes arrived. And while they have long harnessed water buffalo to plow their paddies, they have never used pack animals. Every kilo of rice harvested from their mountain swiddens is carried homeward on their backs. The same may be said for every house post and bundle of thatch, at least until recently. From a young age, someone like Phaivanh would have walked miles every day in the forest, often bearing heavy loads. His ingrained skills are marvelous to behold. I can no more duplicate his grace in this terrain than I might match a Puebloan cliff dweller on the scarps of Mesa Verde.

This nameless stream is as flood-scrubbed and precipitous as the tributaries of the upper Nam Nyang. It holds few patches of mud or sand that might record a track. Still, it seems more promising. Robichaud says it smells right. To my eye, it closely matches the backgrounds of the few photographs of saola that camera traps have caught. The relative dimness, owing to the thickness of the canopy, seems to equal the dimness of the photos. Also similar is the ubiquity of horizontal vines, which, in defiance of gravity, extend laterally and improbably across the streambed like cables. Here the usual palette of greens has shifted toward gray, as though the foliage and rocks in this dank place achieved a kind of kinship. Whatever the secret of the creek may prove to be, we push on with anticipation, climbing a headwall and the ledge behind it, and another headwall and ledge, and on and on, like mice on a staircase.

An hour passes, and finally we face a dripping, moss-hung wall of rock that is double the height of those we've already scaled. Robichaud owl-hoots to Phaivanh, who comes sliding down to the creek. Phaivanh and I will wait here while Robichaud goes ahead "to see if there is anything worth checking out." His foray will be solitary and silent, the kind of reconnaissance he prefers.

A slow rain of leaves trickles from the canopy. A barbet chants *tookaroo*. The forest vibrates with an insect clatter that is like the rattle and whirr of a chain-link assembly line, as though an infinitude of gadgets were being manufactured. And indeed they are: stems, beetles, grubs, leaves, centipedes, eggs, nymphs, molds, turds, photosynthesized sugars, microstomatic exhalations of oxygen, and ten thousand things more. The ecofactory is running full bore.

Phaivanh and I exchange smiles, which, in the absence of a common language, is about all we have the capacity to share. I wonder about his prospects. He is a subsistence farmer, a quondam guide, and a militiaman. He can stay in his village or he can emigrate to Nakai or the poorer quarters of Vientiane. He is a good-hearted and capable fellow, and if he weren't working for us he might as easily work in illegal logging, the wildlife trade, or rosewood smuggling. He likely has dabbled in one or all of these areas already. There are surely other alternatives unknown to me, but not many. At this moment, Phaivanh is the master of an AK-47 and a fifteen-bullet clip. He cleans the surface of his weapon with a corner of his shirt and a spit-moistened twig, which he has chewed into a kind of brush. He picks out grime from the rifle's deepest crevices with the weirdly long nail of his little finger, which, like many of his countrymen, he cultivates for deep and satisfying scratching of the inner ear.

On one level I feel as though I am being held under guard. Phaivanh understands that a central element of his job is to keep me out of trouble. On another level I am more than content. Lazing in a pleasant woods has always been a source of consolation. From the age of twelve onward, I went into the woods behind my house every day after school to have a smoke. A log and a granite boulder made my easy chair. The L&Ms and Tareytons I stole from my parents only partway salved my adolescent insecurities. The calm of the trees, the aroma of leaf litter, and the random sounds of wind and water helped with the rest. So it is now in this forest, as long as we sit still and I am not reminded at every step that the forest and I are strangers to each other.

Robichaud returns. Unfortunately, he has found nothing. No *Schismatoglottis* and no tracks in sand or mud, for there is only stone in the stream channel and leaves and roots on the sides. It is a typical day surveying for saola. We seek the exceptional, the one in a million, the lottery jackpot, and we get the ordinary—a precipitous, rockbound stream in a merely beautiful mountain forest.

Departing the creek by the north wall of the canyon, the side that Phaivanh did not inspect, we soon encounter a snare line that must have been a monster to build. The steepness of the slope would have doubled the physical effort necessary to chop and pack the barriers and install the snares. As the Lao say, the Vietnamese know how to work. Both the Lao and the Cambodians are farming people. They are the *Indo* part of Indochina. The Vietnamese are the other part. They have more in common with their loved and hated Chinese neighbors to the north, who excel at trade and entrepreneurship.

The French noticed the difference between the two groups in the earliest days of colonization. The Lao refused to be good slaves. They might work for themselves, but they wouldn't work for European overlords. In frustration, the French imported Vietnamese into Laos to build a cadre of bureaucrats and overseers who would crack the whip on the peasantry and help squeeze wealth from the country.

And the wealth is still being squeezed, although it is now carried off in new pockets. The government of Laos continues to pay Vietnam reparations for the costs Hanoi bore when it "liberated" Laos from US-backed royalists in the 1970s. In addition, the relations between the two countries feature business concessions and sweetheart deals of every stripe and color, lopsidedly benefiting Vietnamese interests. The same may be said for relations between Laos and China, whose hunger for minerals and timber is without limit. That's at the macro level. At the micro level, the squeeze continues in places like Nakai–Nam Theun, in territory that nominally belongs to the Lao nation but effectively serves Vietnam as a collection ground. The ubiquity of snares and hacked rosewood stumps in the Nam Nyang watershed, to say nothing of the existence of the Rosewood Highway, bear the proof. They testify to the permeability of the border and to the unequal flow of wealth across it. In particular they testify to the nearly superhuman energy and industry of the men who build the snare lines, often in the rainy season, under conditions of astonishing hardship. They also testify to the utter absence of sympathy for wild creatures.

No doubt the poachers, or at least most of them, enjoy a beautiful sunrise as much as anyone. It may even be that they rejoice to hear a chorus of gibbons or the bark of a muntjac, and not because it betrays the location of game. I grant that they may delight in the music of the forest, yet this wins the creatures of the forest no reprieve. The fact remains that the situation is dire. The harvest of wildlife is indiscriminate, wasteful, and relentless. No one for a moment can believe that it is sustainable. We may sympathize with the poachers as individuals — they are poor; they work; they strive — and still blame the soulless system in which they work; we can acknowledge that the familiar rationalization "If I don't do it, someone else will" probably comforts those who regret cruelty while committing it; we can lament the pervasive belief that nothing can brake or halt the inexorable consumption of the forest and so to hold back is only to penalize oneself; but the net effect is that in this place, at this time, not the least shred of a conservation ethic operates in favor of wildlife. The result is a powerfully lethal combination: a dedication to work that would put pious Calvinists to shame yoked to a valuing of nature that counts only dollars and cents, yuan and dong.

A scan of world headlines attests that this bane afflicts places far from Southeast Asia, but Southeast Asia is surely its center. The hunger of the region for exotic flesh — for ivory and other animal parts deemed precious, and for the bones, fluids, and tissues of wild creatures to provide cures, real and imagined — has now spread to some of the remotest recesses of the world. Informed people know that the pursuit of blood ivory threatens the survival of elephant populations across broad swaths of Africa, but few have heard that jaguars in Guyana, in South America's north, now also feed the craving for big-cat *qi* in a growing Chinese colony there. This kind of hunger, to be fair, is not unlike other consumer hungers that draw substance from the planet and leave desolation behind, but it is redder in tooth and claw, for it literally tears flesh and spills blood.

In Vietnam I heard it said, as a point of pride, "We will eat anything with four legs except the table!" Ha-ha-ha. That's a good one. Pass the beer.

One day Robichaud and I had lunch in an open-air restaurant at a crossroads near the Mekong. We watched trucks and buses, in a blue diesel haze, make the turn onto Highway 8, bound eastward toward Lak Xao and Vietnam. The loads were heavy, the traffic constant. Then an enormous flatbed came from the opposite direction, from Vietnam, rattling and grinding to a halt. The driver parked it just outside our restaurant. "Do you know what that is?" asked Robichaud.

I did not. The truck was unremarkable, its load no more than a mass of empty cages, each a cube about three feet on a side, stacked two high and three wide the length of the bed.

"It's a dog truck," he said. "It'll load up in Thailand with strays, kidnapped pets—whatever its people can find or steal—and head back to Vietnam. Each of those cages will be jammed with terrified mutts, which will be sold for restaurant food."

We had just come from the market in Ban Namee, a small community beside the highway, where we browsed a modest selection of comestible and pharmacological wildlife. There were plucked bulbuls and mouse-deer hooves, dried geckos and a pile of bats. There were gaur teeth, monkey hands, and owl feet, all authentic. The biscuit-size squares of elephant skin may have been genuine, too, but one wondered about the tiger teeth, at one hundred dollars each. The rhino horn, price unknown, was undoubtedly fake. One limp corpse looked like a black bobcat in a furry cape: a giant flying squirrel, said Robichaud.

Whether the object of desire is a tiger penis, dog flesh, or a Tiffany diamond, the craving that makes it valuable goes back deep in time to hungers that transcend need. The early Greeks knew something about this. They had a story about ravening hunger, as they had a story about nearly every theme and subject. The protagonist in this case was a Thessalian prince, son of Triopas, who was named (not mellifluously) Erysichthon (pronounced "Erees-*ick*-thon"). It is fair to think of his tale as a parable of consumerism.

Because Erysichthon wantonly felled trees in a grove sacred to

Demeter, the Earth goddess avenged herself by sending Famine to sleep with the young prince. As Erysichthon and Famine embraced, Famine breathed her bottomless emptiness into him. Thereafter Erysichthon had an appetite that no amount of eating could sate. He ate through the storerooms of his father, the king, and when they were exhausted, he sold his own daughter into slavery and used the proceeds to continue feasting. Here one story intersects with another. As a result of other dealings with the gods, Erysichthon's daughter became a shape-shifter and managed to escape her enslavement. This worked to Erysichthon's benefit because now he was able to sell her again and again, and she would escape each time. Erysichthon's story exists in multiple variants, but Ovid, in *Metamorphoses*, tells us that eventually the deception with his daughter wore out, and Erysichthon was reduced to beggary. Even then his cravings did not die. With nothing else to feed him, he gorily tore into his own flesh and devoured himself, perishing not from hunger but from appetite.

At the top of the slope, the snare line we have been following crests the ridge and continues down the other side. No animal traveling the ridge can fail to encounter it. Robichaud and I pause at one sprung trap to examine a snared silver pheasant, a male in glorious plumage, its feathers a speckled snowfall beneath the corpse. Phaivanh starts down the other side, still following the line, collecting every wire noose. Soon he calls to us, with urgency.

He stands beside a red-shanked douc (also called douc langur), snared by one foot, hanging upside down. The limp hands reach vainly for the untouchable earth. The monkey has been dead for several days, possibly longer. Scavengers have torn away the fur and eaten one leg to the bone.

Like saola, red-shanked doucs are endemic to the Annamite Mountains and adjacent lowlands. Doucs range much of the length of the mountain chain, exhibiting intriguing but poorly understood color variation — black-, gray-, and red-shanked forms — from south to north. The adaptable rhesus macaque may travel the world in cages and inhabit many a zoo and testing laboratory, but maintaining a douc separate from its habitat requires competence that few institutions possess, so not many are found in captivity. Nevertheless, fashion designers should note that few creatures in nature, and certainly no other primates, dress with more flair. The basic suit of the douc is gray flannel, with a cape of black. Among the red-shanked, the trouser legs are the color of a Williamsburg brick. The fingers are black, but the hands and forearms are white, an elegant touch giving the appearance of long, fingerless gloves. The tail and rump are cream-colored, and the pretty, snub-nosed face, framed by a white beard and black headband, is mango orange, the color of a dessert.

Doucs are leaf eaters and lead an almost entirely arboreal life. The carcass in the snare before us testifies to the peril of a visit to the ground. The spring pole of the trap that killed the douc is thick, powerful, and tall, and when the monkey stepped into the snare, it must have whipped him into the air as though he were a minnow jigged on a salmon line. If he was lucky, his spine gave way and the snap killed him, but this was probably not the case. There are few vertebrates more supple than a douc, which even by the standards of monkeydom is lank and long-limbed and moves as though made of rubber. Probably the animal bobbed at the end of the wire for a long while, and kept bobbing as he clawed at the metal tourniquet that had seized his ankle. His shrieks would have caused the rest of his tribe to draw near. Perhaps they gathered in the trees above, chattering anxiously, faces contorted with worry. One or two might have come down and gingerly touched the victim, trying to understand his plaint or even comfort him. Perhaps they, too, picked at the wire.

I wonder if at some point the douc managed to right himself and perch atop the spring pole to which he was tethered. The maneuver would have required spectacular athleticism but, once the animal's panic subsided to a dull roar, maybe it was possible. Balancing on an unsteady stick, however, would have been expensive in energy and

Phaivanh with snared red-shanked douc.

concentration. Eventually the tribe moved away, to feed or sleep for the night, and unquiet darkness fell. Pain, exhaustion, and sleeplessness then took their toll. Fear was constant. The moment had to come when the douc could no longer hold on, and he toppled from his perch to hang inverted, gravity working his heart and veins the wrong way, the legs drained, the head gorged. Slowly, too slowly, dehydration and hunger eroded consciousness and pulse, a torture like the martyrdom of a saint at the hands of especially creative centurions.

Robichaud is cursing, stamping around, visibly moved. He's not distraught, exactly, but he has acquired a molar-grinding intensity. He retrieves a tiny video camera from his pack and records the scene, narrating the ghoulish details: "Particularly sad...a douc langur...listed on the IUCN Red List as globally endangered...usually arboreal, this one came to the ground for something and was caught in the snare and hung here until it died."

Phaivanh has found a scrap of trash nearby. It is an empty package boasting MENTHOL CANDY. A few words are printed in English, but most of the lettering is Vietnamese. The brand is Hanoi Capital. We are days of travel from the nearest village, much too far for local hunters to have come to set snares, and if any question remained about the Vietnamese origin of the men who built—and then abandoned—the snare, this bag is a kind of signature. We take pictures of the douc while Phaivanh prevents it from spinning. Robichaud is now silent. His narration and picture-taking finished, he has plunged deep into himself. Abruptly he stows the recorder in his pack and heads downhill, moving fast.

But it doesn't seem right to leave. The douc, a cousin primate, is still dangling. Should we not cut him down? But I have nothing to cut the wire with, and the spring pole is long, the junction of wire and pole too high to reach. Phaivanh is watching me the way a border collie watches a problematic sheep. He will not leave until I do, although he would certainly like to get on with things, gather the rest of the snares, and finish our patrol. I try to remember the Lao word for machete, thinking we could hack down the spring pole, but I cannot summon it. Besides, I don't think Phaivanh is carrying anything but his Kalashnikov. I am at a loss, also tired and hungry, an observer without tools. I take a last look at the douc and glumly follow Robichaud down the slope. Our failure to cut down the douc nags at me—it nags at me still—although I have no idea what I would have done with him once I had him on the ground. Just stretch him out and leave him? Perch him in the fork of a tree? Take him away and hide him, so that anyone returning to check the snares would get no benefit from his skull or hands or genitals, if he still had them?

Our small party is silent on the descent to the next creek and thence to the river, but my mind is churning. Mentally I compose an imagined letter, which grows into a report. Even as I hop boulders and dodge holdfast vines, I am cobbling together—and trying to hold in my memory—the sentences and paragraphs, then whole pages, calculated to alarm the International Environmental and Social Panel of Experts, the Independent Monitoring Agency, the managers of the WMPA, the World Bank, and the readers of *The New York Times*. I lay out the gravity of the cruel war on wildlife being waged in Nakai–Nam Theun and the extreme and poignant threat it poses to one of the richest concentrations of biodiversity on the planet. I persuade myself that if I set out the facts accurately and eloquently, infuse the argument with vigor, and build it step by inexorable step, the decision makers will finally and meaningfully take action. I see matters in sharp definition: the sequence of points to be made, the multiple elements comprising a solution, the ultimate benefits of a secure, well-patrolled protected area. I feel saturated with ideas.

Then we reach the river. We pause by the murmuring water. The air feels soft, the shadows cool and long. We rest, drinking deeply from our canteens. Gradually, cooling and rehydrating, I remember how the world works.

March 5

A Tributary of the Nam Nyang

The camp larder has become a source of mystery. Several days ago, abundance became scarcity. Now scarcity is transforming into abundance.

Simeuang has found a stash of instant noodles, which were previously reported exhausted. Perhaps, now that the idea of an early return to the villages has been quashed, we are not so poor in supplies as had been advertised. Simeuang offers me a steaming bowl in the early half-light, as though delivering an expensive present. The noodles are hot and salty, delicious and fortifying. Simeuang knows I am running on fumes, and indeed I could not be more grateful or relieved. Today we will climb Phou Vat, a lesser sibling of Phou Vang but a steep and forbidding mountain just the same, and I will need all the strength I can muster.

Our plan is to ascend the Nam Nyang tributary on which we are camped as far as terrain permits, and then, when we meet the inevitable headwall, to strike north and west, bushwhacking up the side of what we hope will be Phou Vat. If one is to believe our maps, the crest of the mountain resembles a shallow *M*. We will aim for the dip in the mountain crest. From there we'll descend toward Thong Kouang and our campsite of a week ago, which we hope to reach before dark.

Our collection of snares, including the dozens Phaivanh gathered yesterday, now numbers almost eight hundred, and the guides, led by Viengxai, have lobbied Simeuang hard to let them ditch them. The coiled bicycle cables look like a bundle of abused Slinkies and probably weigh ten kilos. The guides don't want to carry them any farther than they have to, least of all up and over Phou Vat. So far Simeuang has held firm—he wants to take the evidence of poaching back to the WMPA—but the guides won't let up. They are still on his case when Robichaud, Touy, Olay, and I set out at 7:00 a.m. We want to get a head start on the others and cover as much ground as possible without the chatter and agitation of the larger group; otherwise our chances of glimpsing wildlife are nil.

But first the boys and I have something to show Robichaud. We lead him across the river to a gully above camp. A hundred yards up the gully, on a little bench, is the Vietnamese camp a few of us landed in two days ago when we slid down the mountain to the tributary. Robichaud made his descent farther downstream and never saw it. He is impressed. We show him the elaborate tarp shelter, which has a pitched roof, extra high, perhaps to accommodate smoking meat in the rainy season. Next to it is a crib for porcupines, fourteen feet long and as sturdy as a hog pen, the largest we've seen. In the bottom of the gully we find wire tethers, which must have been used for holding live animals, maybe a muntjac or two or even, God forbid, a saola. Across the gully and partway up the slope, we spy a small table, which proves to be an altar of thin poles. On it are burnt joss sticks and the stub of a candle. A cardboard tube, brightly decorated and nearly full of incense, is stored safely under a tarp. The poachers who stayed here made their place of butchery as homelike as they could. Prudently, they burned the occasional offering to keep ghosts and Lao patrols away, not that they had much reason to worry about the latter.

We destroy what we can of the camp, but there is little of value to ruin. Our efforts are symbolic and recreational. It is not often one gets to wreck things guiltlessly. But the tarps that provide shelter are already in tatters, and the wood of the structures is too damp to burn. Still, I dig out a lighter from my pack, and we set fire to what we can, coaxing from the wreckage a pyramid of orange flame and a column of greasy smoke. Robichaud has confided that he, too, is badly troubled that we did not cut down the douc yesterday—"a monumental moment of unconsciousness," he calls it—but for now our little bonfire is diverting. He strikes a pose, and in the voice of Robert Duvall's Lieutenant Colonel Kilgore in *Apocalypse Now,* proclaims, "I love the smell of cheap Vietnamese plastic in the morning!"

The flicker of yard-high flames is on our backs as we exit the mouth of the gully and turn upstream. A stairway of river ledges stretches before us toward Phou Vat.

The river cleaves the forest, soft light filling the breach and settling a golden gleam on the rocks and water. Scores of birds, invisible in the trees, exult. They shriek and scream, raising a tropical hullabaloo. Robichaud identifies the calls of three different barbets, the red-vented, green-eared, and moustached, plus a blue whistling thrush and a pin-striped tit babbler, whose name is longer than its song. I listen to the cacophony like a dog watching television, fascinated but bereft of understanding. I wonder if Robichaud's memory for warbles and chirps and his facility for languages belong to the same cranial domain. By contrast, I am a mediocre linguist, and although I know the calls of the handful of passerines that dwell around my Rocky Mountain home, the profligacy of the tropics overwhelms me. The bird guide for the region runs to three hundred pages and presents half a dozen species per page. In the forest nearly every identification is by sound. The density of vegetation surrenders few glimpses of any animal, let alone a small, flitting bird. Maybe one reason the birds' calls are so insistent and their plumage so often colorful is that they, too, have trouble seeing each other.

The tributary we ascend has carved its way through the same limestone that we encountered on the main channel of the Nam Nyang. We clamber up the same kinds of water-smooth boulders and broken ledges. We peer into similar gravel-drilled potholes. Still, there is a difference. Where the main stem, in the rainy season, was broad and powerful enough to sweep away every fallen tree, on the tributary we find ourselves slowed by mounded debris dams and jackstrawed logs of prodigious girth. One toppled giant, roots on the bank, crown in the river, lies festooned with white orchids twining down its length. Over it we scramble and onto the next, which is a logjam of broken limbs and canted trunks twice as tall as any man. I find a kind of chimney within it and begin to climb, amused when the term *jungle gym* springs to mind.

Gradually we approach the upper limit of saola habitat, about one thousand meters above sea level. (Phou Vang tops out at 1,890 meters.) The lower limit, defined by increasing dryness, is close to four hundred meters in Laos but considerably lower in Vietnam, where the northeast monsoons keep more of the mountainsides moist. The upper limit of saola habitat (as far as anyone can claim to understand it) may also be determined by moisture, but in this case by an excess that produces a shift away from the suite of plants on which saola depend.

I can feel changes in moisture underfoot: humidity rises as we ascend, the canopy becomes shadier, and the microscopic algae on the river rocks thickens and grows more slippery. As the footing worsens, four steps on level ground without sliding or teetering begin to feel like a state of grace.

Far ahead, we hear—what? The murmur of disturbance. Up in the canopy, two hundred meters away, a billow of green leaves quivers. Robichaud already has his binoculars up. "Doucs," he says. "They haven't seen us yet." As I bring my glasses in focus, we hear a commotion to our rear. The guides are arriving, chattering gaily. The doucs vanish in a shimmer of boughs. The guides swarm toward us, up the rocks. Viengxai, no surprise, is in the lead. This is the first day of the expedition that they have set out at an early hour and the first day Robichaud did not want them to. The delicate intactness of the morning has fractured. We'll see no more doucs today. Crestfallen, he looks at me and shrugs.

The headwall blocking our progress has a niche in it, like the sill of a recessed window. Dropping his pack, Viengxai climbs into it. Around him, the headwall is streaked with rivulets of water, hung with ferns and clumps of moss, but the niche is dry. He reclines, stretching his legs, head propped on one hand, the other hand saucily poised on his hip. "Take my picture!" he calls. "Take my picture." I cannot bring myself to train a camera on him, but Robichaud plays along with Viengxai's vanity, coaching improvements to the Lao-beefcake pose. As he snaps a photo, he mutters to me, "I'll never take him on a trip again unless I cut his nuts off first." He snaps another. "If he allows me to do that, he can come."

We take more pictures framed by the dripping headwall: the three militia with their rifles; the Ban Beuk teenagers. Robichaud studies the map. He estimates the top of Phou Vat is six hundred meters above us. We retreat from the headwall a short distance, hunting for a patch where the slope leans back. We find something we think we can climb. Then we plunge from the open ground of the river into the trees and thrash our way into the tangle, clawing for altitude. Upward we flail and flounder.

The border with Vietnam lies a dozen kilometers east of us. It follows the crest of the Annamites, and because the axis of the mountain chain slants to the north-northwest, we would also intersect the border if we flew, crowlike, northward for about fifty kilometers. Then the remotest headwaters of the Nam Theun would be beneath us, and across the mountain divide, on a clear day, we might see the high ridges of Vu Quang National Park, in Ha Tinh Province. It was there, in May of 1992, that John MacKinnon's Vietnamese colleagues discovered saola. Unfortunately, their discovery launched a wave of captures and killings that, in retrospect, appear to have been a calamity for the animal they introduced to the world.

All of a sudden, people far and near, people with ready cash, wanted a "Vu Quang ox," preferably alive. They wanted one to observe and study, film and exhibit, or, in the event of death, dissect and mount. They wanted whole, live animals if possible but would settle for parts. They wanted saola for all the reasons that people want anything that is rare: vanity, novelty, scientific understanding, profit. It was as though the saola had stepped from the mists of anonymity into the glare of celebrity, but not the celebrity of an idol. It was the celebrity of a glamorous commodity. Competing Japanese television crews offered hunters in Vu Quang rewards that far exceeded their annual income just to bring one in.[1] The hunters responded by targeting their hunting efforts — "with alarming intensity," in the words of one observer — on an animal that they had seldom seen and rarely pursued. Previously it had constituted an infrequent supplement to their diet. Now, like tigers and golden turtles, it offered a path to wealth.[2]

In Vu Quang alone, WWF personnel documented seven saola killed from May through December of 1992 (six males lost to foot snares, one female hunted by dogs). Ten more were taken in 1993 and six in the first eight months of 1994 for a total of twenty-three dead.[3] Another estimate for the 1993–94 period placed the total even higher, at thirty.[4] These animals likely represented a substantial portion of the total saola population of the district. Certainly their loss materially depressed the capacity of the population to reproduce itself. And there were no doubt unreported losses as well. The goal in most of these instances was to capture a saola live, but the saola, whether snared by the foot or chased by dogs, failed to cooperate, and died. Many went down fighting. WWF researchers were shown two dogs that had lost eyes to saola horns and heard of others that were fatally gored. The hunters, too, had to respect the saola's fury, and more than once they resorted to the expedient of killing a mother saola in order to seize her undefended calf.

Forestry officials on the outskirts of Vu Quang appropriated one of these orphans in May of 1994.[5] The calf was female, four or five months old, and weighed forty pounds. It stood about two feet high at the shoulder and had large eyes, a fluffy tail, and stubs of undeveloped horns. The saola calf was quickly conveyed to the eight-acre FIPI campus outside Hanoi, where Do Tuoc and his colleagues installed it in an airy shed. The campus doubled as a botanical garden, and after the juvenile saola settled down and adjusted to its new surroundings, its handlers sometimes opened the door of the shed and allowed it to roam the gardens, feeding as it wished. Little was known (then or now) about the saola's preferred diet, but one plant saola were believed to eat was identified as *Homalomena aromatica,* an herb with heart-shaped leaves belonging to the Araceae, or aroid, family. Because of its medicinal properties, *Homalomena* was grown in some abundance at FIPI. The saola's caretakers found additional sources of *Homalomena* and experimented with other browse. The young female began to put on weight.

Meanwhile, a second juvenile saola was captured, possibly near Pu Mat, in Nghe An Province. The authorities seized this one, too, and took it to the provincial capital at Vinh. A WWF contractor, Shanthini Dawson, and Pham Mong Giao, a specialist in large mammals with Vietnam's Forest Protection Department who had participated in the second Vu Quang survey, traveled down to Vinh to supervise its care. This calf was male, younger than the first, and much smaller. Giao and Dawson fed it milk from a bottle. Eventually it, too, was brought to FIPI and placed with the older female.

They were mild creatures, "not very aggressive," said Giao. Together they wandered the FIPI gardens, and when a train rumbled past on the tracks that abutted the entrance gate, they dove for cover in the shrubbery. Unfortunately, the young male never prospered. Perhaps he had been injured when captured; perhaps he was too young to thrive without his mother's care. The female, however, kept growing. By October she weighed close to seventy pounds, a thirty-pound gain. Then both saola fell sick. The FIPI caretakers summoned veterinarians and called as far away as London for advice. The little male died first. The female followed it, having survived since capture four and a half months, still a record for saola. Members of the FIPI staff wept.

The official cause of death, said to be based on an autopsy, was reported as liver flukes, the explanation holding that saola, being native to high mountains, could not tolerate the parasites of Hanoi's

Juvenile saola at FIPI, Hanoi, 1993. (Courtesy J. C. Eames)

low, hot, delta environment. Le Van Cham, however, does not agree. He worked at FIPI in those days and followed the progress of the young saola closely. He felt a personal interest in the fate of the species, for it had been he who first spotted saola horns on the wall of a hunter's shack in Kim Quang, when he and Do Tuoc went looking for vegetables. The two young saola did not waste away from parasites, he says; they were accidentally poisoned. Cham heard (and this was confirmed to me separately by one of Cham's colleagues) that someone fed the saola juveniles *Annona* fruit, familiarly known as custard apple, the black seeds of which are sufficiently toxic for a powder made from them to be used to control head lice. Cham believes that *Annona* seeds poisoned the two young bovids.

The skins and at least parts of the skeletons were retained as specimens. No one openly discusses the fate of the soft tissues, but the assumption, attested to by various reports, is that they were eaten. On a visit to Hanoi, I asked around. At best, answers were oblique, but one of the cognoscenti allowed that "young saola meat is soft, better than older, better than muntjac."

Imagine a ladder that stretches upward until it disappears. Imagine that half the rungs are broken or about to break, but you cannot tell which ones because they are wreathed in vines that bristle with thorns. Such a ladder is the side of Phou Vat we are climbing. The guides, understandably, are unhappy. We are off trail, on an absurd route. Their packs, although lighter than when we set out from Ban Nameuy, are still heavy and snag easily in the crisscrossing growth that riots on the mountain. But no matter: Bone or Meet or Phaivanh, at the first tug of a restraining vine, halts midstep in perfect balance, rocks back an inch or two, and ducks or tilts to slip the momentary tether. Then he completes his step, steady as an acrobat, and engages the next with metronomic poise. I watch them enviously, when I can steal a glance, as I flail and bull upward, lighter-burdened but expending far more energy, a cart horse among Lipizzaners.

We have not battled the slope for long when to our surprise we crest a knifelike ridge. Even here, a snare line follows the blade. Meet says he hears voices. As he speaks, something in the near distance crashes off through the brush, and the three militiamen, shedding their packs, rush to follow. The other guides commence collecting snares while Robichaud stands puzzled, squinting at his maps. We are at the top of something. We aren't supposed to be. Robichaud looks for a vantage point from which to see beyond the ridge. There is none; the trees are too thick. He aligns the maps with his compass and compares them. He looks up, grinning sheepishly. "Maybe I need glasses," he says. "Down there, I read this slope as six hundred meters tall. It is only sixty." Turns out he'd read the close-packed contour lines on the map as a single slope, mistaking those that represented scarps on the far side of the mountain as belonging to the near side, which we had just climbed.

Before the news can sink in, the militiamen are back, winded. Again, nothing. The noise was probably a muntjac or sambar bolting. Robichaud is laughing. Our six-hundred-meter vertical ordeal has shrunk by nine-tenths, and the climb lies behind us. We will soon go down what we had thought we would climb up. I am slow to believe him. Phou Vat cannot be through with us. It is only noon. The day has been too easy. I expected to suffer.

We attack the snare line with more than usual energy. The guides collect the cables. The boys and I rip the bamboo trigger rods from their concealment in the ground, and with their machetes Robichaud and Simeuang hack the spring poles so that they cannot be used again. We encounter the remains of various animals, but most are too decayed to identify. The feathers of yet another male silver pheasant shine from a litter of leaves and rot.

Skidding and sliding, we descend the far side of Phou Vat in little time and strike the headwaters of a lazy brown-water creek, which we follow toward our old camp beside Thong Kouang. The creek deepens as we go. A mile downstream it has become a flooded U-shaped depression sixteen feet deep. We come to a chainsawed stump. A tree has been felled as a bridge. Some kind of camp lies across the stagnant water.

The tree is too long and narrow for me to trust my balance. While the guides glide across, not even breaking stride, I slide down the crumbling bank and wade the thigh-deep, paint-thick water. Robichaud opts to wade, too. We head for steps cut into the far bank, probably the camp's water trail, but Simeuang, who has crossed by the felled tree, looks down and calls our attention to a decomposing carcass, angular with bone, breaking the surface of the water, two meters downstream of us. Simeuang's face is contorted with disgust. He motions to Robichaud to stay away.

The camp is larger and more elaborately outfitted than any we have seen. Essentially it is a processing facility for poached wildlife. It has a chest-high butchering table decked with planks and a roasting pit large enough for an entire muntjac. It has a smoking rack two yards square woven from bamboo slats and set above several charred logs and a deep accumulation of fire ash. Other logs, four inches thick, are laid up like a small cabin to form the walls of a live-animal crib. The usual frames for hammocks and tarps, however, are absent. Instead there is a proliferation of posts, tables, stands, and rails, high and low, that radiate backwards from the slough and the fireplaces. Some of these skeletal structures no doubt served domestic purposes while some served the processing work, but there is no time for further analysis because Robichaud, Simeuang, the boys, and most of the guides, machetes in hand, are slashing the bamboo wraps that bind the joints of the structures and are rapidly throwing them down, pole by pole.

Our wrecking of the butchering camp gave vent to our anger, but the damage we produced was trivial. A returning crew might rebuild the camp in hours. Nevertheless, we walked away convinced that the carnage we had seen in the Nam Nyang was equally virulent on the north side of Phou Vat, even though we were now much closer to the villages.

The guides hurried ahead to make camp, leaving the slow foreigners to look at birds and odd features of the land. Simeuang and the boys lingered with us. Phaivanh, ever bemused, kept guard.

Our dawdling brings a reward. In a seasonally flooded wetland, now a dry meadow, we find the tracks of at least two gaur, one large, one small, presumably a mother and her calf. Seeing the big one's track, preposterous in its size, is like seeing the print of a Kodiak bear or some other remnant of Pleistocene megafauna. It harks back to a time when nature's most extravagant experiments shook the ground; when only insects, not humans, numbered in the billions. The tracks are weeks to months old, perhaps as old as the ashes in the fire pits of the butchering camp, which lay no great distance away. Gaur are a dwindling reminder of the former abundance of big animals in NNT. We wonder if these two giants succumbed to the smoking rack.

When we reach camp, Bone is stirring a pot of rice pudding with a stick. The pudding, which Mok Keo has seasoned with a handful of herbs, is made from regular (dry) rice, not sticky rice, a staple we earlier believed had been consumed. The magical reappearance of food continues. I feel pampered to arrive in camp, hot and hungry, and find a meal waiting. Even better, the meal consists of something other than fish bones and a cue ball of sticky rice.

As we did on our outbound journey, Robichaud, Simeuang, the boys, and I will camp apart from the guides. Lugging our gear to the *thong*, we check the death site of the snared muntjac that Simeuang and I had inspected a week earlier. Jungle fowl crow cock-a-doodle-doo from the forest edge. The body, foul though it was, has been removed. Only a black, maggoty grease spot and the shanks of two hind legs remain. Simeuang reminds us that there is value in the antlers, head, and larger bones. The lone bicuspid that I had considered taking is also gone.

We realize that we have been circling poachers, and poachers have been circling us, for a week.

A pair of brown hornbills yelps from distant treetops as we pitch our tents, the sky vast above us, the claustrophobic forest held at bay. Robichaud comes over. His shirt is plastered to his torso with sweat. He is gaunt, and the dishevelment of his hair recalls snarled fishing line. In a voice borrowed from Humphrey Bogart in *The*

Treasure of the Sierra Madre, he growls, "I know you've got a half bottle of Scotch in that pack. Viengxai told me so."

If only it were true.

Guides drop by. Bone says he lately turned fourteen and claims to remember Robichaud passing through Ban Beuk when he was five. He beams with goodwill. He says he wants to continue guiding until he gets old. We make tea. Phaivanh and Viengxai arrive, the former amiable and silent, the latter brimming with complaint. Viengxai scolds us, particularly me, for failing to appreciate what a nuisance my pack is, how it catches on the vines, how hard it made the journey for him. No one pays him attention, but we give both him and Phaivanh cups of tea. Bone has left, and there are now seven of us. We pool what we have: a small bag of dried cranberries, a handful of nuts and raisins, and some dried mushrooms from Luang Prabang. We are far from replacing the calories we spent this day—or any day in NNT—but the morsels amount to a feast.

Robichaud has formed a decision over the past days. Originally he thought we might set up one or more camera traps near Ban Kounè and leave them in place to last through the upcoming rainy season. But now he's not so sure. No site in that area seems particularly promising, and the cameras would be vulnerable to theft. Robichaud also considered establishing traps in the Nam Nyang, but the Nam Nyang's remoteness would make servicing the cameras—renewing batteries and memory cards—too difficult. Another site, instead, has come to the fore. He wonders why he didn't think of it weeks ago. It is a mineral lick, a *poung,* high up on a river called the Nam Mon—Mulberry River—in the northern reaches of NNT. Saola are said to frequent the place, and two years ago Robichaud may even have bagged two camera-trap pictures, seconds apart, of a saola there. He's not sure.

The pictures show a large mammal, certainly an ungulate, with its head down, nearly facing the camera. Unfortunately, a large, broad leaf has spread in front of the camera, screening the animal's head so that no horns or antlers or any facial markings can be seen. Is it a sambar? A muntjac? A saola? The camera was installed, at Robichaud's direction, in March of 2009, but he was elsewhere in the protected area when the work was carried out. The camera snapped the pictures on the afternoon of April 20, after plenty of time had passed for a plant to grow into view and spread its leaves.

With Rob Timmins and Will Duckworth, Robichaud has pored over the images, comparing the mystery animal to shots of sambar and two species of muntjac taken at the same location during the same period. The rounded withers and thick barrel of the animal seem to favor a saola more than any of the local deer, which have a rangier build. Timmins, who has squinted at many thousands of camera-trap photographs, says he is 95 percent sure the animal is a saola: "I can't think of it being much else."

If it is a saola, the animal at the *poung* of the Nam Mon is the first of its species to be photographed since 1999.

Moreover, when a joint team of villagers and WMPA staff approached the *poung* in March of 2009 to install the camera trap, they claim to have surprised a saola at a bend in the river. The animal quickly bolted for the forest, but at least one, maybe two members of the group got a fleeting look at it. The first in line says he saw the extravagant horns. He swears it was a saola.

Robichaud wants to retrace their journey. Since we are nearly out of food, we will return to Nakai, where Touy, unfortunately, will leave us (so that he can bid good-bye to his Java-bound girlfriend). We will obtain fresh supplies and return as quickly as possible to the protected area, this time traveling to the Nam Mon by way of Ban Navang. We'll install multiple cameras at the *poung*. It will be a good test of the cameras and our best chance yet to photograph — or to glimpse — a saola.

The saola's discovery in 1992 — on the evidence of horns and hides — launched a race to capture the first photograph of the living animal in the wild. But the inaccessibility of saola habitat and the cumbersome equipment then available guaranteed that the race would be slow. Early camera setups were clumsy contraptions. The first system was deployed in Vu Quang, site of the initial discovery. Its trigger was a pressure-sensitive mat, modified from a burglar alarm. A footfall on the mat sparked a flash unit, specially altered to conserve battery power, and caused a motor-driven 35mm camera to expose several frames of film. All the gear was off-the-shelf consumer stuff, good quality and dauntingly expensive, but hardly designed for the rigors of a Vietnamese rain forest.

Six of these contrivances were installed on game trails in the Vu Quang forest. And pretty much everything that could go wrong did. The units leaked. Moisture shorted and corroded the batteries, even though they were packed in silica gel. The energy-conserving flash conserved too much battery power, and nighttime photographs were uselessly dark. The burglar mats, meanwhile, stayed dry, thanks to encasement in rubber sheeting, but termites found both the sheeting and the mats to their liking and ate holes through them, shorting the mats and causing the cameras to use up their film on rapid-fire pictures of nothing. To top matters off, the rubber sheeting emanated a pungent, durable stink that seemed to keep wildlife away.

Vu Quang researchers also experimented with systems triggered by sensors that responded to sound or touch, such as that of an animal brushing by. It turned out that a good breeze and dancing, scraping leaves were sufficient to set them off. More nothing.

In January of 1998 a saola was cornered by dogs and photographed only fifteen kilometers from the citadel of the ancient Vietnamese capital of Hue. Some might argue that the incident produced the first image of a wild, living saola, but the dogs had chased the saola into a rice field—hardly its natural habitat—and it did not survive the ordeal.

Photographic success finally came in October and November of 1998 with camera traps set near a presumed mineral lick in the Pu Mat Nature Reserve (before Pu Mat was a national park), in Nghe

An Province, Vietnam. Five separate photographs, three of them taken at night, show either one or two animals. The triggering device was an infrared beam transmitted from a generating device to the camera. The camera fired when an animal stepped into the beam.

Even better images appeared a few months later in Laos. Robichaud, then working for WCS (with support from IUCN), instituted a program in a proposed northern extension of Nakai–Nam Theun under which five participating villages stood to receive rewards of approximately two hundred dollars for each camera-trap photograph of saola they secured. The camera-trapping began in late 1998, but for reasons never made clear, the governor of Bolikhamxay Province soon banned Robichaud and his colleagues from returning to the study area. (Most likely the governor did not want them to see something—perhaps logging trucks where logging trucks should not have been.) Robichaud then entrusted care of the camera traps to two young men who had been assisting him, Saykham and Kambai, both from the Toum ethnic group. They rendezvoused each month in Lak Xao, one or two days' walk from the young men's village, to exchange film and replacement batteries. The cameras they used marked another step up from previous models—their sensors could detect both motion and body heat, and they were self-contained; there was no separate beam generator that had to be installed.

Late in the dry season, only four cameras still operated, but Saykham and Kambai kept at it. They placed the cameras according to their own judgment and not, says Robichaud, "where I would have placed them." In April, at the conclusion of the project, the cameras were duly retrieved and delivered to Lak Xao. Their developed film showed two excellent images of saola, taken in separate locations, including one shot that has since become iconic in the small world of saola conservation. The photograph shows a burly animal, probably a pregnant female, hock deep in a pool of water. The saola, standing broadside, has turned its head to face the camera and appears regal, defiant, and supremely wild.

Camera-trap photograph of possibly pregnant saola, Bolikhamxay Province, 1999. (Ban Vangban Village / WCS, courtesy William Robichaud)

After that, a decade of nothing. No camera-trap photographs, no captures or sightings save for the reports of village hunters. Granted, only a handful of field biologists were plying the dank habitats of Vietnam and Laos, but they all came up empty. The long drought of information made saola conservation seem, more than ever, a futile enterprise.

Finally, in August of 2010, word raced from the Bolikhamxay hills to Vientiane and thence to the rest of the world that a saola had been captured alive. According to sanitized reports, a group of men were walking through the forest. Their dogs caught scent of a saola, gave chase, and brought it to bay. At the risk of goring, the men wrestled the saola, bound it with vines, and held it in a hastily constructed pen.

Not everyone believes this. An alternative interpretation holds that the story about the dogs was invented to obscure the fact that the men caught the saola in a snare. In any event, a runner was dispatched to alert the authorities, but heavy rains slowed communication. The area of the capture being closed to Westerners, district officials, with support from WCS, rushed to the site. When they arrived late on the fourth day of the saola's captivity, the traumatized animal was already in steep decline. It died the following morning. Someone, however, took a picture. It shows the saola lying belly down on folded legs, in a small corral or sty, tethered by several thin cords. The saola looks abject, but it is a fine specimen, with horns twice as long as its head. Although the capture proved fatal, it nevertheless demonstrated that saola were still out there, that the long-horned will-o'-the-wisp remained corporeal, that there was something yet to save.

A short time later a second report came in from Bolikhamxay. A hunter, checking a trapline only fifteen kilometers from the previous incident, found a live saola in one of his snares. He raced back to his village for help, but returned to find that the saola was gone — broken free, he said. One hopes it escaped with all its feet intact. The patch of forest separating the sites of the two encounters is regarded locally as a "spirit forest" and rarely hunted. It was subsequently declared a protected area, and since then, Olay, in conjunction with a WCS-organized survey, has documented tens of additional saola encounters in the vicinity.

Evidence exists that saola survive. Exactly where and in what number no one knows. After the Nam Nyang, perhaps the most promising location in NNT is the *poung* of the Nam Mon, where the frustratingly ambiguous images of 2009 were captured. Finally, we are mere days from getting new cameras into this old place and perhaps days from our own best chance at seeing the animal itself. The Nam Nyang may have disappointed us, but our hunt has far to go.

March 6

Thong Kouang

Gibbons call in the dawn haze. All manner of owls, barbets, and laughingthrushes hoot, thrum, chunk, and whistle. Touy, by his tent, sings softly.

Viengxai, the human toothache, appears by the tents and ruptures the morning peace. He says *phi kong koy,* the wild man of the forest, was calling in the night. Robichaud hears him out and thinks he might be genuinely spooked, not just putting on a show. I don't care. If he had conversed with the Virgin of Guadalupe or the living Siddhartha Gautama, I still would not care.

We retrieve the camera traps from the *poung* where we left them a week ago, and Robichaud returns across the veld of Thong Kouang with the cameras in a plastic bag emblazoned with the Australian flag and the word SALE in giant red letters. He looks like a vagrant fleeing a shopping mall.

We remove the memory cards and place them in our digital point-and-shoot cameras for viewing. The guides are intensely interested and crowd close to see. I step out of the throng for a moment to put my camera's memory card in a safe place, and Viengxai immediately seats himself on my camp stool and starts tinkering with one of the cameras. When I return, I take him by the upper arm and lift him from the stool. For someone who has weighed us down so heavily, he is surprisingly light.

Robichaud loads the cards from the first and second cameras, but neither took a picture. This is a disappointment, not just for want of game but also because of concern for the reliability of the cameras. I load the card from the third camera, and it has something. I need a moment to read the picture. There is glare on the screen, then too many heads blocking the light, too many fingers pointing.

The camera snapped two images. In each, a long, snakelike thing crosses the field of view. It barely enters one picture, but in the second, which was taken within an instant of the first—before or after is not immediately clear—it extends across most of the scene. The lighting is poor and the focus fuzzy, but the creature appears to be a big snake, a cobra or python. The guides whoop. It must be a python, they say. Only a python is that big. A dozen heads strain to see the tiny screen. A python would be a weighty portent. A dream of a dangerous animal, especially a snake, is considered a powerful harbinger of good fortune. A picture, especially one taken remotely, as this one was, is something like a dream. The guides are jubilant.

Robichaud is not so sure, however. The camera sensor responds to heat. It is supposed to detect warm bodies moving across a cooler background. A snake is cold-blooded, the temperature of the environment. How would it trigger the sensor? "We'll figure it out in Nakai, on the computer screen," he says. In the meantime, the guides celebrate the advent of the putative python as the best possible news.

The patter is merry as we set out for the villages. Tonight the guides will sleep under their own roofs. They are horses headed for the barn. We all are.

Robichaud has taken a separate route down the length of the *thong,* cruising the east side of the grassland while the rest of us follow the trail on the west. Years ago he flushed a covey of quail there. He wants to see if he might find the birds again. But meanwhile he has spotted a crested goshawk cruising the forest edge. He whistles for us to stop and be quiet. Raggedly the line comes to a halt, but not the noise. Viengxai jabbers loudest. The goshawk flies out of sight, and Robichaud resumes walking. So do the guides. Soon we reach the edge of the *thong*, and the guides continue into the forest without waiting for Robichaud.

He waves at them and double-times to catch up. He shouts for them to come back. They assemble, indifferent, at the entrance to the forest. Robichaud's outward calm contains a vibrato of anger. "I only ask two things: silence, and that the person most capable of identifying birds and other animals goes first." The veins stand out on his neck. "This is a wildlife *survey*. You never know what you will see. It could be something important, something we need to see. But we won't see it if people are talking, and we won't see it if the right person isn't where he needs to be. In this group, I go first. It's that simple."

We start again, but within a kilometer, a hubbub of chitchat rises from the line. In frustration, Robichaud sends the guides ahead. "We'll let them go as fast as they want and hopefully create a gap of peace and quiet between us and them. By the time we get down the trail, maybe the birds and critters will have settled back down."

If they did, we didn't see them. The next fifteen kilometers are hot, strenuous, and empty of wildlife or diversion.

Every hour we stop briefly to rest. Simeuang, despite the heat, wears his usual turtleneck and wool pants. Touy has stripped down to a T-shirt, but Olay, lest the sun darken his already dark arms, remains enveloped in his broken-zippered raincoat as we toil up and down the hills. Late in the afternoon, when finally Olay steps out of his coat, his T-shirt is completely dry. Robichaud's shirt is damp in patches, betraying the heat only modestly. My saturated clothes, meanwhile, have become a badge of ill adaptation.

At the first rice paddies, we hear the cry of a baby from a distant thatched hut. We come to a fence, a planting of cassava, a patch of banana trees. We come to our guides, sitting under a shade tree by the trail, playing cards.

Phiang, the quietest of the Ban Beuk teens, is said to be related to someone in a nearby hut who is alleged to be boiling a pot of cassava. The guides, all but Viengxai, are waiting for their snack.

Viengxai has gone off on his own. He has taken my pack. It is ninety-one degrees Fahrenheit in the shade.

Robichaud sits. We all sit. A half hour passes, and nothing changes. "These guys are supposed to be working for us," he says. "They said they needed an early start this morning so they could get home, and now look: they're having a picnic."

Mok Keo has just won a hand. "You go ahead," he suggests. "We'll bring the packs later."

Robichaud has had enough. He had intended to continue on to Ban Kounè today, but precious time is slipping by. We won't make it now. He thrashes through the piled equipment, searching for his gear, which has been distributed among several loads. Finding his tent and sleeping bag, he rams the missing items into his larger pack, which he quickly shoulders, then puts on his daypack backwards, across his chest, and sets off, muttering that this is the worst crew he's ever had. Simeuang, the boys, and I follow.

"Where's my pack?" I ask. Touy says Viengxai has it at the house of the woman cooking cassava. Simeuang says he's taken it to his paddy. Robichaud says he's gone to the village with it. The pack could be anywhere. If Robichaud is frustrated, I am ready to strangle Viengxai, or anyone.

A kilometer down the trail, a woman in a conical hat tends rice stalks in a flooded paddy. A naked, muddy toddler with red insect bites stippling her chest stands in the trail, staring at us in bewilderment, not sure whether to cry. Beyond the paddy is a house. My pack leans against a house post. Simeuang calls to Viengxai. We hear him shout back something that includes the words *kin khao*, then he hurries from the door and across the porch, hopping on one foot as he pulls on his pants. Soon he is trailing behind our moody group with my pack on his back, singing incongruously, unable as ever to remain silent.

When we arrive at Kong Chan's, the porch bitch is guarding the top of the stairs. I have a pole in hand ready to whack her. She calculates the odds and, as we march up, dashes down the stairs and disappears, growling, under the house. We unpack a little and drink tea. We rest. Soon Kong Chan appears. He already knows about the photograph of the python. In his loudest Wolfman Jack voice, he proclaims the appearance of a great snake to be an omen of success. "The next animal that camera photographs will be a saola!"

Bone with snared ferret badger. (Courtesy William Robichaud)

Eventually the guides straggle in with the rest of the gear. Last up the stairs is Bone. The vile bitch darts from ambush and attacks him, avenging her displacement. She gets him on both legs. The bites streak his legs with blood but do not bleed enough to cleanse the wounds. Touy administers first aid, and I contribute a Betadine swab and some surgical wash, although neither is effective against a closed puncture. The danger of infection looms, for the bitch no doubt has mouth flora to match a Komodo dragon's.

At the other end of the veranda, Simeuang and Robichaud hold court as paymasters. Each guide gets forty thousand kip per day, plus a share in the aggregate reward (at fifteen hundred kip per snare) for collecting 970 snares. Split nine ways, the snare bounty equals pay for four extra days' work—about twenty US dollars—and brings each man's total to almost half a million kip, or slightly more than sixty US dollars. Smiles are broad and the banter light-hearted as bills are dealt like playing cards. As soon as each man has his wad, he takes off. Everyone has a family to see and beers to buy. Tonight will be a night of celebration.

When the porch has emptied, one of Kong Chan's daughters goes under the house to collect the sulking black bitch that bit Bone. She hauls her up and locks her in an airless cabinet on the porch. The dog intermittently howls and scratches for a span of hours, then nothing.

III

Circling Back: Nakai, Again

March 7

Ban Nameuy

Inky night has settled on the village. Music and loud voices echo. Sometimes running feet patter past the house. Finally sleep comes, but not for long. In the wee hours a voice speaks:

"Wil-yam, are you asleep?"

Silence.

"Are you asleep?" A little louder.

Viengxai's older brother, who speaks fair English, has the expressionless gaze of a stoned cat. Earlier, he had attended a meeting with Kong Chan that lasted most of the evening. At last everyone left, including Kong Chan, and the house became quiet. Now Viengxai's brother is back. He squats outside the mosquito net like a cat at a mouse hole.

Robichaud stirs.

"Wil-yam, are you asleep?"

"Huh?"

"Let's go partying."

"Too tired."

"Let's go partying."

"No."

"Let's go where Simeuang went."

"Don't know where he went."

"Let's just go. We'll find out."

"No."

"Wil-yam..."

Viengxai's brother has run out of money, a misfortune because parties have broken out in Ban Nameo, Ban Nameuy, and Ban Beuk to celebrate the expedition's return—or, more particularly, the guides' payday. This far from Nakai, beers aren't cheap—about three and a half US dollars for a 750-milliliter bottle—but with nine men carrying sixty new dollars apiece, the brew has nevertheless been flowing.

Unfortunately, this late in the evening no one seems to be giving it away, at least not to Viengxai's brother.

"Wil-yam..."

Robichaud burrows deeper into his sleeping bag. Viengxai's older brother studies him a few minutes more, then rises silently and leaves.

He returns within the hour, accompanied by several others and a quantity of clinking beer bottles. The party has come to us, but we remain in our sleeping bags. Simeuang and the boys, who have recently come in and gotten settled, do likewise.

Eventually the loud voices and clacking bottles retire to the kitchen, leaving the main house a little quieter.

When finally the party moves next door, a baby in one of the sleeping closets begins to bawl. After it calms, the dogs, pigs, and chickens under the house take up the cause, and their hubbub sizzles through the floor. I feel like I am being fried in a skillet of noise. I have no idea what is disturbing them.

Then Kong Chan crashes up the stairs. He stands at the porch railing and declaims the imperfections of the world in an angry, stentorian voice. Judging by the length of the oration, his docket of complaint is comprehensive. No one in the village can have failed to hear it. I look at my watch: 3:45 a.m.

Kong Chan comes inside, still spewing.

His wife stage-whispers from their sleeping closet, "Be quiet! You'll wake the foreigners."

He growls back, "It's my house. I'm the village chief! I have the power!"

"But you'll wake the foreigners!"

"It's my house! I'll do what I want!"

. . .

Impressively, Kong Chan betrays no sign of hangover or weariness when we meet with leaders of the village the next day to discuss saola conservation. Elders they are not. None of the five men whom Kong Chan has invited—and they are all men—is older than forty, and one is barely twenty. All are active hunters or have hunters in their households. Robichaud wants to sound them out on an idea.

In two days we will meet a boat in Ban Makfeuang that will take us back to Nakai to resupply. This leaves time for a round of conservation diplomacy. Many people in Ban Nameuy and its sister communities consider rare creatures, like saola, a liability because their presence sometimes brings restrictions, including more policing. Robichaud wants to turn that liability into an asset and improve the odds for rare species. He would like to set up a network of camera traps close to the village cluster, tied to a system of rewards similar to the system that helped net photos of saola in Bolikhamxay in 1999. If one of the traps, say, captured the picture of a saola or a tiger, something like two hundred US dollars would be paid into a fund for the villages. If a large-antlered muntjac were photographed, a reward of perhaps one hundred dollars would be paid, and so on down the scale of rarity. The money might go to schools or to any project valued by the community. Robichaud wants to gauge whether people would support such an arrangement and, if certain animals were consequently worth more alive than dead, whether it would change how people hunted. Would they avoid certain areas, use dogs less often, or set fewer snares?

But Robichaud is cautious and doesn't present his proposal in full. He reasons that if he suggests, no matter how speculatively, that money might be paid for photographs of animals, the suggestion will be taken for a certainty, and expectations will soar. Any failure to fulfill those expectations might then destroy the utility of the program as well as his personal credibility. So he speaks in general terms, asking hypothetically—*We're just talking as friends here*—what form should those benefits take if somebody, the government or an NGO, were to design a program to reward the villages for saola conservation?

He is still elaborating his ambiguous question when a figure fills the door. Robichaud looks up and says in English, "Ah, Mr. Ka flies in on his black wings." Ka—Mr. Crow—the redoubtable hunter from Ban Kounè, joins the circle on the floor. His presence is puzzling. We have sent word to Ban Kounè requesting a similar meeting tomorrow, so why did Ka trouble to come to Ban Nameuy? Does he intend to monitor all talk of saola and conservation? Ka sits and instantly composes himself, eyes alive but otherwise as motionless as a post.

Simeuang and Kong Chan have opened notebooks and are taking notes. Olay, like me, sits outside the primary circle. He also scribbles away. Perhaps his observations of the meeting will find their way into his thesis. The village men whom Kong Chan has gathered—Sunya, Ping, Tong Ka, Pone, and Tien—listen with varying levels of concentration. Pone, alone among them, reports that he has actually seen a saola. It was a decade ago, when he was a boy, in the forest between Ban Nameuy and Ban Kounè. "Are you sure it was not a serow?" Robichaud asks. "I am sure," he says. "I also checked the tracks, and they were saola."

Pone and the others are not restless, but they shift position now and again, idly scratching, stifling yawns, solemnly observing the proceedings. In the half-light of Kong Chan's house, I shoot a few photographs, careful to turn off the flash. Only the immovable Ka sits still enough for the long exposure.

When Pone has spoken, the others briefly take their turns.

Robichaud attempts to draw them out: What do people want? Is something needed for the school? What about an easily accessed water tap where everyone might fill their jugs? What about piping spring water to the paddies? There is equivocal assent that all Robichaud's suggestions have value, but none elicits a strong response.

Improved irrigation for the paddies would be good. Also a secondary school for the village cluster. Also a road.

With no women present, one wonders how fairly the community's views are represented. Even more, with Kong Chan present, one wonders how fairly anyone's views are represented. It is common knowledge that Kong Chan will interrupt, out-argue, and out-decibel anyone who contradicts him. Indeed, the other men have not been speaking long before Kong Chan closes his notebook, stares long and hard at Robichaud, and, nodding to the last speaker, begins to argue his case. The villages are poor, he says, but cash is not the problem. People can get cash by selling pigs or a buffalo. What keeps them poor is the difficulty of bringing things to the village, essential things such as salt, metal roofing, and rice when they need it. The problem is isolation and access. What they need is a road.

"I am seventy years old," he says. "Before I die, I want to ride to my village on a road."

His eyes are fixed on Robichaud. "Look, you're an American. You've been to my village. The Soviets have been to my village. The Vietnamese have been to my village. You've been to my village five or six times, and you have seen how poor I am. My own district governor has never been to my village to see how I live. They should have built this road twenty or thirty years ago."

Kong Chan is just warming up. He soon points out that other village clusters are more favorably located on deeper rivers or easier ground. He adds that the hypocritical government showers favors on such places not out of concern for the people but because they are easier to show off to visitors from the World Bank and other outside entities. Eventually he asserts that the priorities of the WMPA are wrongheaded and its employees are lazy. And that the World Bank has no idea what goes on in the protected area and someone needs to tell them. He details his grievances with ever greater emphasis and volume, omitting neither the smallest point nor the slimmest rationale for outrage.

And he concludes his speech, smiling, with a personal appeal to Robichaud:

"Wil-yam, you are my *seo,* my compadre. You have been coming here ten years, sleeping in my house, learning about our problems. You must go back to them—the government, the WMPA—and tell them to bring us a road."

Robichaud, of course, protests. He is nobody, he says. He doesn't work for the government. He doesn't work for an organization. He has no influence. He is a guy interested in wildlife who scrapes together money from here and there so that he can work in NNT. He could not build a road if he wanted to.

Kong Chan rejects this posture of humility. "You can go to the district governor! You can go to the provincial governor, and you can talk to the American embassy, and tell them to build us a road!"

Even if he had the clout, Robichaud has no desire to see more roads in the protected area. He well knows that the merest dirt track will accelerate the extraction of rosewood and wildlife from the forest, speeding the delivery of illegal goods to Vietnam or to buyers in Nakai. But he must approach the subject delicately, not angering his host. He poses a question: "Kong Chan, don't you think a road would lead to more things leaving the villages, more smuggling and more violations in the protected area?"

"No, no, no," the old man growls. "The road would not be used for that! We would not allow it. The rosewood would be safe. We would control all that."

Mr. Ka, for the first time, moves. He nods his assent. "That would not be a problem," says Ka.

Robichaud has previously confided to me that he believes Ka conspires with Vietnamese smugglers to sneak rosewood—or something—past the Ban Kounè border post. No road is there: no road is necessary, but if a road stretched out from these villages in any direction, the idea that Ka, Kong Chan, or anyone might restrict its traffic is absurd. Ka is a man of secrets; Kong Chan a man of ambition. Kong Chan may see a road as the crowning achievement

View from Kong Chan's porch, Sone's house at left-center.

of his political career, but surely he knows how mixed its blessings would be.

Kong Chan presses on: "Wil-yam, listen to me: *2015*. I'm giving you a deadline. If we don't have a road by 2015, I'm not working with you anymore—on conservation of saola or anything else."

"But Kong Chan, I don't build roads."

"You can suggest to people. I've been telling you, you have until 2015 or we're through. You're my compadre, you're my *seo,* but I'm telling you, that's the date."

March 8

Ban Nameuy

Robichaud, Touy, and I leave Kong Chan's house at the first hint of light. A drizzle falls from a dark sky—it is saola weather. Wary buffalo watch us pass the last paddies and cross the broad, flood-torn channel of the Nam Pheo. Dawn does not advance; the sky remains leaden as the trail winds into the forest.

Olay and Simeuang are already in Ban Kounè. They went last night to arrange a meeting for this morning. We would all have gone except that Simeuang was AWOL for the last hours of the afternoon, throwing us off schedule. We waited for him. Well after sundown, he reappeared, contrite and well lit—he'd bumped into old "friends," gender unspecified, and could not refuse their hospitality.

At the forest edge, Ban Kounè materializes from a gray cloud, hovering on stilts above its muddy sward of beer cans. The eaves drip with rain. Pigs scatter, and the usual curs come snarling. The vale echoes with the *thump-thump* of a rice mill.

Simeuang and Olay descend the ladder of the headman's house. The meeting will begin in two hours, they say. Its purpose will be the same as yesterday's—to discuss rewards for protecting saola. This meeting probably matters more than the earlier one because Ban Kounè matters more to saola conservation than any of the Sek villages. It is located squarely in saola habitat, and its Brou inhabitants hunt more frequently and range deeper into the forest than do the Sek. In the past they have crossed paths with saola more often. Also, differing ethnically from the rest of the village cluster, they are

236

less inclined to follow Kong Chan's leadership. On certain issues, men like Mr. Ka quietly, perhaps furtively, go their own way.

We pay calls on three households known to have saola horns. In each case the master of the house generously permits us to drill a sample of bone for genetic analysis. Mr. Vong shows us an ancient frontlet that once belonged to his grandfather. No, he says, he has not personally seen a saola. The trophy belonging to Mr. Giang, meanwhile, has not been moved from its place on the wall in many a year. As Robichaud turns it over, gecko eggs roll out of the skull.

Mr. Giang's four children stand in a line, youngest to oldest, heads like stair steps, as Robichaud guides Olay in measuring the length, circumference, and width of the rack. It is not exactly known if saola horns are sexually dimorphic; that is, if a female's horns are different from a male's. If they are, Robichaud expects that the male's are apt to be more parallel, the female's more splayed. Two more children appear, clad, like the others, in soiled T-shirts and shorts. Now there are six stair steps in the solemn line.

At Louey's house we meet an old man, Louey's father or father-in-law, who is too weak to walk to the clinic in Ban Nameo, and no one is willing to carry him. This does not trouble Louey, who says, "They just give you pills that help for a day or two; then you are the same again. Better to get medicine from Vietnam." While Robichaud, with the help of the boys, samples saola horns, I wait on the porch. The slope down to the rest of the village is a mosaic of dead batteries, crumpled cans, old sandals, manure, and cellophane wrappers. Tobacco grows in a side garden. An abandoned satellite dish, trailing wires, lies canted nearby.

Soon we cross the valley to the house of the headman, Phone (pronounced something close to "fawn"). Phone, among other things, is a honey collector. When we have settled in his dark shack—lit feebly by a smoldering cooking fire—he passes around a bottle filled with the fruit of his labor. The honey looks black in the dimness and flows slowly from the bottle. Its sweetness is heavily perfumed. Phone collected it in April of the year past, just before the rains. He

237

finds hives in a tall tree or in a cleft of rocks on a cliffside. He builds a fire close below the hive. When the smoke has calmed the bees, he cuts away the honey-heavy comb. It is simple work, he says, as long as you are a very good climber and can build a fire in a tree or on the face of a cliff where there is no place to build it. A beer bottle filled with honey sells for fifty thousand kip, slightly more than six dollars.

Prodded by Robichaud's questions, Phone explains, with the ever-present Ka nodding agreement, that saola used to be found in the forests around Ban Kounè, but "bad people"—otherwise unidentified—came to the area, and the saola vanished. Maybe, Phone continues vaguely, the saola are hiding. They are too clever to catch with snares. You only find them with dogs. But now, even with dogs, you don't find them.

A large bottle of rice whiskey has followed the honey around the circle, and Simeuang provides a chaser of instant coffee, nine cups made from our last three packets, Simeuang abstaining. Four men from the village are present, including Phone and Ka, and one woman, whose presence is unexplained. I wonder if she is a healer or a shaman.

The chatter dies away until only Simeuang is speaking. His voice is low and uninflected as he intones an official greeting from the WMPA and calls the formal meeting to order. Outside, the faltering day wears a shroud of gray, and within the dim house the embers on the hearth tease no detail from the faces in the circle.

Robichaud asks about the needs of the village. Phone answers that the WMPA and its backers are always offering irrigation projects and other improvements, but the projects come with the onerous condition that villagers must provide labor, and the pay is never enough. So no one is interested in those kinds of projects anymore.

It is an interesting answer, not just in the way it rejects the idea that those who benefit from such projects should help to build them. By painting public works as a burden, Phone may have another goal: to keep the government and its representatives out of the village.

Ban Kounè, lying close to the border and a whisper away from Vietnamese traders, has much to conceal. It is plain to see that cash flows copiously through the village—the ubiquitous beer cans and bottles, all Vietnamese brands, are flotsam in its wake. The status quo is apparently good.

Pressed by Robichaud, Phone concedes that he has a vision for the future. He says there are three things he would like the village to have: "good food, enough food, and good eyes." The last item stumps Robichaud. At first he thinks Phone wants eyeglasses. Simeuang and Touy offer a translation—"Eyes to see good"—but even that remains cryptic. Perhaps something was lost when Phone internally translated his idea from Brou to Lao. With discussion, his meaning emerges: he wants to see good things, beautiful things. It is a poetic vision, seemingly at odds with the squalor of Ban Kounè. But no, he doesn't care to specify what those things might be.

The discussion returns to criticism of the WMPA and of the soldiers at the border post. Everyone joins in. The complaints spiral like water down a drain, around and around, until nothing is left. Only the woman remains silent. Because Brou men learn Lao as they travel to other villages, and because women stay at home, lacking comparable opportunity, Simeuang later surmises that the woman was embarrassed to speak her pidgin Lao in our presence.

But she, like everyone, appears to support the unremarkable consensus that it is too bad what happened to the rosewood, and it is too bad what has happened to the saola. It is also too bad that years ago the WMPA brought goats to the village instead of cattle. Nobody liked the goats: they wandered too far and they were a nuisance to keep track of. Why didn't the WMPA have the sense to give them cattle?

Robichaud sees an opening. "You want cattle. I want saola," he says. "We can trade."

Phone refuses the bait. He replies, "We are afraid if you don't see saola, you won't come back. You are the saola expert."

239

Under his breath, in English, Robichaud mutters, "I am the expert of air, of dodos, of nothing."

The meeting ends by midday, resolving nothing. Rain falls steadily as we depart, and the trail back to Ban Nameuy is as slick as a ski jump. Olay slides anxiously down one slope. Touy snowplows after him, totters, falls, and stands up with one hip coated in mud. Even Robichaud goes down in a bath of greasy clay. He curses and stalks onward. His mood is dark, like the day. He prides himself on his gift for hanging out, for chatting, joking, and passing the time, but the meeting in Ban Kounè discouraged him. The gap between what was said and what was held back felt uncommonly wide. "I don't know how many more times I can sit in dark rooms like that, saying and hearing the same things, getting nowhere."

We slog on, and a chill settles on the forest, along with heavier rain.

Our immediate challenge is logistical. In twenty-four hours a boat will arrive in Ban Makfeuang to pick up Touy. Robichaud and Simeuang arranged the rendezvous two weeks ago. Given the unreliable radio communications in the forest, not just Touy but all of us need to meet that boat. It is our best chance to get back to Nakai.

We had planned to accomplish the first stage of our journey to Ban Makfeuang by boating downriver this afternoon to Ban Tong, but the boatmen in Ban Beuk demanded almost double what we could pay. So we decided that we would hike overland instead from Ban Nameuy to Ban Thongnoy, where Simeuang might report to a WMPA post, as he is required to do. Thongnoy lies half a day away if the trail is dry. With the trail now as slick as eel skin, Thongnoy is hours farther off.

When we arrive in Ban Nameuy, Kong Chan bellows with laughter when he hears we want to walk to Thongnoy. "That trail! In rain like this? The leeches will kill you!"

Like it or not, we are stuck where we are. The weather is in charge.

"That leaves plan C," concludes Robichaud. "We marry here and stay forever." He turns to me, grinning. "You get first choice."

The rain now pours in sheets from the eaves of Kong Chan's house. Simeuang and Touy have come back soaked from Ban Beuk to report that neither porters nor boats — at any price — can be hired.

We still have a kilo of rice. What we mainly lack are luxuries, like instant coffee, tea, and energy bars. We would buy a chicken if there were one to be bought, but another mysterious disease, like the one that decimated the pigs, has killed the hens and chicks of Ban Nameuy, leaving only a few scrawny roosters to argue with the dawn and each other.

Our immediate problem is staying warm. The clothes we washed when we returned from the Nam Nyang have yet to dry, and our last change of clothes, worn today, is now wet. We retreat to our sleeping bags. Robichaud and I swap baseball stories — Orioles in my telling, Brewers in his — while the boys lie next to us, shivering. Their rain gear leaked more than ours, and their bags are not as warm. So we get up and add our bags to the pile of quilts covering them. Simeuang, meanwhile, remains impervious to the weather — any weather. He has gone to visit a pretty young woman who made him a gift of fried snails on our return from the forest. When he reappears, at dinner-time, he has another gift: dried skin of water buffalo.

The boys, hungry for its warming fat, quickly fry it up.

It has the texture of harness leather and evokes a memory of pork rind. As one chews (and chews) it breaks into resistant nodules, upon which continued chewing has no further effect. Ultimately, one swallows the musty nodules as one would swallow pills. The rain pours down, and the day, like us, is now exhausted. We need boats. We need traveling weather. We need to get to Nakai so that we can gather supplies and start for the Nam Mon.

March 9

Ban Nameuy

Pinholes in the bamboo-mat gable shine yellow. And yellow light leaks between the planks of the walls. The gauze of our mosquito netting grows luminous. The rain has stopped, and gusts of the wind that chased it away roll through the village like breakers across a reef. In darkness a half hour earlier, Robichaud and Simeuang left for Ban Beuk to hire boatmen, resolved to employ whatever combination of entreaty, cash, and promises proved necessary.

Notwithstanding the insect bites covering my torso, a result of warming myself in one of Kong Chan's quilts the day before, the luminous morning feels joyous. Robichaud and Simeuang presently return with two boatmen close behind. "We can go as soon as we are packed."

By 8:00 a.m. we are on the river, alternately floating past flood-torn banks or shoving our two boats, scooterlike, through shallows. We see crested kingfishers, common kingfishers, wagtails and fork-tails, two species of heron, and, perched in a towering snag, a crested serpent eagle. The sky lifts, yielding hints of blue, as we speed downstream. A male jungle fowl flies across the widening channel, the red of his comb and mantle brilliant, his wing strokes powerful and bold. It is hard to believe that a bird nearly identical to the chicken can look so good.

The river rocks us, and the *chak hang* screams. The odds of meeting our boat in Ban Makfeuang improve every minute we are in motion. Nakai beckons. The Nam Mon and its mineral lick are waiting.

In two hours we reach Ban Peu. We muscle our gear in double loads to Ban Tong, where we hire motorbikes to carry it to Ban Makfeuang—Star Fruit Village, as I now have learned. We follow the motorbikes at a quick march. The rain was light here. The footing is good.

The boatman from Nakai, true to his word, awaits us at the appointed place. By a quarter past one we are stowed and settled in his craft, headed for the reservoir. Even above the engine noise we hear the whistle of hill mynahs from either shore.

I am facing backwards, reclining into the V of the bow, watching the forest recede. How different to see it from a boat! Where the forest climbs the hillsides, it reveals its now familiar variations of texture and color. But as the river broadens, the forest that was so large when we were in it seems to shrink. The sky swells with volume, dwarfing the trees that earlier seemed majestic. With distance, the forest becomes a fragile thing, its span from soil to treetops no more than a coverlet on the undulating hills, a membrane between rock and air.

We pass stands of dead trunks by the water's edge—the beginning of the drowned forest and a reminder of the unrequited treasures that the forest has surrendered. For a moment I picture the exodus of those marvels as a parade in a children's book, a Disney procession of exotic animals in single file, head to tail, exiting the forest. Some of the species are gone for good; some are going; all are on the march. Rhinoceroses, banteng, and tigers lead the throng, then golden turtles, leopards, elephants, and gaur. White-winged ducks flurry overhead. Pangolins sniff the air as they waddle onward, otters and big-headed turtles awkwardly trailing them. Now come the clouded leopards, padding furtively, and golden cats and marbled cats, packs of dholes, and herds of at least three jumbled species of muntjac. Ragtag gangs of doucs and gibbons chatter as they pass. On a snaking line of a thousand bearers, an overburdened train of eaglewood and rosewood also follows, raising dust that dims the day. The dust has not settled when ghostly figures appear within it:

243

saola, half seen and nearly incorporeal. They might have taken their place far up the line of disappearance, but they tried hard to stay behind, hidden from all but a lucky few. Shy and exquisite, they trot in the wake of the others. Then a cloud drifts before the sun; the light shifts, and the saola, too, are seen no more.

The forest pours out its wealth, emptying in spite of an alphabet soup of managers, experts, and monitors—WMPA, POE, IMA, ADB, WB, WCS, WWF, and plenty more—a modern equivalent of all the king's horses and all the king's men, charged with repair and maintenance of the now fracturing ecosystem. The king, of course, is the NTPC, the sovereign of hydroelectric commerce, which indeed commands its realm with monarchical power but whose reign, like that of every sovereign in the history of Earth, will not last forever.

The boat plows downstream, engine roaring. Behind the racket, I hear a plaintive, desperate wail, a cry of grief, coming from the forest. Probably only cicadas, I tell myself. It can only be cicadas.

Some conservationists argue for the preservation of places like NNT on the basis of the value of biodiversity. They maintain, for instance, that the chemistry of Earth's biota may hold the key to new chemicals or cures for disease. There is truth enough in this, as many studies make clear—the story of Taxol, derived from yew bark and effective in treating breast cancer, is one of them—but such breakthroughs are episodic and unpredictable. They make a frail foundation for a muscular ethic of protection.

Another, stronger, utilitarian argument centers on "environmental services"—the prevention of erosion, moderation of climate, purification of water, and other benefits that healthy ecosystems provide. The society that drains its wetlands or levels its forests soon finds that it must pay handsomely to replace the flood protection or water yield it formerly received for free. Or, more commonly, it learns to scrape by in a degraded, more miserable, and more hazardous world.

All true. But a forest does not have to contain tigers and saola in order to fulfill its vital hydrological functions, and a wetland need not harbor a white-winged duck in order to modify a storm surge. There are other functions, pollination being one, that more clearly rest upon a foundation of diversity, but the arguments that make the case for ecological complexity, notwithstanding the wonders they recount, put the rank and file of humankind to sleep. A defense of the intricacy of the web of life demands another banner.

Some religionists will say that God's creation is a sacred thing and must not be diminished. By this reckoning, "Thou shalt not kill"—an injunction common to all great religions—might be thought to apply to the protection of species, too. But the contrary view, voiced loudly in certain corners of Christianity, but known, as well, from other monotheisms, is at least as widespread, namely, that God put man at the center of creation, giving him dominion over all else, so that if a species flickers out it is His will. Unfortunately, God has remained lamentably silent on the subject and appears unwilling to break the tie.

If you probe deep enough among the people who labor in the vineyard of species protection, you find another answer, another motivation. It goes by many names, and it often goes unmentioned, ceding primacy in formal publications to the usual quasi-economic analyses of costs and benefits or to the unprovable umbrella argument that small tears in the fabric of life will lead to big rents that endanger humankind. Robichaud, like many others, says that what gets him out of his sleeping bag in the morning is something different and simpler. It is beauty.

No matter how it is parsed or how much it resides in the eye of the beholder, no matter how its elements might be divided among delight, awe, surprise, or inspiration, beauty moves the heart as reason moves the mind. Imagine a world deprived of the tanager's colors, of the hummingbird's whirr, of the mad shrieks of a rookery of seabirds. Imagine the Arctic without its fearsome white bear, Bengal without its tiger, the Serengeti without its prides of lions (*pride* being an ancient and meaningful term). We are entranced by beautiful creatures not just because they give pleasure and inspire awe but because they carry a charge like an ionized particle. Beauty excites and glows. Put a horse in an empty meadow, and the meadow becomes animate. Put a saola, even a saola you cannot see, in a forest, and the forest, as though it held a unicorn, acquires an energy that cannot be named. It becomes numinous; it gains the pull of gravity, the weight of water, the float of a feather.

March 10

Nakai

The culprit, I am sure, was the fried egg. Or not quite fried enough, as it now seems.

We were famished when we reached Nakai and repaired straight-away to Trung's restaurant, a plank-and-sheet-metal shack on the dusty main road. Our hunger was not the hunger of a single day or even of a day of hard travel by foot and boat. It was the hunger of two weeks of deficit, gaining less from food than we put out in energy, our trousers fitting looser, the tails of our belts ever lengthening.

Trung, who is Vietnamese, lounges in his hammock by the chat-tering TV as we come through his doorless entry. We order one or two servings of everything he has on hand: ant-egg soup, mounds of rice, fried pork rinds, small sweet bananas, noodles nondescript, chew-forever chicken, and a platter of eggs. We gulp down two rounds of sodas before we take to our red plastic chairs and start on beer. While we wait for the food, we gaze at the traffic outside—trucks, chickens, dogs, pedestrians, and the occasional aimless cow. Trung's place hasn't windows so much as a gap of three or four absent planks in the front wall, which he has covered with clear plastic sheeting and chain-link mesh. Dust flows in along with light, leaving on everything a film that Trung and his indefatigable wife are forever wiping away. We wash our hands at a tiny basin by the door, near a shrine replete with joss sticks and an offering of bananas. Then we settle anew at our table while Trung hurries from his stove with a succession of plates and bowls. From advertising posters papering the walls, pretty Thai models, Photoshopped to an unnatural whiteness, smile at us as we dig into the food.

A few hours later, having checked into a modest guesthouse managed by Olay's uncle, Robichaud and I eat again. Simeuang has gone to his home, and, after the briefest of good-byes—we are all too tired and dirty to wax sentimental—Touy and Olay have departed for the bus (Olay, like Touy, felt compelled to return to Vientiane; he promised to rejoin us in Nakai two mornings hence, when we depart for the Nam Mon).

Robichaud and I feasted on our second dinner, not far from Trung's, at the Houaphou Restaurant, the lone outpost in Nakai offering Western food. It is the creation of a French engineer who came to Nakai to work on the dam and his Lao wife, who has more than mastered French cuisine. We ordered steak au poivre and a bottle of Bordeaux. Life was good.

Until it wasn't.

I will spare the details, but suffice it to say that I later lay down to sleep with apprehension in my innards. Something was amiss. I blamed the not-quite-fried egg, but it could have been many things. Sleep did not come. What came instead were successive paroxysms of ejection such as I had never before experienced. I feared the bursting of an artery or the breaking of a rib. Every orifice took part, except that my brains did not come out my ears. I spent the night in the bathroom, periodically crawling back to bed and briefly closing my eyes. But no comforting darkness descended. Instead I beheld a vision of glutinous hell. I saw, on the backs of my eyelids, as it were, vast prairies of sticky rice, brilliantly white, puffy, and repugnant, a Great Plains of undigestion stretching to an infinite horizon, the sight of which hastened my return to the plumbing.

I was surprised that my involuntary racket did not wake Robichaud, who was next door. Gratefully, when light at last began to tinge the sky, I felt the paroxysms ebb and was able to remain in bed. But I could not rest easy. We were due to take to the trail again the following day, beginning our ascent of the Nam Mon, and here I was, voided, feverish, light-headed, and as weak as a dishrag. I could barely walk the room, let alone resume the labors of the trail. I was also parched. I found a bottle of water and took a sip. It was alpine cold and felt like starlight on the tongue, then radiated through my core, the finest drink that ever passed my lips.

Nakai, newly hacked from the forest, has the look of a town that is angry at the land, and the land is angry in return. Only a few ragged trees survived the clearing. They rise like the crooked pillars of an ancient ruin. Some exhibit prodigious kinks and curves, which give them the knock-kneed look of a naked beauty trying to cover herself. The shanties and bungalows they shade, clad in red dust, are set every which way, as though they had dropped from the sky.

I am upright, and we are driving to a meeting. Robichaud and Simeuang are obliged to debrief the managers of the WMPA. As I am known to have been present on the expedition, the managers expect to see me, too, at least what is left of me. I am woozy but stable. I took an antibiotic once I thought I could hold it down, and the effect has been salutary. My principal duty is to avoid passing out.

The WMPA offices sit at the edge of Nakai, on a slight rise above the reservoir. The new and handsome building sports a red tile roof that curls up, pagodalike, in swallowtail eaves. The grounds around it, bereft of vegetation, exhibit the rawness of a construction site. We shed our sandals on the broad stairs leading to the entry and go in.

The air in the lobby is faintly scented with formalin and decay. A glass aquarium the size of a fat man's coffin lines one wall. It is lidded, but not tightly enough, and contains an immense fish, five and a half feet long, belly up in a lake of yellowing preservative. The legend on the tank proclaims that the pickled creature weighs eleven kilos and is a *balai fafa*—an electric fish. The people of Ban Thameuang (our next destination, en route to the Nam Mon) caught it in 2008 and made a gift of it to the WMPA. Fish experts have opined that it might have been forty years old and that it migrated up the Mekong, the Nam Kading, and the Nam Theun all the way from the sea. If so, it was among the last of its kind in these precincts. The NT2 dam now bars such journeys.

We wait for our audience with the managers. Windows above the fish allow us to peer into the next room, an office where stern-faced women labor under the sterner glare of portraits of Lenin and Marx. Shortly we are led upstairs to a long, narrow conference room. Ten or more ornate wooden tables, arranged in a horseshoe, nearly fill the room. Several dozen thronelike chairs range beside them. The director is there, in the alpha position at the head of the U, somewhat dwarfed by his throne, which is larger and more grandiose than the others. Four lieutenants attend him, two on either side.

The director, smiling, bids us sit. He is a slight man with a grave manner, but amiable and kind. I don't know where he hails from, but long ago he became native to rooms like this one, a veteran of a thousand tiresome meetings. Although he is a man of power, he operates under much restraint. There is always pressure from above and resistance from below, which runs strongest on his staff among those he cannot fire, who owe their jobs, and their loyalty, to other thrones. If the director is not an ironist, he should be.

He explains the purposes of the WMPA and the agency's great concern for wildlife. His monotone suggests that we are not the first persons to hear this speech. When the director is finished, he asks the head of enforcement to describe the number and accomplishments of recent patrols (very few) and the number of patrols contemplated for the future (a great many). The head of enforcement then adds, "We are ready to coordinate our efforts with the district government. We are also building additional ranger stations as a way of increasing our enforcement capacity." These words are uttered with as little emphasis and inflection as the director had used.

Next, the head of biodiversity conservation invites Simeuang to make his report, which Simeuang does in his usual drone, duly noting each of our councils with village chiefs and the messages they directed him to carry back to Nakai.

Finally it is Robichaud's turn. He speaks partly in Lao, partly in

English, so that I may follow along, which does not disadvantage the director or any but one of his lieutenants, who command the language fairly well. Robichaud is serious in his delivery, as befits his account of the saola's precarious hold on existence, but also at moments mirthful. He has collaborated and negotiated with these men for years. Their wan smiles suggest that they enjoy his cajolery, or at least that they are used to it. He describes the evident influx of cash to the villages, the ubiquity of poaching camps, and the prevalence of snares. He makes them laugh about the poacher's phone number posted on a rosewood stump and suggests they make the call. He says he has never seen Vietnamese camps so close to the villages before, which he takes as a sign of collusion between poachers and some element of the village hierarchy. His account is vivid and direct but also tactful. He says nothing shaming or accusatory, nothing that blames. He closes with a grim description of the biota of the Nam Nyang being sucked from the forest and carried over the mountains to Vietnam.

And then he asks for my comments. He warned me he would do so, but nevertheless I am dry-mouthed at the prospect. Throughout the meeting I have greedily eyed a glass of tea that was placed before me, but I do not trust my innards sufficiently to take a sip, lest it trigger something uncontrollable. I feel ghostlike, as though I might float away. Robichaud told me the director might listen more acutely to a foreign journalist than to someone like himself, whose concerns he has heard many times before. An hour ago, the idea made sense. Now it seems absurd. Why should the director listen to anyone so obviously immaterial? Besides, Robichaud has said everything in need of saying.

They are looking at me. One more beat of silence will embarrass everyone. Thick-tongued, I begin to speak. Recalling that compliments seem to introduce every statement in this part of the world, I praise the beauty of NNT and the vibrancy of its communities, but I overdo it and quickly sense the cloud of tedium, already heavy in the room, thickening further. I change course and pursue the first intelligent-sounding thing that comes to mind, which concerns the burgeoning population of the villages and the consequent strain on resources, as the six thousand people now living in the watershed become sixty-five hundred, then seven thousand. But I am quickly in over my head in front of people who know far more than I about birthrates, death rates, and emigration, and so I veer toward the safer ground of my own reaction to the carnage of the snare lines. Now I seem to be getting a little traction: my auditors' eyes narrow with concern. So boldly I continue, asserting the urgent need for forceful patrol, that not a moment should be lost, that the remote extremities of NNT have been surrendered to poachers, that this is a betrayal of the promise of NT2, that concerned people throughout the world, were they to learn of this, would...

Robichaud kicks me under the table.

I glance his way. He is smiling mildly. Have I been untactful? Perhaps he was just shifting in his chair.

I begin to add a verb to my incomplete thought, and Robichaud kicks me again, harder. The thought is left unbuilt. I have gone too far. I retreat. "You can see that these matters are very worrisome to me," I say, and thank them for their attention. They nod. Everyone looks relieved. The director intones a few summary comments and tells us our comments are gratefully noted. More nods and smiles. Meeting over.

On our way out, the odor of formalin in the lobby incites in me a surge of sympathy. I feel a sudden affinity with the giant electric fish. All I want to do is return to the guesthouse, take to my bed, and lie belly up, immobile, unfragrant, and grateful for onrushing sleep.

March 11

Nakai

Early in our conversations about saola, Robichaud told me that many villagers ask if the animal might also be found in the United States. He said that when they learn saola are unique to their own home ground, their responses are surprising. So it was when Robichaud, Simeuang, Olay, and I, near the close of our explorations in NNT, visited an elder in the village of Ban Fangdeng.

His name was Siengtho, and he was close to my age. Chanphan, the young headman of Ban Fangdeng, guided us to his home, where we huddled on the porch, hugging ourselves to stay warm as a cold mist blew through the village.

Siengtho retrieved a saola frontlet from inside the house and showed it to us. A loop of string hung around one horn—to bring good luck. Age had darkened the horns, and they were light and dry. Siengtho explained that he shot the animal in 1975, when he was a soldier and had a gun. Traders of all kinds—Lao, Vietnamese, and Hmong—have tried to buy the frontlet from him. He hasn't wanted to sell.

With Siengtho's permission, Robichaud drills a sample of bone from one of the horns. Olay, as usual, assists. While they're at it, Chanphan the headman asks, "What other countries have saola?"

"No other countries have saola," Robichaud answers. "Except Vietnam. Saola only exist here"—he gestures with a sweep of his arm—"in these mountains, in Laos and Vietnam. This is the only place in the world that has saola."

Chanphan reflects before asking, "Would you like us to catch a saola for your zoo?"

If Robichaud had affirmed an interest, Chanphan would next have asked how much we might pay. After all, we had come to Ban Fangdeng from halfway around the world. If our country had none, didn't we want one?

In Vietnam in the early 1990s, at Vu Quang and Pu Mat, it had been the same. The readiness of mountain people to catch saola for outsiders ultimately prompted Vietnam to ban the killing or capturing of saola early in 1994.[1] (In Laos, the targeted taking of wild saola continued through mid-1996, partly thanks to General Cheng.)

Other early actions by the Vietnamese government in the name of saola protection included tripling the Vu Quang reserve to 136,000 acres (55,000 hectares) and the prohibition of logging within its boundaries. Similar measures were taken at Pu Mat and other locations where saola were reported.

But the wildlife trade continued to boom, driven by the expanding economies of Vietnam and other "Asian tigers," especially China. Demand soared for every kind of meat, every putative medicinal cure, every animal talisman, trinket, trophy, and decoration. Out went the old, laborious way of setting snares with cords of vegetable fiber. In came spool after spool of steel bicycle cable. The new snares were stronger, surer, and faster to set. And many more people were now positioned to set them.

Because Vietnam's lowlands, especially in the north, had long been overcrowded, the government encouraged migration of Kinh villagers from coastal lowlands upslope into the less densely settled mountains. People also moved from the north into the mountains of what used to be South Vietnam. New territory for northerners was one of the prizes of the American war. And no one in the government regretted it if Kinh people infiltrated the territories of mountain ethnics—montagnards, in the language of the day—many of whom had sided with the United States or whose loyalty to the party was suspect.

The mountain ethnics, of course, continued to hunt and trap in the forests around their villages, as their forebears had done, but now, as the empty places filled, they had more neighbors—and competition. Some of that competition came not from new settlers but from large teams of men, drawn by the rewards of the wildlife trade, who traveled hundreds of kilometers to live in the forest for months at a time, hunting and snaring. These were not farmers putting meat on the family table or killing wild pigs that preyed on their rice crop. These were men engaged in a commercial enterprise. They employed scouts to search for new territories. They made careful plans and carried them out. Many of them came from Nghe An and Ha Tinh, provinces located at Vietnam's narrow waist, where the mountains come close to the sea, provinces whose storm-battered farmlands are plagued by famine when typhoons flood the paddies with salt water. Nghe An and Ha Tinh share a reputation for producing indomitable people. Long ago, their lands were shorn of all but the most rudimentary resources, and they began producing people with the grit to do anything that survival might require.

Vietnam's nature reserves and national parks may have looked good on paper, but year after year, the forces that stripped them of wildlife outmatched the intentions of their creators. Without adequate funding for patrol and law enforcement, the taking of wildlife raged on. The unrestrained hunting and trapping spilled across the border into Laos and raged there as well, where enforcement was equally lax.

Conservation groups, sometimes allied with international lenders and foreign governments, tried to stanch the bleeding. They contributed funds, underwrote management plans, and conducted studies; they strove to enhance livelihoods and alleviate poverty. But as much as they gave advice and wrote checks, they refrained from law enforcement. They had no choice. Activities that might lead to arrest and seizure were solely the prerogative of the government.

In 2010, in Vietnam, these issues came to a head as a result of a murder and a giant corpse.

Cat Tien National Park lies slightly more than a hundred kilometers northeast of Ho Chi Minh City (formerly Saigon). Despite defoliation by Agent Orange during the American war, which left some sectors almost treeless, Cat Tien supports forty species of animals on the IUCN Red List that are considered globally threatened. These include Asian elephant, sun bear, and gaur. The park's Cat Loc sector was specifically gazetted as a rhinoceros reserve in 1992, following the discovery (in which the ubiquitous George Schaller played a role) of the lesser one-horned, or Javan, rhino. It became a source of national pride that Cat Tien harbored the last population on the Asian mainland of so impressive an animal.

The Vietnamese rhinos were the last remnant of a subspecies (*Rhinoceros sondaicus annamiticus*) that once ranged through Indochina and south along the Malay Peninsula.[2] Their only close relatives were forty or so Indonesian Javan rhinoceroses (*R. sondaicus sondaicus*) in a small park at the extreme western tip of Java.[3] Although the Indonesian rhinos face multiple threats, they appear to be protected from poachers. Not so their cousins in Vietnam.

On April 29, 2010, in the Cat Loc sector, local people informed park rangers of a large jumble of skeletal remains at the bottom of a ravine. It proved to be what was left of a rhinoceros.

Initially park officials reported that the rhino died of natural causes, a comforting notion suggesting that nature had taken its course. All comfort was banished, however, when WWF staff examined the bones of the dead beast. They discovered a bullet buried in the ulna of the left foreleg. The news for this particular animal had been trending badly for some time. In a novel program that had commenced the previous year, WWF, in cooperation with park management, had used "detector dogs" to census the rhinos of Cat Tien. The principle behind the dog program was simple: you train an energetic dog to seek out rhino dung (ideal candidates work feverishly for rewards as small as the throwing of a ball), and then you turn the dog loose in appropriate habitat.

According to Sarah Brook, a coleader of the effort, "Most people thought we would find three or four rhinos remaining and that then we would decide the best course of action." Through the fall of 2009 and the following winter Sarah and her colleagues found modest amounts of dung and plenty of fresh tracks. But after the Tet holidays of February 2010, they found no more of either. The implications were ominous.

Genetic analysis confirmed that all the dung they had collected belonged to one individual—the rhino whose skeleton was discovered in April.

A forensic examination of the bones and close investigation of the death site told the story. The rhino did not die of old age. It was only fifteen to twenty-five years old, whereas rhinos are believed to live to around forty. At least two months prior to the animal's death, someone had shot it in the leg with an AK-47 or a rifle of similar caliber. (It may have been shot more than once, but bullets lodged in soft tissue would have been lost as the carcass rotted away.) At a minimum, the leg wound became inflamed and the bone abscessed painfully. In mid-February, the rhino, by then physically unstable, lumbered down a trail toward water. Perhaps the bad leg, which was on the downhill side, bearing lots of weight, buckled. Perhaps a poacher who had staked out the water hole opened fire.

The rhino collapsed and rolled, crashing through a wall of bamboo, and came to rest at the bottom of the ravine. If it survived the fall, its maimed forelimb would have prevented its getting up. Because of its weight, breathing while prostrate was difficult, and finally impossible. After the rhino died, someone—possibly the original shooter—decapitated it, dragged the head to an open area, and hacked off the horn.

Ground into powder, the horn would have fetched prices as high as sixty-five dollars per gram, making it worth literally more than its weight in gold. Although a tea made from human fingernail clippings or any other source of keratin would have the same dubious medical effect,[4] people buy the powder to cure a range of ailments, including fever, rheumatism, gout, hallucinations, typhoid, headaches, carbuncles, vomiting, food poisoning, "devil possession," and hangover.[5] In many cases the motive for using rhino horn includes ostentation. Dearer than cocaine and just as illegal, it is the ideal consumer item for demonstrating how rich and untouchable you are.

The death of the last Javan rhinoceros in Vietnam—and of the last exemplar of the Vietnamese subspecies—was an international embarrassment for Vietnam. It rightly stirred the government to a flurry of compensatory activity, some of which was intended to benefit saola. For years, a proposal to create a new "saola reserve" in northwest Quang Nam Province, adjacent to the Laos border, had been stalled. When combined with another saola reserve across the provincial boundary in Thua Thien–Hue Province, and with an expanded Bach Ma National Park, the new reserve would complete a contiguous 91,400-acre protected area. Now, finally, the proposal won approval.

Perhaps more important, the post-rhino possibilities for meaningful law enforcement suddenly grew robust. The Forest Protection Department accepted a WWF proposal for joint supervision—actual decision making and management—of patrol activities in the saola reserve in Thua Thien–Hue. Subsequently, in little more than a year, forest guards removed more than 12,500 snares and destroyed nearly 200 illegal hunting and logging camps from the protected area.

Unfortunately, the change of heart may have come too late. If saola still exist in Vu Quang or Pu Mat, their populations consist of small numbers of isolated individuals, like the last lonely rhino of Cat Tien. Considering the pressures brought to bear by Vietnam's ninety million people, the best prospects for the species' survival may now lie on the less populous Lao side of the Annamite divide. And the best prospects within Laos probably lie within the country's largest swath of "protected" saola habitat, embraced by Nakai–Nam Theun NPA. Unfortunately, as we had learned, on-the-ground protection in NNT remained thin to nonexistent.

• • •

The chicken soup at the restaurant beside the guesthouse tastes not unpleasantly of dead twig. Robichaud and I sit in the open air under a thick thatched roof. Mr. Keo, the proprietor, watches a Thai soap opera on the TV at the bar. If the soup settles in me, perhaps I will dare a scrambled egg.

Robichaud has calculated that we can burn one day—today— for rest and recovery, but tomorrow we must return to the watershed if we mean to reach the mineral lick, the *poung,* of the Nam Mon. When I tell him that I will be ready, I hear more confidence in my voice than my gut approves.

Robichaud and Simeuang are listing the supplies to be bought at the market when Olay suddenly appears. He accompanied Touy to Vientiane, dallied for a day, and rode the night bus back to Nakai, a nine-hour grind, arriving only an hour ago. His hair is more disheveled and his eyes sleepier than ever, but it is a joy to see him and, absent Touy, to feel the reassembly of our little family of trekkers. It is also a joy to see what he has brought: three entire boxes of granola bars. Robichaud gives two to me. "Fuel for the Nam Mon," he says. It may seem laughable to attach importance to so small a matter, but I am elated.

Robichaud commences discussing yesterday's meeting at the WMPA. Biological conservation, he argues, started out as the agency's number one priority, while its parent, the NTPC, carried out the theoretically humane relocation of more than six thousand people whose homes the reservoir would inundate. Unfortunately, attempts at quick-fix poverty alleviation gradually trumped the WMPA's conservation mission and monopolized the agency's attention. It is easy to see why. The protection of biological diversity involves holding on to what you have. It comes down to maintenance. When you do it right, you avoid change and come away with little to show for your efforts—just the continuation of what was there before. Almost always, if change occurs, it is negative.

Poverty alleviation operates in the opposite way. Change is good, and you demonstrate it with tangible results: more tractors, more metal roofs, more electricity, more income. Even in an administrative system where a punch list of achievements is not always the summum bonum of performance, results ultimately matter. You get to carve a metaphorical notch on your pistol. Rewards follow.

It is an axiom of politics that you get more credit for building a new road than for filling potholes in an old one, and the director and top staff at the WMPA are reminded of this every time they report to the higher-ups in Vientiane and the provincial capital. Economic development is noncontroversial; you can measure it and get praised for it. It is also a national priority. Having formally adopted the UN's Millennium Development Goals, the government of Laos expects every agency to do its part.

By contrast, the patrols and arrests that attend serious enforcement work lead to conflict. The difficult task of leaning on the army or the district authorities to control Vietnamese penetration of the border is even worse, as it touches sensitive political and diplomatic nerves. The upside of such toil, beyond pleasing a few foreigners, is limited. The downside is nearly infinite.

Back at the inception of NT2, when management structures for the project were still being designed, quite a few people, including some at the World Bank, said that the job of protecting biodiversity in NNT should be contracted to an independent, mission-driven NGO. The idea was abandoned early, however. The highest level of management and planning determined that the "optics," as appearances are called in public relations, would be terrible. Ceding such authority to outsiders would be an affront to Lao sovereignty, as though the Communist Party and the government lacked the substance to execute the task. True enough. But events have proved that strong medicine was needed. Lately, says Robichaud, some of the solons who originally rejected the idea have begun to advocate it. They are near to admitting that continuation of the present course can only result in a colossal conservation failure—and that, too, would be bad for the optics.

In 2009, Robichaud worked for the WMPA as a technical adviser. He analyzed data from twelve thousand days of camera-trapping and concluded that the implications for wildlife in the protected area were dismal. Unfortunately he could not immediately schedule a meeting with top management, and finalization of the work plan for the coming year was imminent. In haste he wrote a memo to the WMPA director emphatically describing the decline of NNT's wildlife populations. Undiplomatically and naively, he sent copies to the Panel of Experts as well as staff at the World Bank. His timing was hardly shrewd. He distributed the memo five days before his contract was to be renewed. It wasn't.

The crisis is now worse, although warnings have continued to rain on the WMPA. Robichaud, who has been roving the protected area since 1995, asserts that until the past two weeks he never previously observed such dramatic changes in the watershed. The differences were material—more motorbikes, more beer, more stuff from outside—but also intangible: the seemingly new attitude, so pronounced in Ban Kounè, of "go away and send us more money." Change is now pervasive and profound, the situation unstable. The WMPA would have to be extremely agile and energetic to keep up with the tide of transformation, and presently it gives little sign of rising to the challenge. These concerns visibly weigh on Robichaud as we sit at Mr. Keo's table, finishing a late breakfast on a sunny morning.

Oh, he says, and there's something else. The camera-trap photos from Thong Kouang? That was no python, no snake of any kind. Yesterday he enlarged the images on his computer screen. The long, smooth, snaky thing that we thought might be a giant reptile appears to be the tail of a civet. The animal must have passed right under the camera, and by the time the trigger went off, every inch of it, except the tail, had slinked through the field of view. Our exotic, portentous serpent has shrunk to an ordinary, catlike forager. So much for our omen of good luck.

IV

Upriver:
The *Poung* of the Nam Mon

March 12

Nakai

Mr. Phouvong, Olay's ever-smiling uncle and the proprietor of the oddly named Wooden Guest House, refuses to let us pay for our lodging these past three nights. Poised on his wrist like a hunting hawk is the enormous green moth I discovered this morning on the wall beside my door when I went out to test my step.

Robichaud and I have used our rooms rather hard. I have cleaned up the evidence of illness as best I can, but the pile of soiled towels and linens will surely dismay the housekeeper. Robichaud, for his part, has endowed his room with a powerful stink, having filled the closet with biological specimens in various stages of decay, including the skull of the juvenile large-antlered muntjac that fed our crew on the Nam Nyang. Despite Mok Keo's efforts to rid the head of brains and flesh, it has turned maggoty.

Robichaud remonstrates with Phouvong, insisting that we pay, but Phouvong, deeply grateful for Robichaud's tutelage of Olay, makes a shallow bow and says payment is impossible. The struggle is quintessentially Lao: two people bent on outdoing the kindness of the other. Phouvong wishes us well, shakes hands, and walks away, gazing fondly at the insect on his arm. Man and moth make a curious tableau. "Lao falconry," Robichaud quips, and Phouvong, still admiring the moth, closes his office door.

The moth was the size of a small bird, fully six inches from wing tip to wing tip. I measured it with a ruler. The four delicate wings (two fore and two aft) were nearly translucent. Each had an eyespot that peered toward the furry thorax. Most exquisite were the fan-shaped antennae, a lattice of orange filaments that stood out from the head like solar panels from a satellite. After my initial surprise at seeing it on the pale red bricks beside the door, I wondered what message it might bear.

I suspect that Mr. Phouvong read the arrival of the moth as a friendly omen, a harbinger of luck, as did I. In the extremity of my sickness, crawling from bed to toilet, I had thought of my wraithlike friend Mary, who wrote in my notebook, "Just call for me if you need a guardian spirit." When I was lowest, I sent her a mental scream. The frail moth seemed her reply, a gift of beauty and reassurance. Yet I worried, too, that it might be a dispatch from her departing spirit, signaling her death. While in Nakai I had heard from Joanna that things were well at home, but there was no chance of a quick reply to any query I might send now. Within hours we would be across the reservoir and again beyond the reach of messages. I packed my gear feeling light and heavy at once.

At the boat landing, Simeuang enacts a metaphor of saola conservation. The boatman has gone to fetch the motor oil he forgot, and while we wait Simeuang fishes, in vain. His casting net, a purse seine, is different from the nets the guides dragged through the water of the Nam Nyang. It has a light chain around the skirt, which sinks the net, dropping a dome of nylon mesh around the fish—if only a fish were there. When it settles, Simeuang pulls the lanyard of the net, which closes the skirt, and hauls it in. He sees it is empty and patiently casts again. And again. Robichaud says he has watched thousands of such casts and witnessed the catching of only one or two fish. But those who are fishermen to their hearts, as Simeuang is, keep casting.

Our trip up the Nam Mon is another long cast, too—for saola— and we set out in a *chak hang* that is dangerously small and overladen. We have scarcely a knuckle's worth of freeboard. A significant swell would swamp us, but for now the lake is glassy and flat. We roar on, or try to roar. Periodically the engine coughs and nearly quits. The boatman is impassive. We have three hours to go.

· · ·

It turns out that even before the MacKinnon expedition to Vu Quang in 1992, knowledge of saola was not always restricted to the Annamites.

The Dong Son people, who occupied Vietnam's Red River delta during the first millennium BCE, decorated their exquisite bronze drums with images of people and animals. Among these animals is a deerlike creature with long, straight horns. It appears to be a saola.

Roughly contemporaneous, the Sa Huynh culture prospered farther south, in central and southern Vietnam. They were evidently seafarers, for archaeologists have detected their presence even in the Philippines, on the far side of what the Vietnamese call the East Sea (and most US atlases call the South China Sea, an abominable term from a Vietnamese point of view). Notably, the Sa Huynh cremated their adult dead and buried the ashes in large jars. The grave goods recovered from such jars feature glass and stone beads and, in the late stages of the culture, jade ear pendants, which were probably worn by influential or ritually important men. The pendants are the only representational artwork known from the culture. They depict matching animal heads that face outward from the point of attachment to the ear. The animal, which is apparently always the same, has a deerlike face and possesses long, pointed horns. Some say it represents a saola.[1]

Even in modern times, a glimmer of the existence of saola flashed on the wider world. In 1912, the lexicographer Théodore Guignard published his *Dictionnaire Laotien-Français,* in which he listed the word *saola* as "species of antelope, antelope of the rocks."[2]

Then for eighty years, beyond the confines of saola habitat, the word and the animal were forgotten.

The motor has quit again, and as we drift upon the lake, the boatman sucks and siphons it back to something approaching life. Finally we stammer across the remaining flat water and up the broad, drowned Nam Xot, beaching at the sprawl of Ban Nahao. We pile our gear onshore. Our immediate destination is Ban Navang, on the Nam Mon, the next drainage southeast. Again we will send our goods ahead by tractor or motorbike, and we will follow on foot. Simeuang and Olay will make the arrangements. Robichaud, as usual, has a call to make.

He directs the boatman to cross the river to a set of steep bluffs, the landing for Ban Thameuang, a hodgepodge of resettled Vietic tribes. Robichaud wishes to visit a friend.

Ban Thameuang is a village built on a complicated mix of values and emotions. Shame is one of them. The mavens of world economic measurement have long termed Laos "underdeveloped," "least developed," even "primitive," a word rarely spoken but often thought. Laos ranks low in all the conventional indices of material progress, from adult literacy to televisions per capita, and it is cushioned from the abject bottom only by an unfortunate few nations that include its regional neighbor Cambodia and the failed states of sub-Saharan Africa.

A low position on the ladder of economic advancement easily translates as *backwardness,* and the shame of backwardness breathes its infection into one of the least ventilated corners of Lao national life—the treatment of "ethnics." In conventional thinking, backward people hold back the nation to which they belong. They score low on the metrics of modernity. They hobble their country's advancement.

In order for the state to progress, so the argument goes, such people must be hauled from their dim pasts, by force if necessary, and brought into the enlightening glare of modern life. They must be persuaded to live in proper houses, and they must learn to grow rice and own things. Ultimately, like everybody else, they need to hunger for cell phones, motorbikes, televisions, and even "jobs." This, at least, is what a Lao official might be inclined to think after he has been snubbed at yet another international meeting, viewed as representing a weak sister among the giants of the world, a country that is less a nation than a melting pot of ancient ethnicities. Such thinking can color a government's treatment of its least modern people.

The other side of the coin, of course, is that Laos is a world leader in cultural intactness, linguistic diversity, and the preservation of ancient ways of life. Such qualities, unfortunately, are rarely measured and less often ranked. Counting TVs is easier.

The Sek and the Brou grow paddy rice, which is a mark of relative advancement, but they also create swidden, a practice generally deemed backward, and so they somewhat contribute to the belittlement of their country. The "worst" offenders, however, are the Yellow Leaf People, those who wander the forest shunning agriculture in all but its most rudimentary form, the people whom anthropologists term "nomadic foragers" or "hunter-gatherers."

The term *Yellow Leaf People* has a revealing etymology. In the forests of Laos, nomadic foragers typically roof their temporary shelters with palm or banana leaves, but they rarely stay in one place for long. By the time the leaves turn yellow, they have moved on.

On one occasion, a colleague said to Robichaud, it was "very embarrassing" to have people "living in the forest." Another official, elsewhere in the government, asserted, "These people have a *right* to be civilized!"

"A right?" Robichaud replied. "Translocation is killing them. What good is civilization going to do for them if they're dead?"

The resettled misfortunates of Ban Thameuang include remnants of several Yellow Leaf tribes. One of these is the Atel, who formerly roamed a portion of the upper watershed of the Nam Xot, deep in saola country. They neither built villages nor accumulated goods. Each day their principal occupation was to secure the food they would eat *that day*. The next day, and every day, they did the same. For ten months of the year they slept in palm-leaf shelters that were little more than lean-tos, and every few days they would move to a new location, across a ridge or up a canyon, to see what food they might find. Only in the depths of the rainy season did they root themselves in place, with sturdier huts, to last out the worst of the weather.

Probably no one outside Ban Thameuang knows for certain how many Atel survive—certainly less than two dozen, perhaps half that, which renders them at least as endangered as saola. By means unrecorded (I heard the word "captured" in one account; "encouraged" in another), the government caused them to relocate to Ban Thameuang in the late 1970s and 1980s. At the time, the traumas of war and revolution were fresh, and the new Lao government was anxious to consolidate control of its people.

Among the Atel who came to Ban Thameuang were an elder known as Touy (another Lao "Chubby") and a younger man named Bounchan, who by the mid-2000s was "fiftyish."

In 2006, Robichaud arrived in Ban Thameuang and asked Touy and Bounchan to take him to the Atel homeland, in the headwaters of the Nam Xot. Robichaud would cover the expenses. They readily agreed. Like the rest of their people, Bounchan and Touy relished any opportunity to go home.

Going home meant being able to honor their ancestors with offerings of food and tobacco in exactly the places where such honoring was most meaningful. It meant gathering rare herbs and longed-for foods. It meant contact with the place spirits that knew every Atel person individually, spirits that were the guardians of Atel culture and resided where each person had been born.

Robichaud, Touy, and Bounchan traveled by boat for a day up the Nam Xot until impassable rapids stopped them. Then they walked along the river, eventually branching up a tributary, the Houay Kanil (*houay* means "stream"). They visited a gemlike waterfall, swapped stories, and roamed the country. Robichaud surveyed for wildlife, as usual, but was no less interested in learning how a small band of people possessing almost nothing and speaking a language known to no one else once inhabited their territory. For three days at the headwaters, Touy and Bounchan introduced Robichaud to the world they had lost. They came to a pomelo tree, a variety of citrus, growing beside a big rock. They sat and ate pomelos (which taste much like grapefruit), and Bounchan said, "This is where my old uncle, who planted the tree, would sit and eat the fruit, just as we are doing." Touy and Bounchan told Robichaud how the Atel used to use the bark of a certain tree[3] as a poison, throwing it into pools to kill fish, which they collected and ate, and they told how they pounded the tree bark into sheets that they wore as clothing, because whatever toxin killed fish also kept mosquitoes away. One day Robichaud witnessed Bounchan kindle a fire starting with nothing but a knife. First he found a certain kind of dead, hard bamboo and split a length of it in thirds. He bored a hole through two of the pieces and placed tinder between them, making a kind of sandwich. While Touy stood in the background offering advice, Bounchan wedged the third piece in a notch in the trunk of a tree to hold it fast and sawed the sandwich back and forth against it. In moments the tinder began to smoke and then to flame.

Bounchan said that when he was young, the only metal known to anyone was a single machete shared among twelve families. He recalled that the big knife was especially useful when they built shelters for the rainy season.

He and his people roved the forest, always on the lookout for scavenging birds. A raucous flock of crows might show where a pack of dhole had made a kill. People would rush there and with spears of sharpened bamboo drive off the wild dogs. (They lacked bows and arrows.) They would take the carcass, leaving a leg or some other portion as an offering to the pack. They would do the same with a bear's kill or even a tiger's. Every day the paramount task was getting food, and the Atel had many ways to get it. Few plants or animals escaped their attention, and they could make a meal of tubers or termites with equal ease.[4]

Bounchan is now dead, a few years gone. It is Touy whom Robichaud has come across the river to see. He brings photographs of the now distant trip to Houay Kanil, and gifts of food as well. We tie the boat at the foot of a tall bluff, said to be the approach to Ban

Thameuang. The trail is indistinct and fiercely steep; with difficulty we scramble up the sandy bank. It is the heat of the day, and the village bakes on its barren plain above the river, a shamble of dwellings and hacked stumps. Not a soul stirs. No children call or play, and not even a cur comes forward to bare its teeth. We approach a sleepy-looking house, and Robichaud calls out, asking for Touy.

A woman's voice answers from within the doorway, "He has been sleeping in his swidden. I don't think he is here. But you can ask his niece. She lives over there." An arm projects from the door, pointing.

The indicated house boasts a few scraps of sheet-metal roofing, the only metal on any house in view; the rest of the roof sags under aging thatch. The walls are mats of bamboo, woven in diverse patterns. The house perches on skinny stilts and lacks a porch. Its flimsiness and the several small pigs asleep beneath the entry ladder bring to mind the children's tale of the big, bad wolf, who huffed, puffed, and blew down shacks like this.

Again Robichaud addresses the darkness beyond the doorway. We are invited to enter, but the ladder is spindly, and I fear the frail rungs will not bear my weight. I climb with my feet at the edges, near the dubious support of the rails. Inside is no better. Broomstick poles and cracked slats comprise a floor that is as much holes as wood, as much gap as substance. Robichaud settles himself carefully. I am a little heavier, certainly clumsier. Were I to lurch sideways, I might fall through the wall. I pray we do no damage to this structure.

Touy's niece sits with her infant son beside the pool of light spilling through the doorway. Her husband, shapeless in a dim corner, reclines on a pile of bedding. He seems to nod to us, perhaps lifts a hand (my eyes have not adjusted to the dark), and does not further stir. The clay hearth behind the niece is cold on this hot day, but everything within the hut—quilts, clothes, baskets, and walls—is tinged with soot. There are no windows, only the doorless entry. Myriad pinpricks of light, like a crowded galaxy, leak through the wall mats.

Yes, says the niece, Touy is at his swidden. She has a pleasant smile. Her mahogany skin is lustrous. Her uncle, she says, is unlikely to return soon.

Robichaud asks about the baby, and she holds him for us to see, a toothless, grinning, jolly fellow in a dirty brown shirt. He might be seven or eight months, old enough to be amused by odd-looking, whiskery, pinkish strangers. The child is plump, but his mother says he has been sick, shitting water for three days. She doesn't know what the matter is. He is her only child. She had another baby a few years ago but lost it.

Touy's niece speaks Lao haltingly. Even I can tell it is not her native tongue. She might be within a few years of twenty, which would put her among the first generation of Atel children born in Ban Thameuang. I cannot see any food in the house, although surely there must be some.

All that the outside world knows of the Atel would fit in a small notebook — some scraps of language, a pittance of lore, almost nothing of their cosmology. Among the few items that have been recorded is their belief that wild foods and domestic foods must not be eaten at the same meal.[5] To mix, for example, ant eggs and rice at one sitting would be poisonous, and if the combination did not finish you on the spot, it would cause much suffering. The resettled Atel of Ban Thameuang walk a perilous line in their striving for subsistence. They grow rice, cassava, and other crops, but not enough to live on. Some of them labor for the Brou of neighboring villages, who work them hard for meager pay — sometimes rendered in kip, sometimes in opium, which the Brou get from the Hmong to the north. The Atel also forage as best they can, but the land near Ban Thameuang, unlike their lost homeland, is continuously scoured by many hungry eyes, leaving little to be found. The Atel do not prosper. They fall ill in body and soul, and they die young.

In at least one place elsewhere in Laos, the government allows other clans of Yellow Leaf People to continue their nomadic ways, even providing depots of food to help them through times of shortage. But NNT lies in Khammouane Province, where the authorities prefer their people planted, like rice, in fixed places. Again, the correspondence between NNT and the nineteenth-century American West bears noting. Ban Thameuang recalls the early years of American Indian reservations, where lives were also short and heartbreak epidemic.

Robichaud shows Touy's niece photographs he took of her uncle on their 2006 journey to Houay Kanil. She smiles appreciatively, perhaps out of politeness. It is not clear to me that she reads the photo as a photo, which is a knack no one is born with. Surely she has seen few such images before, and the first view of a relative reduced to an inch-high image on a piece of photo paper is not always comprehensible. Robichaud also gives her candy and a few packets of dried jackfruit and other edibles. She asks him what to do with the contents of the packets—plant them or eat them? Robichaud explains that they are food, not seed. We prepare to go, and as I stand on stiff legs, bent low beneath the roof, I am again fearful of stepping on a weakness in the floor or of having to grab a door frame that cannot stand a tug. The kindly niece and her ailing son watch us as they might watch water buffalo lumber away. They are patient and calm of gaze. Much like Martha, the saola, in her grotto in Lak Xao, they live in a place not of their choosing, subsist on a diet as foreign as moon rocks, and are observed by outsiders, like Robichaud and me, in their naked vulnerability.

Electricity is coming to Ban Navang. Lines of bare poles angle through the village, soon to be wired to a small hydroelectric generator on the river and soon to enable a long-awaited inrush of modernity: pumped water, refrigeration, lightbulbs, cold beer. It is already sundown. We overlook the village from the second-floor veranda of the new WMPA building and witness one of Ban Navang's last journeys into natural darkness. The roofs are a mosaic of old thatch, blackened with age, and new thatch, yellow and plump. A man in blue undershorts squats to bathe at a fountain. The usual dogs bark.

Ban Navang.

The expected boom boxes, powered by solar chargers, tangle their songs. Hills rise into the mist beyond the village, foliage stacked on foliage, a confusion of canopies smoothed by gentle light.

We traversed those hills not much earlier in a three-hour trek from Ban Nahao, at first zigging and zagging along the rims of dry paddies, then tunneling into the forest. The way was flat, the footing solid, the trees alive with sound. At every squawk or warble, Robichaud named the bird that made it: a racket-tailed drongo, a greater coucal, and many others. We lingered amid swiddens at a towering snag where a coppersmith barbet hammered out its *tok, tok, tok,* metronomic and unfading, two hundred identical *toks,* ringing like a copper bell.

It was a fine walk, made finer by drugs. Still weak from my rodeo of purgation, I indulged in a remedy that I hoard in my kit. It is intended for migraines but bows only to coca leaves and amphetamines as a corrective for hard hiking. It quells pain with large doses of aspirin and acetaminophen and adds a jolt of caffeine to keep the legs moving. I floated down the trail.

Climbing the hill in Ban Navang to the WMPA quarters, we met a Vietnamese trader on a motorbike. He was handsome and affable, sporting torn jeans and a mouthful of crooked teeth. He had *putt-putted* down from Lak Xao, in the north, ferrying his bike and goods across the Nam Xot. In Saigon and Hanoi, his countrymen make an art of overloading motorbikes. You see mountains of chicken cages and towers of cartons roped, bungeed, and delicately balanced on two frail wheels, with no outriggers or sidecars to keep the peace with gravity. The young trader who bantered with us was well along in the art. Nested basins stood like a radio dish above what was left of his taillight, and a brimming crate of pots and miscellaneous knives rode at the small of his back. Big wire baskets flared to either side, filled with buckets, cheap metal bowls, machetes, and the kind of gizmo clutter you see in a sale bin at a hardware store. The young man had the manner of someone easy to amuse who was no less practiced at amusing others, someone hard to threaten and harder to bluff, a man sharp in trade and ready to trade anything he had for anything else if only he might squeeze a margin from the swap. Buried in the hodgepodge of his side baskets were several wicker canisters, and I wondered whether a turtle or a pouch of dried monkey hands had found their way into one of them, or would soon. Despite all his goods, the only thing he might have had that we wanted was information about the traffic in wildlife in the villages where he traded, and we knew that was the one thing he would not sell. We bade him good-bye and watched him coast down the hill and disappear into the thatch of the village.

Our business this evening, after a meal of sticky rice and little else, is to visit the *nai ban,* or village chief, of the Ban Navang village cluster. A friend of Simeuang's, a fellow employee of the WMPA, guides us in darkness to the house of Sai, the headman, down narrow lanes where the murmur of family talk drifts from windows overhead. Sai's main room is crowded with sacks of rice and crates of Beerlao. Sai's wife operates a little store, and they have returned this day from a buying trip to Nakai. We sit in a circle on the floor —

Robichaud, Simeuang, Olay, and me, Simeuang's friend, and nearly a dozen adults of Sai's family, including a handsomely gaunt old man, a seeming patriarch, who sits next to me and watches me closely. My beard has grown in, and it is all white. I surmise that the old man sees me as someone as antique as he is.

New wires and light sockets are stapled to the rafters, awaiting electrification, but tonight three dim bulbs linked to a motorcycle battery are all that push back the gloom. The light glints on the eyes of several children who peer from behind rice sacks in the depths of the room and hide when we look their way.

Simeuang buys two large bottles of beer from Sai's wife, and we drink in ritual fashion. Sai listens solemnly as first Simeuang and then Robichaud explain our desire to ascend the Nam Mon, our need for guides, and our intention to leave camera traps at the mineral lick. Sai is impassive but alert. He is perhaps in his late forties, square-shouldered, not big, but taut and solid, like a wrestler. He and Robichaud are old friends, having traveled together to the upper Nam Xot in 1997. He sits grave and patient, a Brou Buddha. When Robichaud appears to be finishing, Sai nods as though asking for more. At last Robichaud has nothing more to tell him, and after a long pause, Sai speaks.

He says he will provide the guides. He would like to send Phok, because it was Phok, two years ago in March, who saw a saola at the bend in the river, just before the *poung*. It was four o'clock in the afternoon, on a clear day, and after the animal fled, Phok and the rest of the party examined its tracks carefully. Phok, in particular, is sure the animal was a saola.

Unfortunately, Sai continues, Phok is in the forest on survey work and is not available, but there are other guides he can lend us who have been to the *poung*. It is an interesting area. A little farther along the river is the WMPA's new ranger station, placed to keep an eye on movement across the border. And not far away is the grave of a Vietnamese border crosser shot dead by a Hmong hunter. The Hmong wasn't supposed to be there, either—no one from outside the protected area is authorized to hunt within it—but people say that the Hmong regularly hunted the mineral lick and did not like competition. Since the shooting, Vietnamese have been scarce.

The second beer is empty when Sai returns to the subject of Phok's sighting. Modestly he explains that he was also there, behind Phok, as they came to the bend of the river. Robichaud and I exchange a glance. This is news. We had not known Sai was among the group. Phok, he says, had a good look at the animal before it bolted, but Sai himself saw only a fleeting shape. Nevertheless, he examined the tracks, traced them with his own fingers, and he heard Phok describe what he saw while it was fresh. Phok is certain, and Sai believes him, that the creature by the river was a saola.

March 13

Ban Navang

The guides have gone ahead. We follow upriver through a tangle of villages, paddies, and buffalo pastures. At the edge of settlement, where fields give way to river and forest, an old, bent woman stands beside the trail making the *nop*—the shallow bow of head and shoulders over praying hands. She blesses each of us as we file past: "May you go well and return safely." *Nop* to Robichaud, *nop* to Simeuang, *nop* to Olay, *nop* to me. Thank you, Auntie, we say. *Khop chay, khop chay.* The fields behind the old woman hold craters the size of swimming pools, the work of American bombs. The sun is high, the sky clear, and the soil of the fields, beneath rice-stalk stubble, is strangely purple. On a far mountain, a tree with lavender blossoms dazzles like a jewel.

The river flows shallow on a gravel bed. Soon after crossing, we overtake the guides. The trail weaves across the river and back again. With each crossing it narrows and deepens, pebbles replaced by cobbles and then by boulders. The land steepens, and we rise into moister environments, the forest thickening with thorny vines, the trail all but invisible, the silence perfect except for the chants of cuckoos and barbets. Then, abruptly, as though a switch were flipped, a whine of cicadas erupts, like the shriek of a dentist's drill. The sound bores in, deafening and hostile. I feel the energy go out of me and the jungle close in.

Hot now, it is past time for lunch, but stopping for food amid the screaming cicadas would afford no rest, so we keep on. I am behind Robichaud, struggling to keep up, when suddenly the foliage ahead of us parts and a man appears, hustling down the trail at a burdened trot. We stand aside to let him pass, and his eyes widen as he sees us—foreigners!—but he does not slacken his pace. He hurries onward, dripping with sweat and audibly panting. It is plain to see what the rice sack on his back contains. It is a single long block of rosewood, thick as a railroad tie. Contraband. Robichaud turns and fixes a stare on Simeuang, who stands just behind me, but Simeuang will not return the look. He wants no confrontation with the smuggler, no complications. Eyes down, he makes a shooing motion with his hands. "Bai, bai," he says: go, go. The huffing rosewood porter has disappeared behind us, enveloped by the forest. Robichaud looks again at Simeuang but receives no acknowledgment. He harrumphs as though to himself, but loud enough for me to hear, "If a staff member responsible for the protection of this place doesn't blink an eye..." Leaving the thought unfinished, he plunges up the trail.

At last we stop. I throw down my pack and gratefully sprawl in a patch of shade. The head of our new team of guides, a comical fellow named Khamdy, with whom I have not yet exchanged two words, makes a fire, and before the water has fairly boiled—or anyone notices what he is up to—he raids the food reserves and stirs up a single bowl of instant noodles, which he proceeds to eat. Only hours earlier, back in Ban Navang, Robichaud had set forth the camp rules, specifically stating, "No one has special foods unless everybody does." Now Robichaud, exasperated, explains the rule anew, and Khamdy grins back, a noodle on his chin. The rest of us make do with canned fish and the inevitable cold sticky rice, the sight and smell of which make me queasy.

Khamdy seems a sly clown. Stretched to maximum height, he might come to my shoulder. His oversize camouflage shirt is new, the cloth still stiff from the factory, and it hangs on him like a dress. Beneath the shirttails he wears a pair of shorts so ragged they would flutter, if only the air would stir. Khamdy's lower lip juts out in a wry leer. He finds the day, the food, and Robichaud's consternation equally amusing. I am sure he finds my evident exhaustion amusing as well. White guys in the forest: What could be funnier than that? Robichaud and Simeuang may think they're in charge, but nothing happens without Khamdy; he's the squad sergeant, the hub of the wheel. And he's got the gun. I am not sure if Khamdy is officially militia, but he carries a weapon—an ancient carbine with a folding bayonet, the blade of which is deeply chipped and as dull as a cobble. Etched into the barrel in Arabic numerals is the date 1952 together with the five-pointed star of the Red Army, placing it in the era of the Korean War. It is the only armament our group carries, a far cry from the three assault rifles that guarded us on the Nam Nyang, when we were closer to Vietnam and at greater risk of running into poachers.

Khamdy might be in his thirties, barely. The other four guides are teenagers. Thii (pronounced "Tee"), who carries my pack, would look only slightly overgrown snuggling on his mother's lap. Moment to moment, he seems to metamorphose: one minute a sweet-faced innocent, the next, cigarette in hand, a haughty Huck Finn disdaining the world. There is magnetism about him, and Thii knows this. He smiles when he knows he is being watched.

The other boys are painfully reserved. Around his neck Vieng wears a blanket, to which he seems particularly attached. His voice is high and squeaky. At least he speaks. Khum never utters a word. His sideburns, as fuzzy as the thatch atop his head, give him a blurry, out-of-focus look, which his silence reinforces. And Sai (again that name) sits alone, thick-shouldered and morose, avoiding eye contact with everyone. Moodiness aside, Sai and his comrades win my admiration. They are half my size, a quarter my age, and carry twice my load.

I am asleep in the grass when Robichaud spots three great hornbills, birds the size of eagles. "Good omens," he tells me later—perhaps they indicate that hunting pressure on big animals is relatively muted here. Soon we move out, ahead of the guides.

If the hornbills signaled luck, it was a peculiar kind. We have scarcely gone a kilometer when Thii overtakes us. Sai is sick, he says. He can't go on. Nonsense, says Simeuang; he is only hungover and underslept. Olay mentions that Sai told him he'd been drinking at a *hiit* the night before. Robichaud instructs Thii to go back and tell Sai and the others to come up; we'll rest half an hour and see if he can go on.

But Sai doesn't come up. Nor does Khamdy or any of the others. We wait. And wait. Robichaud, his face a mask, sits utterly immobile, as though jostling would crack his self-control.

The friction with the guides on the Nam Nyang disappointed him mightily, although most of the difficulty was attributable to Viengxai. The tensions were an exception to most of his experiences in NNT. But now, with our schedule tight and every delay a threat to the completion of necessary work, our failure to cover ground is particularly vexing.

I stretch out on a long, smooth boulder, feeling disloyal. Limp as string and too tired to sit up, I am content to doze again.

When Thii next appears, Vieng and Khum are with him. Extra loads are tied to their packs. "Sai puked," Thii reports. Khamdy has taken him back to Ban Navang.

We have no choice but to camp where we are and wait for Khamdy to arrive with a new recruit in the morning. Robichaud is glum. "I will never do this again without my own team," he mutters, yanking gear from his pack. "I am tired of ten years of this, tired of rushing. Guides make you rush. They eat up the food so you have to rush to get back. They get sick so you have to rush through a ten-hour day to get to where you need to go." He throws down his bundled tent. "I am sick of it."

I jot notes beside my tent, which I pitched beside the river on a slanting table of bedrock. Robichaud, still frustrated by the day's lack of progress, strides past with fishing pole in hand, headed upstream. "Therapy," he says. "I am getting therapy." A day ago, Sai, the Ban Navang headman, predicted we would need three days to reach the *poung*. By the map, Robichaud judged only two, but now Sai seems prescient. I cannot say I am disappointed. My strength has not returned since my illness in Nakai. It wanes quickly when we are on the move. I try not to think about it. There is nothing to be done except to admit a terminal weakness and go back, and I will not do that. When we stop and rest, I feel at ease, and the forest, in the present clear, if steamy, weather, is glorious to behold.

Beside our camp, slate-gray water twines past boulders sculpted by Henry Moore, between mountainsides painted by Frederic Church. Downstream, the sunlight diffuses into a misty yellow gauze, and the riotous vegetation pillows upon itself. Far in the distance a bluff stands silhouetted against the sky. On it a solitary tree, as tall as the canyon is deep, soars above the usual canopy. Its long trunk is a sinuous improbability. It slaloms upward through deep curves, bending horizontally left and right, and ends in an emerald halo of foliage. I cannot fathom how it might have formed or how it can stand without breaking. A growing trunk might bend if crowded or injured, but left alone, most trees strive toward the sun. This tree defies that notion as it also defies the force of gravity. Its singularity stirs me from my lethargy. I photograph it multiple times. Although I am no artist, I attempt to sketch it in my notebook, but nothing I do captures its peculiar grandeur. I wonder that I never saw it as we came upstream. Viewed from the lower river, it would have presented the shape of a question mark looming above the land of our destination — a question mark hanging beneath an umlaut of greenery.

March 14

Nam Mon, Camp 1

In the birdcall racket of first light, Thii and the other boys tromp past my rock to check their nets upstream. Thii peers in the tent, a cheeky act, and smiles cheerfully when he sees I am awake.

We linger over breakfast and take our time packing tents and gear. The boys stoke the fire and smoke the fish they've caught. Robichaud stitches up a tear in his trousers. I write some, doze some, and wash a shirt.

We wait for Khamdy and the replacement guide.

I again attempt to sketch the tree that towers above the downstream bluff. The result is unsatisfying, but the effort to *see* the forest, in the slanting morning light, excites me. For whatever reasons of illumination or clarity, the textures and hues of the trees seem suddenly exclamatory. Vines wreathe the treetops in bold, strong lines. The forest today seems a sea in which every figurative wave and whitecap possesses an identity distinct from every other. Yet oddly, the strongest impression I have is one of unity, of the whole forest existing as a single, enormous organism, a blanket of life, a factory of photosynthesis, enveloping the geologic ground. The competitive energy within it seems to me no different from the manic pulse of Mumbai, Jakarta, Hanoi, or New York: the Darwinian clawing for light and space, the constant churning of mutual aid, aggression, and injury, the ceaseless experimentation in form and function. And then I realize the irony of the construct I have made. In earlier times, when large conurbations were new, people compared cities to the jungle. Now, as an emissary of a city-driven world, I have built the image in reverse.

• • •

At ten o'clock, still no Khamdy. Had he started early, traveling light, he and his new recruit would be here by now. Our plan was to reach the *poung* today, work there tomorrow, and return downstream the two days following. This now appears impossible, and Robichaud has the look of a man in pain.

Finally, at nearly eleven, Khamdy marches into camp, his grin lascivious and triumphant. Mr. Voy, the new recruit, blinks shyly behind him.

There was a wedding party in Ban Navang last night, explains Khamdy. Much to drink. Slept late. All is good.

Suddenly he is staring at me, peering closely at my neck. He steps close, still staring. Our faces are inches apart. His fingers probe my throat. His immense brown-toothed smile seems momentarily carnivorous. He has spotted an insect bite, and he tweezes it with his fingernails. Then he attacks another on my elbow.

The bites must be burst and squeezed out quickly, he says. Otherwise they fester into boils. They are the work of the cat-tailed fly and another anesthetizing biter, neither of which exist in the village. But they are here, and very vexing. One must be careful.

"*Khop chay*," I say, grateful if I have been spared a minor grief yet still uncertain if the bites were as he said, for I never felt a thing. Either way, Khamdy has diverted everyone's attention from the lateness of his arrival.

The canyon has narrowed, and the river collides now with this wall, now with that one, so that we must cross it with increasing frequency. We jump from boulder to boulder, and the boulders are like ridge-backed tortoises, except that their shells are greased, and—I swear—when they feel my tread upon them, they shrug. I am soon well bruised and excessively bathed.

At one crossing I find a pole to steady myself, but Simcuang looks at it with disapproval and draws his machete. He chops through a

285

green stalk of bamboo at the river's edge, and a pint of clear, fresh water runs from the hacked cylinder. He hands me the walking stick with a tolerant smile that says, *Good luck; you'll need it.*

The pole is light and strong, a pleasure in the hand. I stump along more steadily now, and more amused: the staff is like a physical koan. When it strikes the rock, its hollowness makes the rock sound hollow, as though the staff were not.

We come to a waterfall fifteen feet high and climb it on a ladder of faint toeholds and brittle vines. At the top we pause to watch finger-size silver fish shoot up the cascade like missiles, flailing desperately, none succeeding in topping the falls.

The cobbles of the river channel have changed. Many are pocked with igneous bubbles and shot through with air holes, signs of volcanism. Soon we encounter a lava flow that presses the river against the opposite canyon wall, enclosing it in a chasm. We climb away from the river, scaling the face of the lava, and work our way in and out of timber along a narrow bench of tilted, broken bedrock. The rock crumbles underfoot, and fragments clatter into the nerve-tingling void. Each challenge seems a little harder than the one before, but each brings us closer to the *poung*—and, we hope, to saola. Our journey feels like a poker game, with the stakes rising hand by hand, the possibility of gain and loss racing upward.

Beyond the lava, we stop and wait for the guides to catch up. An hour passes: still no guides. Did they stop to fish? Simeuang thinks not. Did they leapfrog us, taking a trail we missed that detoured through the forest? Simeuang thinks not. If one of them were hurt or sick, would they not have sent a runner?

Then laughing Khamdy heaves into view, the ancient carbine slung on his shoulder and hanging nearly to his heels. Thii is behind him, dwarfed by my pack and looking as lighthearted as his leader.

We climb a second waterfall, slick with moss, and then a third, where a strangler fig provides the only passage. Its tangled arches and buttresses afford handholds, and we squeeze ourselves like reptiles through its twisted apertures.

We see the tracks of a water monitor, a lizard that can grow more than two meters long. We come to a broad rock ledge heavily spotted with macaque dung. We see muntjac tracks and scat. We flush four jungle fowl, which flee in a drumroll of wing beats. We hear a crash in the forest as a large animal—muntjac, sambar, saola?—bounds away. Then comes a fourth waterfall, which we struggle past by chinning our way on tree roots.

The guides are lagging again as we reach the Houay Mrro, a drainage that joins our westerly course from the south. The lavas we have been traversing evidently flowed to the Nam Mon by the canyon of the Mrro. As soon as we cross the creek, we are back to familiar limestone.

The canyon encloses us as though it were a prison, its walls nearly vertical and the river flooding its narrow floor. Were the river a foot higher, there would be no passage. We lurch from boulder to boulder, or, forced by deep water, climb a rock face to seek a ledge swallowed in thorns and vines. When at last we come to a place wide enough to sit down, we wait again for the guides. Robichaud is restless, impatient to go on.

Khamdy arrives and flatly announces we must camp where we are. The next place wide enough for sleeping, he says, is a great distance away. Robichaud, stunned, appeals to Simeuang for a contrary opinion, but Simeuang shrugs. Anywhere else he might offer advice. Simeuang retains a nearly photographic memory of the many trails he's walked in the watershed, but he has never before tramped this reach of the Nam Mon, above the Houay Mrro. We have no choice but to accept Khamdy's guidance.

As though to mollify Robichaud, Khamdy makes a show of clearing the leaves and smoothing the sand of the small flat patch of ground where he bids Robichaud and me to pitch our tents. His anarchic cheerfulness is irresistible. The bon vivant who started late from Ban Navang has now become a pampering, lunatic butler. He runs back to the other guides, fetches Robichaud's big pack, and deposits it with a flourish at the spot he has picked out. Thii, joining the farce, does likewise with mine. They stand behind the now

Back row, left to right: Simeuang, deBuys, Khum, Olay, Khamdy. Front: Thii, Vieng, Voy, Robichaud. (Courtesy William Robichaud)

leafless patch of sand, grinning proudly, as though to ask, "How do you find your room? Will you take tea here or in the parlor?"

Robichaud, fighting laughter, asks, "How far to the *poung?*"

Chipper and authoritative, Khamdy fires back, "If we leave early, we'll be there by ten."

Robichaud is astounded. "I'll believe it when I see it," he says to me in English.

Khamdy needs no translation of Robichaud's doubt. He points to his tattered camo shorts, which hang below his knees. "If we get there when I say, you can buy me a new pair of pants in Ban Navang!"

"It's a deal," Robichaud agrees.

I am pitching my tent when Khamdy skitters by in his undershorts, fishnet in hand. By the time the tent is up and I have unrolled my sleeping bag, Khamdy is headed the other way. A dozen small fish quiver in his net.

Suddenly someone calls an alarm, and Khamdy comes running back, gripping his machete. Thii is running downstream on the far side of the river, leaping from boulder to boulder, shouting and pointing at something midstream.

A small, furry head, dark-nosed and whiskered, breaks the surface. An otter! At first it seems that Khamdy and the boys, all brandishing knives, are out to slay it, but no, they only want to clear their valuable nets from its path.

In a moment the alarm has passed. The nets are intact, the dark head is seen no more, and a general feeling of elation pervades the camp. The sight of an otter confirms Robichaud's growing sense that the biota of the river is reasonably intact. Evidently Vietnamese hunters have not lingered here. Otherwise otters would have been stripped from the streams, early targets of poaching. We've also encountered no snares in the forests of the Nam Mon, not that we would have expected to see them along the river's edge. But neither have there been any when we've clambered up slopes seeking passage around a defile, and this is a heartening sign.

If indeed the hills are free of snare lines, the causes may be multiple. Perhaps the army post at the head of the river is effective in keeping Vietnamese out of the watershed. Perhaps the notorious murder of a Vietnamese poacher counts for even more. Or perhaps the big, organized hunting and trapping gangs mustering out of Nghe An and similar places haven't yet targeted the Nam Mon. Whatever the reason, the result is good for otters, for saola, if they are here, and for all the other creatures of the forest.

Consider extinction: It is an abstraction, unexplorable by the senses. It is an absence, a vacuum, a negative space. Although the fact of extinction is more durable than diamonds or steel, it is as incorporeal as smoke.

For people to care about extinction, it needs to have a face. For many, that face is the tiger's.

Tigers are extinct in 93 percent of their historical habitat. Their wild populations in China, Cambodia, Korea, Laos, Vietnam, and Myanmar are, at best, in the low two digits. Of the roughly 3,200 wild tigers believed still to exist, approximately half survive in India.

The threats to this remnant population are the work of humans. Demographers tell us that India will pass China as the most populous nation on Earth within a year or two of 2030. Forty-one people are born there every minute. The pressure to find space and resources for the country's swelling population dwarfs most other concerns and produces habitat fragmentation and degradation, encroachment on protected areas, and depletion of prey species (which, if it does not result in starvation or reproductive failure, leads to predation on domestic livestock, with ultimately disastrous consequences for the tiger). Most pernicious of all is the omnipresent trade in animal parts. In the folk medicines of East Asia, tiger bone is penicillin, interferon, and Viagra rolled into one. The hunger for it has left vast swaths of viable habitat bereft of its most stunning denizen.

The saola, as Robichaud likes to point out, does not have a price on its head. The tiger, by contrast, is "most wanted" on every poacher's list, rivaled only by golden turtle and rhinoceros. A few ounces of its bone, or a claw or a tooth, can fetch thousands of dollars. With prosperity increasing throughout East Asia, the ranks of those who can afford high-priced "treatments"—or merely flaunt their wealth— swell year by year. Demand only rises, even as the source animals grow scarcer.

These days, the conservation of the world's most charismatic species, in many places, is won only at the point of a gun. Animals such as tigers, rhinos, elephants, and many more, all with bounties on their heads, require the protection of armed guards—squads of militia, rangers, and wardens on constant patrol.

A tenet of modern conservation is that community support is key. If elephants are to survive in Kenya, say, then the Maasai, Samburu, and other tribes who live in proximity to them and bear the difficulties of that closeness must want them to survive. They have to think of elephants as assets, not just as crop raiders and competitors for badly needed land. And so shared revenue from ecotourism becomes a priority, along with quick-response management, democratized decision making, and, where necessary, elephant-proof fencing.

Community support remains vital wherever people are in contact with wildlife, which includes every place where important wildlife populations can be found, including Nakai–Nam Theun. And yet far too often, it is not enough. When gangs of armed men infiltrate an area to strip it of its tigers, ivory, or other animal-based riches, they have to be met with force. They and their masters, who may include international criminal cartels, have to be defeated. This means encircling the animals in a metaphorical ring of guns.

It is not hard to imagine a dystopian future in which the great forests of the world become empty of the species that earlier generations referred to as their "royalty." No more King of the Jungle. Instead, one day not long from now, children may think of T. rex, tigers, and elephants as co-occupants of a single, distant Lost World, accessible only in dreams and storybooks. The prospect is desolate. Sure, some of the megafauna will be bred forever in zoos, or for as long as society produces enough luxury to maintain zoos, but even the best zoo is a faint simulacrum of wild habitat and a zoo animal a ghost of its free-roaming forebear. Uncounted species—not just charismatic animals like tigers, gorillas, rhinos, and saola but an even larger number of obscure rodents, amphibians, birds, and reptiles—have been pressed to the brink. We hardly know them, and yet within the vastness of the universe, they and the rest of Earth's biota are our only known companions. Without them, our loneliness would stretch to infinity.

March 15

Nam Mon, Camp 2

Robichaud is up by half-light and packing at high speed. He says he's skipping breakfast with the rest of camp—"gonna burn a Clif Bar instead"—the better to see what he can see. "You are welcome to come if you want," he tells me. I say I hate to miss my portion of sticky rice, but yes.

The river narrows between steep walls, forcing us to cross and cross again. We try to avoid water deeper than mid-thigh, but the possibility of doing so declines with every twist of the channel. In the water or out of it, the footing is bad and the banks often impossible to climb. The Nam Mon in this reach is as heavily scoured as the tributaries we explored on the Nam Nyang, and there are few patches of sand or light gravel that might show a track. We find scraps of otter scat, conspicuous on boulders, but little else. The usual birds clamor, and the heavy green weight of the jungle leans over us.

By nine I am worn. The river flows in a rock cradle, and we cling to its sides, inching along toehold ledges, seeking the slightest concavity or moderation of slope to belly along the wall. Failing that, we go into the water or tempt fate by jumping boulders. For some there is no challenge. Olay and Simeuang, who will soon catch up to us, dash balletically across such boulders, caroming without pause from angled face to angled face. Were I to try to match them, I would crash on the third landing.

I joke to myself that river crossings now come more frequently than Don Giovanni ever had sex. The algae on the boulders is a miracle of lubrication. More and more I stick to the water, wading belly deep across submerged, shin-banging boulder fields until finally there is no choice but to climb the exposed rocks (an exhausting task) and leap across some fast channel or bottomless pool. The difficulty wears on Robichaud, too. He calls out that the rock hopping is "very stressful," an understatement of the first order. I cannot help reflecting that every step made today will have to be won back tomorrow or the next day, when we head for the villages.

A racket-tailed drongo screeches and churrs as we wait by a long, flat pool for the others. I wash down two caffeine-and-analgesic pills, noting with concern that only a dose and a half remain in the vial. I would rather run out of food than those pills. Soon Simeuang, Olay, and the guides come up, and we start again, but we gain only a few hundred meters before Robichaud and Simeuang, in the lead, simultaneously freeze.

High above the river's edge, in the top of a spindly tree, a bulky black ball is stirring.

The creature is so uniformly dark that I cannot tell head from rump. Then a leg moves, separate from what now appears to be a bushy tail. Two eyes shine dully from a mass of hair. The movements are ponderous, as of a creature barely waking from slumber, or stupidity.

"Binturong," announces Robichaud.

The word means nothing to me. I ask him to repeat it.

"Binturong. It's a kind of civet." The animal is backlit by the sky, almost impossible to see in detail, but Robichaud nevertheless takes photographs. He explains that the Lao call the binturong a perfumed bear because of its heavily scented musk and ponderous, ursine behavior. Zoos, I later learn, sometimes use them for school education, for if unprovoked, they remain nearly somnolent, even in a noisy classroom. To North American eyes, they are as improbable as a Dr. Seuss creation. The binturong has a bearlike head, the body of a wolverine, the claws and temperament of a sloth, a prehensile tail, and double-jointed ankles that allow it to descend trees

293

headfirst. Much like a human, it eats anything: fruit, eggs, small mammals, fat insects, and birds. Once Robichaud came upon a group of hunters who had killed one. The meat, he said, was heavily aromatic, as though seasoned with Indian spices—not bad at all.

We watch the binturong lurch above our heads from one frail, sagging limb to another, remarking that although we are lucky to see it, the binturong is luckier still. Any other group of humans on the Nam Mon would have shot it instantly for their supper pot. Or cut down its tree and clubbed it to death. Slowly and awkwardly the binturong clambers away into denser treetops, branches bobbing, until finally it fades from sight, never having uttered a sound.

We resume our upriver march. I flounder, wet to the waist, while others spring from rock to rock. The day grows hot. We keep going, back and forth across the river, then up a vertical bank, thrashing along a ledge of jungle, and down another bank to the rocks. I've made it a point of pride on the Nam Nyang and here never to ask for a halt or rest. Keep moving, I tell myself, just keep moving. I do not want to make myself an issue, for I fear the concern of the group will shrink around me like a smothering shawl and that their attention, ticklike, will suck out the last of my strength.

Even so, I have noticed that Simeuang often has me in the corner of his eye, and Olay sometimes walks close behind me, like a spotter in a gym: if the old man begins to totter, he'll try to break the fall. His attention is comforting, and I appreciate it all the more that it is unspoken. Unfortunately, no amount of comradeship can return vigor to my legs. They feel sodden, inside and out. Meanwhile, the lightness in my head tells me that I am dehydrated. Heavy and light, both at once. Usually I find a paradox amusing, but not now.

Another crossing. Another shin-banging slide into deep water. Another field of submerged boulders. Sometimes I wonder if the guides aren't laying bets about whether—or maybe just when—the guy with the white beard will break his neck. It takes more energy by far to walk badly than to walk well, to borrow balance instead of own it, making a hundred ungainly adjustments where others glide.

Up the canyon of the Nam Mon.

At last, dripping, I stagger out of the river to face the bank, a vine-hung, nine-foot wall with no evident handholds or footholds. Robichaud lunges upward, grabs a root, hauls himself up. Simcuang does the same. My turn. I lunge for the root, grab it. It breaks. Down I go, but Olay saves me from toppling backwards. I take aim at another root and lunge again. This one holds. It takes everything I've got to chin myself up and grab for another, then pull again, and again, to the top. I am on my knees, winded, heart pounding, but Robichaud and Simeuang have already disappeared down an invisible path, bobbing like boxers through the trees and vines. I lurch after them. And am tripped by a vine. It is never the first trip that gets you; it is the second or third, like a series of jabs before the knockout. I catch my foot on another vine, maybe a log. Falling, I curl my shoulder into a tree, which is wreathed in the band-saw teeth of holdfast vines. Entangled now. Pausing, panting. A deep breath. Two breaths. I need to collect myself, but everyone is moving forward. Hey, Robichaud, what's the fucking hurry? I feel anger welling up. The words to call a halt rise in my tightened throat, sure to sound peevish if I release them. Suddenly Robichaud, invisible in the thicket ahead, says, "Hey, look here!"

He has stopped. I can stop. We have all stopped.

Robichaud has recognized a campsite from a trip two years ago. He and Simeuang had come to this reach of river by a different route. Simeuang confirms Robichaud's judgment and says we are an hour from the *poung*. And if Simeuang says it, an hour it will be, for we are now within the map of Simeuang's indelible memory.

Our proximity to the *poung* requires a new level of care. We must not camp too close lest we disturb the wildlife. Simeuang says we can install ourselves at a good site not half a kilometer upriver.

When we arrive, Simeuang asks leave to fish while we wait for the guides. "I like to fish," he says, grinning. "I know," Robichaud replies.

Simeuang casts and recasts his net. Olay scratches through the last of his snack food. Robichaud looks for animal sign, then stretches out in a patch of sunlight and closes his eyes. I sit against my pack, immobile, too tired to find a spot to lie down but satisfied that from this position, I cannot fall. An Indian cuckoo chants, "One more bottle, one more bottle."

I sleep sitting up and dream of beer.

Imagine a zoo.

It is an excellent zoo, with naturalistic habitats—the savanna, for instance, is an archipelago of tawny islands bounded by dry moats that the animals cannot cross. Gazelles on one moated island, wildebeests on another. Lions on still another. The animals drift through the savanna in seeming freedom under an open sky.

Ambling along, you round a turn on the macadam trail, and suddenly before you, across a moat, stands a copse of giraffes, treelike in their height, heads slightly bobbing like boughs in the wind. They are taller and more brightly colored—custard yellow, spangled with chocolate—than you ever imagined giraffes to be. They move with sleepy grace. One of them looks quizzically your way, blinking its long-lashed eyes. Its sides swell with breath. You see the bristly mane, the stubble on the not-quite horns. The sun, close behind its head, is a little dazzling. The tower of flesh fixes you with a birdlike stare, and you feel unsteady.

In that moment, something shifts. The moats disappear. All barriers fall away. Now suddenly the lions are free to prowl the territories of their prey. The gazelles wheel as a group, scanning for threats. The wildebeests trot beyond the horizon. The giraffes, whose number includes a wobbly youngster, lose their zoo-bred complacency and become hyperalert. Their new attention is electric, and they seem suddenly larger, necks and bodies rocking as they begin to lope away, their animal architecture exquisite, surprising, sublime. For the first moment in your life you feel you are really *seeing* giraffes, and the intensity of their beauty is almost unbearable.

You continue through the charmed zoo. You marvel at the china-blue feet of the blue-footed booby, the limpid eyes of the snow leopard, the shaggy beard of the bison. Part of the charm of this perfect day is that you—only you—are safe from predation: no lion or bear will harm you. Equally, you pose no threat to the other creatures, so you can linger by the gorillas and admire their prehensile feet. You can stroke the stiff and bottomless white cloak of the polar bear, and when you later find yourself among the antelopes, you can read, close-up, the painted face of the oryx and marvel at the sculpture of its horns. For once your mind is not cluttered with borrowed images. You are seeing each animal de novo, as though you had never before beheld its likeness in a photograph or painting, let alone in cartoonish advertisements. You are eye to eye with the real thing.

But this is just a fantasy.

We are rarely so lucky as to see things unfiltered by memory and experience. A lifetime of television and issues of *National Geographic* helps us paint our expectations. And where the documentaries leave off, Tony the Tiger, Simba, and Babar nudge our sensibilities more than we know or dare admit. And if not they, then the Chicago

Bears, Panda Express, Curious George, and the whole bestiary of popular culture. We rarely slip free of our baggage. In the field, I catch myself bending the images of the birds I see to match the pictures in my field guides. I cannot seem to help it.

Once, though, I blundered into a kind of freedom. It was almost forty years ago, but the memory remains vivid. I was at home, in mountain country. A wet snow had fallen, and a heavy sky blotted the sun. No shadows betrayed the passage of time. No wind disturbed the silence. I was prowling around, purposeless, binoculars in hand. I glimpsed a bird darting into the canopy of a snow-covered juniper. I circled around to approach from the opposite side. A jiggle of twigs told me the bird was still there. I crept nearer, but I could not see through the foliage. I ducked under the first branches and crouched within.

Inside was dim space, leaving the outside world muffled, suddenly distant. From a branch four feet away, the bird watched me with a cold black eye. I did not recognize the species. It was new—a find! I held still, on bent, trembling knees, and I marveled that the bird did not fly off. Perhaps the strange day had cast a spell on it, as it had on me. Close-up, the bird's dorsal feathers gleamed like satin. Their hue was part gunmetal, part tree bark, a shade of dusk. The beak was the dun of deer antler, and a white ring encircled the eye. From the throat to the downy feathers of the belly, the bird seemed nearly to glow. Its breast was the orange fading to russet that you see in the last moments of tropical sunsets, a color lurid yet delicious, like the flesh of an exotic fruit.

The bird stared at me and I at it. It twitched its head and hopped one branch farther away, the russet of its underside still shining in the half-light. A minute passed, and I realized I had ceased to care about what species it was. The bird was so profoundly *there,* so close and alive. I began to feel the hard completeness of the bird's separate being. The feeling was strong because I could not place the bird in a category—it was neither sparrow, finch, nor dove. I had no name and no template for it, and so it was just *bird,* fresh from creation and marvelous.

Then, with a cackle, the bird burst from its perch and flew away. The sound and movement woke me from my trance, and I realized what sort of bird it was. It was an American robin, *Turdus migratorius,* the commonest of the common. I felt embarrassed and thick-witted—I'd become a satire of myself! But then I recalled how striking and vivid the bird had looked and how it felt to have that black eye bore into me. Never before had I sensed the presence of another creature so strongly, and, I am sorry to say, I rarely have again. Oddly and eerily, in that moment an ordinary robin seemed as great a miracle of nature as a saola, a tiger, or a bird of paradise.

The last push. We drop most of the gear and leave the guides at the sandy riverbank where we will camp. Only the four of us go on. No need for extra trampling at the *poung.*

The river runs flatter now. Although the crowding forest hides the shape of the land, we seem to be on an immense shelf of the mountains, and the way grows easier. Robichaud moves stealthily forward. At a screen of trees he motions for silence. Slowly rounding the trees, we stand before a broad, abraded bend in the river. Light floods the scene in an abundance we have not seen in days. I feel a cool, mild breeze. At the apex of the river's arc, past several twining sandbars, the bank is steep and raw and stained with minerals. It was here, whispers Robichaud, that Phok, with Sai behind him, glimpsed a startled saola. It bolted up the bank and dissolved into forest. The men stood in stunned silence where we now stand, the image of horns, hindquarters, and a burst of movement fading in their mind's eyes. Shocked, they stood right here, their feet on these stones, as the last pebbles kicked up by the saola drizzled down the riverbank.

We stare at the place where the saola disappeared. No fleeing ghost has broken the stillness. All is quiet. There is only the shadow of a saola long gone, the rain-erased hoofprints, the echo of borrowed memory. Still, we stand awhile and contemplate the place where the vision was glimpsed. Each of us, I suspect, prays in some way for the moment's reenactment, for the return of saola to this bend of river, if not now, then after we are gone, and forever and ever, amen.

A red ooze, evidence of mineralization, seeps from the raw bank that the saola dashed up. Trails of bubbles rise through the river pools, and mats of scarlet algae paint the rocks, gas vents spitting at their center. The place feels charged, electric.

One more bend of the river, and we sight an immense tree rising double the height of the surrounding forest. Below, sloping to a shelf of rocks at river's edge, is an oddly barren patch of ground, which we approach. The dust is thick with animal tracks and the occasional turd. "Macaques," announces Robichaud. "This place is their clubhouse."

To one side of the macaque playground and still within the shadow of the great tree, a thin rivulet angles to the river. In the present dry season it is a mere seep, a corridor of mud and fallen leaves at the bottom of a draw. Here, close to the river, it brings salty water to the surface, an upwelling from the dark earth that wildlife travel far to sip. The bitter liquid is a candy, a vitamin pill, an answer to a craving. This bath of muck is our money spot. We have arrived at the *poung*.

It appears to be a busy place. The heavy presence of macaques affirms its attraction. So does the game trail that follows the rivulet down from the hills. Where the seep is wettest, the hill trail meets a second path that parallels the river. Robichaud will concentrate his cameras on this junction. We set to work.

The plan is to aim the two Reconyx cameras, our best and most reliable, at the intersection of the trails. We'll also set a Bushnell to take ten-second videos of the intersection and place another Bushnell back some distance to take stills across one of the approaches. Robichaud and Simeuang set about barbering the site with their machetes, trimming any plant or branch that might grow or droop into the cameras' view. While they are at it, Simeuang finds the shed exoskeleton of a large cicada and places it on his nose, giving him an elephantine proboscis. Olay hugs himself to stifle his giggles, but Robichaud, intent on work, notices nothing. He places large stones in the ooze at the foot of one of the trees where a camera will be strapped. Nothing must take root that might grow up to obstruct the lens. At last he looks up, sees Simeuang, and acknowledges the comedy of the cicada shell with an unwilling, exasperated smile. The joke has failed.

I inspect the enormous tree that lords over the place. Its trunk is easily six feet in diameter; it looks to be 120 feet tall or taller. "What kind of tree is this?" I call to Robichaud.

He briefly glances my way. "It's a Big Tropical Tree," he says. Evidently I am not alone in feeling tired.

Fastening the cameras to trees is a slow process. Simeuang cuts wedges to adjust their aim. We stage walk-throughs to confirm that camera alignment and trigger sensitivity are correct. Again and again, we take down the cameras and program them anew.

I record the coordinates of the site:

Latitude 18° north and so many minutes and seconds.
Longitude 105° east and so many minutes and seconds.[1]

An hour passes, and still not one of the cameras is set to Robichaud's liking. His standards are necessarily exacting. The effort to get here has cost days of hard travel, and now the worth of all our time, sweat, and not a little treasure (our hard-won grant funds) hinges on the operation of a few quirky and expensive instruments. Even when we get them set, the labor will only have begun, because after the coming rainy season, someone—probably Simeuang— will have to return to this place and, at a minimum, swap out the memory cards and batteries. Then he will return at least one more time to retrieve everything, or multiple times if the project continues. Camera-trapping is an expensive means for collecting data. Even so, it offers only one-sided information. When it works, it can confirm that an animal was present, but it cannot confirm that the animal was absent, for a camera's view is limited. In the case of saola, which are so thinly distributed in their territory as to be virtually undetectable, getting no pictures will change nothing. If we come up empty-handed, we will know only what we knew before. The one thing that will materially boost our knowledge is to capture a photograph of a saola. We've come all this way to hit a home run. Nothing else will do.

I asked Simeuang what would happen if we got lucky and landed a photo of a saola. He said the WMPA would certainly organize a big celebration in the nearby villages, a festival involving all the headmen. On the heels of that bash, the agency would greatly ramp up its protection efforts, probably establishing a restricted area around the *poung* and declaring new rules for the broader surroundings. Patrol efforts would intensify, making it between hard and impossible, at least in theory, for poachers, whether Vietnamese or Hmong, to penetrate the area. If they did, penalties for violations would likely be made more severe—perhaps comparable to the twenty-four-year mandatory prison sentence for killing an elephant elsewhere in the protected area. Beyond that, the WMPA would certainly show more support for saola research and protection throughout NNT. He said he personally would relish an opportunity to go into Bolikhamxay Province, beyond the boundaries of NNT, and find out who the Hmong are who hunt the upper Nam Mon in the rainy season.

One of the savvier apparatchiks of the WMPA later confirmed Simeuang's forecast. Phoukhaokham Luangoudom, who directs ecotourism for the agency, thought a saola photograph would be an immense and much-needed blessing for NNT. It would rekindle enthusiasm at all levels of management for wildlife conservation in the protected area. In fact, he said, everything depends on that. In a grave voice he asserted that we only have "a few years" to stem the tide of destruction. After that, he said, "It's over."

. . .

Rob Timmins expressed a mumbling pessimism about saola when we rendezvoused at an airport after my return to the United States. "I might be the only person who thinks that the chances of us detecting saola are less than fifty percent at this stage." Which was to say that "with whatever means we try to detect saola, it is more likely that we won't detect them." Saola are that much a will-o'-the-wisp, that much a phantom, even in the places most hospitable to them. "And that's kind of scary," he said. "Because without detection of saola I just don't think there's a chance in hell we can save saola."

Or at least not save them intentionally. Another school of thought maintains that the saola's best prospects for survival may lie with the general protection of nature reserves—the removal of snares and enforcement of hunting prohibitions that benefit all species. Perhaps saola, left alone to steal through the twilight background, will enjoy peace and relief enough to carry on unbeknownst to their admirers. Such a proposition may be consoling if unprovable, a sort of last stand for the advocates of hope.

Nevertheless, the value of detection remains immense. With proof that saola are present, the odds of securing enforcement of protective policies, not to mention public support for those policies, rise precipitously. But saola hardly make their cause easy. They occupy some of the most difficult terrain on Earth. They are preter-naturally (and justifiably) skittish. And now they are so few that, like the unicorn, they seem to have melted into the air. They are the quarks of the wild world, particles so small and fleeting that they defy our powers of seeing and measuring. We know them better in theory than we do in fact, and in our effort to detect them we may even nudge them away from us in a macro demonstration of the "observer effect"—the distortion of data by the act of measuring. What we know, compared with what we want to know and have con-vinced ourselves we need to know, is pitifully small. At the *poung* specifically, and in saola research generally, we have come a long way and striven hard to place a few large but doubtful bets.

Fortunately, however, we are not at the end of our options, and new detection possibilities remain. The Saola Working Group has investigated using dung dogs like those that sought out the last rhino of Cat Tien in Vietnam. The dogs would have to be trained to locate other scats in addition to those of saola, for they cannot search the forest day after day without reward. Perhaps they might be trained to seek out serow or muntjac scat to keep their motivation strong. Their trainers would still face a difficult challenge in keeping them interested in saola dung when they seldom or never encounter it, and unfortunately, not much saola dung is available to support the training. Only a small amount was collected from the few animals that were briefly held captive. Most of it was swept away or mishandled. And saola dung surely does not persist long in the muggy forests where it is likely to be found. Overall, the prospects for such a program are at best fair—an effort to find saola with detection dogs could wear out a lot of dogs and a lot of handlers—but if funding can be found, it may be worth a try.

Alternatively, advocates for saola might invest in leeches. Truly. The wormy bloodsuckers can go without feeding for months at a time, and while they are fasting, traces of their last meal persist within them. Researchers in Denmark have successfully extracted the mitochondrial DNA of leech victims from the innards of more than two dozen species of leeches—both in the laboratory and in the field. With the help of Nicholas Wilkinson, a young British doctoral candidate who has doggedly researched saola in Vietnam, the team analyzed twenty-five leeches that Wilkinson collected along the Annamite cordillera. Twenty-one of the samples yielded nonhuman mammalian DNA. Animals identified from the recovered sequences included cows and pigs (no surprise), serows (in three leeches), and ferret badgers (in six).[2]

Most interesting among the identified DNA sequences was that of a muntjac in one leech and Annamite striped rabbits (*Nesolagus timminsi*) in four. The Danish researchers assert the muntjac to be the Annamite, or Truong Son, muntjac (*Muntiacus truongsonensis*), but because the status of *truongsonensis* as a distinct species is unclear, identifications in its name remain ambiguous.[3]

The range of the Annamite striped rabbit, meanwhile, widely overlaps that of saola. Rob Timmins discovered the species based on dead rabbits offered for sale in Lak Xao in 1996, and a Russian team derived a formal description of the animal from collections made in adjacent areas of Vietnam in 2000. Now the evidence of four leeches, which Wilkinson gathered by merely walking through the forest, demonstrates a way of detecting the rabbits that is infinitely easier than physical capture or camera-trapping. What works for rabbits might work for saola, too.

The scientific paper describing these breakthroughs is almost gleeful in its celebration of the leech, particularly the family of jawed leeches, Haemadipsidae (the name translates as "blood thirst"), which is widespread in the Asian tropics.[4] Haemadipsidae are ideal for latent genetic analysis, say the authors, "due to their diverse prey base and readiness to attack humans, making them easy to collect."

Alas, no saola DNA emerged from the distillation of the leeches, but no one really expected there to be any. This was a first try, with a tiny sample. The point was to determine whether the method would work, and it did. If it can now be implemented more broadly, perhaps the presence of saola will be confirmed often enough and over a large enough area to suggest that one or more breeding populations exist and that so beautiful and enigmatic an animal may still have a fighting chance to survive.

The branches of innumerable saplings have been cleared away and the broad leaves of swamp plants clipped back. Stones now form a landing under each of the cameras, and each has been double- and triple-checked for the correct settings. Olay, shedding his famous gray raincoat to increase his heat signature, has hopped and crawled through the cameras' fields of view at least twenty times, and for good measure Robichaud and Simeuang have followed with their own imitation of a wary, mineral-hungry ungulate. These rehearsals have sparked realignments of the cameras more meticulous than the aiming of a satellite dish. The wedges that effect the fine-tuning have been cut, deployed, rejected, and replaced with tedious repetition.

The sun is low. No more than half an hour of light remains. Olay and I exchange a glance. It would be nice to get back to camp and off the trail before full darkness has settled. Robichaud inspects and tightens the bungee cords that hold each camera to its tree. He doesn't like the way one of the Reconyx models is aimed. He takes it down and straps it to another tree trunk. Then he lumbers through the field of view not once but twice. It fires both times. He checks the double set of cords that bind it. "Okay," he says. "I guess that does it."

Simeuang hefts the duffel, now almost empty, in which the cameras traveled and sets off on a faint trail leading downstream from the *poung*. It's a trail we have not used. Robichaud leans the other way, shoulders turned toward the macaque playground and the way we came. "Hey, where are you going?"

"This trail is quicker."

"It's late. We don't have time to try a new trail."

"This trail is quicker." And Simeuang fades into the darkening trees.

We follow. Where pathfinding is concerned, there's no point in arguing with the woodsman from Pakxe.

March 16

Nam Mon, Camp 3

We have a morning to burn. Robichaud plans to visit the new ranger post by the border, a kilometer past the *poung*, and to recheck the cameras along the way. I would go with him, not least to explore again the turn in the river where Phok saw the saola, but my endurance is shot. For the first time I beg off, saying I'll stay in camp, the better to muster energy for our afternoon start downriver.

At camp the previous evening, I pitched my tent in the dark and crawled in, hardly able to move. An hour later I straggled out, famished for a cup of something hot. Khamdy, with a scarf wound around his head, was at the fire stirring rice. In the flickering light, he looked like the Sheik of Araby. Dinner was the usual sticky rice and small fish, mostly head and bones. Occasionally the wind gusted, blowing fire into the brush around us, lighting a crackling blaze. No one paid attention, and the errant flames soon burned out.

We lingered an hour in the firelight. Khamdy told us he had never seen a saola. He knows of the animal, as he knows of tigers, but he has never seen one of them, either. He was born in Ban Navang thirty-two years ago and has four children. He'd like to get married but lacks money for a proper celebration. He looked up from the fire, his lower lip drooping. "But there's no hurry." He grinned.

When the time came to turn in, Khamdy spread out the largest of the tarps, and he and the teenagers wrapped themselves in their blankets, side by side, on half of the tarp. They pulled the bottom half over themselves, and their bivouac was set: five peas in a tarpaulin pod.

Later, I woke to the sound of a violent wind battering the trees. I went out, scanning with a light for snags that leaned toward our sleeping places. The temperature had dropped; the weather was changing. If rain came, the slickened boulders would make our river route a torture, but I crawled back into the tent, too weary to dread it.

Come morning the wind is calmer and the sky only brooding. The temperature has dipped to the midfifties Fahrenheit, seriously chilling by the standards of the place. Robichaud, Simeuang, Olay (in his armor of leech socks and raincoat), and Khamdy, shouldering his carbine, set off for the border post at 7:30. I go back to the tent and sleep two more hours.

When I wake, Thii and the other boys are downstream fishing, pulling their nets through yet another pool. I have the luxury of time on my own. The strip of sand and brush where we are camped feels claustrophobic, hemmed in by the canyon wall. Across the river, though, I see a patch of land that looks flat, perhaps even spacious.

I pick my way across a bridge of boulders and push through a curtain of bamboo at the river's edge. I step into cool, dim understory.

I am in an alcove hollowed into the mountain. Although the wind growls high in the canopy, all is hushed below. The ground is soft, the air musky with leaf mold. Somewhere, water is dripping. At one side of the alcove a rock bluff descends in a series of wet ledges, hung thickly with ferns and something like watercress. A tunnel of light has bored through the canopy to fall on the green cascade, like light from a clerestory.

Years ago, in the mountains where I now live, I used to come to glades like this one hoping for revelation. I especially prayed for an elk or some other large animal to appear. I knew my hopes were greedy, but I waited just the same, sometimes a long time, as a hunter would wait. The elk and the bear never came, of course, not to my summoning, but the waiting proved rich with gifts I did not

The forest of the Nam Mon.

seek. One time I leaned back from where I was sitting and felt something under my hand. It was a long-dried-out nugget of carnivore dung. It sounds disgusting, but it wasn't: the dung had become a crust of crumbling earth, nothing more or less, and it contained a surprise. In it were the hock and hoof of a fawn or perhaps a bighorn lamb. The digestion of the carnivore, probably a mountain lion, had bleached the bones, but the shrunken shell of the hoof remained black. I did not know what to make of my find, except that it was a powerful token of the fierce business of the woods. I kept the relics as a talisman.

I wait now. The fern-hung bluff glows with a shimmery luminescence. In ages past, Flemish and Tuscan painters, depicting the miracles of the Bible, tried to capture on canvas such a light. Against my will, I imagine a saola materializing from the shadows and walking into the glow by the bluff, its head high, ears forward and alert, enacting the kind of miracle I used to wish for.

I tell myself not to wish for something absurd. But I wonder, half dreaming, if I were capable of waiting here indefinitely, like a dryad or an ent out of Tolkien, how long would it be before a saola stole through this silent space? How long has it been since the last time? A year? Five years? Ten? Within the past decade, tigers would have prowled the canyon of the Nam Mon, perhaps lingering in this bottom, observing much, fearing only humans and their rifles. On occasion, a lone rhinoceros might have lumbered through these damps, the rhinos of these parts being forest animals, unlike their African relations. A clouded leopard might have lounged on a low, thick branch, might even have hunted from such a perch, staking out a trail, although nobody really knows how clouded leopards hunt. For that matter, nobody really knows, in depth, how life goes on here. This alcove being a place of deep waiting, the clouded leopard might have waited for a muntjac, or a young saola, or any living thing to pass near. Perhaps a pangolin trundled into view. The pangolin wears an armor of horny scales and possesses the digging claws and humpbacked posture of an anteater. It zaps insects with a gluey tongue and, when attacked, rolls into a ball and exudes a vile stink. No more improbable an animal exists anywhere.

The progress of creatures through the alcove, in slow time, would have delighted Darwin and astonished Noah. Furtive civets would have slinked by, and the tiny spotted linsang would stalk lizards and other prey. Overhead, I imagine a binturong bumbling in the crown of a tree, and on the forest floor a python, like an animate log, gliding through the tangle. My imaginings play on as badgers and pigs of various species snuffle by, rooting in the leaf rot. The treetops hum with the gossip of doucs and macaques. A gibbon comes looping through the branches, lank arms fast and deft, and a slow loris blinks sleepily at the commotion. Suddenly, out of the firmament falls a bundle of light as a silver pheasant flutters to the ground like a ball of fallen moonbeams, there to scratch in the duff. Periodically, packs of dhole course through the alcove, a half dozen or more ranging together, lean, tireless, and always hungry. And people, too, a band of Yellow Leaf People, as lean and hungry as the canines, who perhaps shadow the dhole in the manner of the Atel, hoping to claim a haunch of muntjac. Perhaps hunters or honey seekers from the settled villages drift by, hardly leaving an imprint, at least in generations past, for their numbers and firearms are few and they lack wire for "modern" snares. They also lack connection to distant markets, so they kill only for local use. At intervals long enough to try a dryad's patience, the alcove may even witness the ghost of the forest, the little red *phi kong koy*, shuffling bowlegged through the half-light and uttering his unearthly shrieks.

The abundance and diversity of the past seem magical today, although such wonders are scarcely past. Fifty years ago, when I was a boy learning to fish and shoot in tame old Maryland, the Annamite Mountains still brimmed with an almost full complement of native biota: only rhinoceroses might have been ecologically extinct, though a few no doubt hung on here and there. Years later, these mountains remained mostly intact when, fresh from college, I tried to learn the ways of the southern Rockies, which by then were generations removed from their grizzly bears and wolves. Sad to say, even the diminished diversity now found in the Annamites may well seem magical in some near tomorrow.

The bald facts bear repeating. About half the world's people live in Southeast Asia or the adjacent countries of China, Bangladesh, and India. Southeast Asia (including Indonesia and the Philippines) leads the rest of the world in the proportion of its birds and mammals that are found nowhere else. It also leads the world in the proportion of its biota in grave, current danger of extinction. No part of the region has a tradition of effective biological conservation.[1]

Within this matrix of value and loss, the Annamite Mountains, as one conservation manager put it to me, are "up there competing for the number one spot" in terms of their importance to biodiversity. Within the Annamites, Nakai–Nam Theun is similarly superlative, being the largest and most species-rich protected area in the range. It also has good, if unrealized, prospects for effective management, thanks to the assured twenty-five-year income stream from NT2 power generation. Doucs still troop through its treetops, and the diligent searcher, with a modicum of luck, may yet hear the outlandish cry of the crested argus. The sambar, binturong, and colugo remain. A cacophony of birds prevails. The large-antlered muntjac sounds its bark in the night. The python, although lamentably rare, keeps its place, and at least a few streams, like the Nam Mon, retain their otters. Surprising to relate, in a far corner of NNT, elephants continue to wear paths through the forest. Despite the riot of wildlife wealth, however, a theme of loss plays on.

One fall morning in New York I spoke to Joe Walston, a Brit who directs the Asia Program for the Wildlife Conservation Society. He remarked that someone from Roman times glimpsing the dewy hills of contemporary England would shed many a tear, appalled at the transformation of the land. The vast, primeval oak forests have all been cut. The big mammals, from bears to pigs, are gone. In their place are red foxes, hedgehogs, and a largely nonnative environment, which nonetheless has been immortalized in the literature and music of a great culture. If anyone cries over the English landscape nowadays, it is over injury to the storied green hills, not to the biota they replaced. Transformation now similarly sweeps the developing world, although much faster, and it affects ecosystems that are incalculably richer. What took the Romans and ancient Britons several centuries to accomplish now gets done in decades. "Our role," said Walston, "is not to prevent change but to guide it." The best that can be hoped is to effect a sort of triage, painful though it is to watch. A country that today has 60 percent of its land in forest may soon be whittled down to 20 or 15 percent. "Our job is to guide where that remainder percent is going to be, to keep those areas representative of the indigenous flora and fauna, and to assure that they are of a size suitable to protect those species."

Triage is a principle of emergency medical care. After a battle or a great disaster, attention and resources go first to those who are badly wounded but have a chance of surviving. The mangled dying are left to die. The politics of extinction assert similar priorities, and on the battlefield of the present, unlimited crises, finite funding, and uneven government capability and commitment force a torrent of anguishing decisions. George Schaller decided long ago to stop working in Laos. "The government is not serious about conservation," he concluded, and so today he devotes his energies to places such as Tibet and other areas of western China, where good intentions, in his view, have a better chance of translating into facts on the ground.

The fate of the saola hangs by a thread, and by the principles of triage, it might be abandoned. Yet a fragile, hopeful logic favors it. Its genetic distinctiveness places it in a special category: it is its own species, its own genus, and perhaps even its own tribe within the subfamily Bovinae. Moreover, so little is known about the animal that no one can say for sure that its game of survival is past winning. For nearly a century, Edwards's pheasant, another denizen of the Annamites, escaped detection in spite of much looking. Many gave it up for lost. And then, in a desperate last effort led by WWF, it was found again in hidden retreats, where it still presumably clings to life. The saola, like the pheasant, may yet have a surprise for its advocates. More important is its significance to its biome. The saola's defenders like to say that it is the "flagship species" of the Annamites; if its mystique and charisma can be used to rally support for vigorous protection of large tracts of the mountain range, then many other species of mammals, birds, reptiles, and amphibians—the whole remaining Noah's ark of the region—will benefit immeasurably.

And finally there remains the fact, which is enough for me, that the saola fascinates. It enthralls. Like the unicorn, it combines enigma with beauty, which are perhaps two sides of the same coin.

The alcove is still. The winds in the canopy have paused, and the only sound is the drip of water down the face of the green bluff. Imagining the past of the forest has felt filling, like a deep inhalation, a breathing in. My flight of fancy leaves me invigorated, and in a way more hopeful, as though it filled the forest itself.

To imagine the future yields the opposite sensation. It is a breathing out, a long exhalation, an emptying of the land. At the thought of it, the alcove seems to darken.

Breathe in, I think; breathe in.

Hours later, it is raining enough to darken the river rocks. Then Robichaud and the others reappear.

At the ranger post, a modest rectangle of poles supporting a corrugated roof, they found no one and not much sign of recent human presence, only a sleeping bag hung out to dry. Optimistically, one might conjecture that the rangers were out on patrol, a prospect more cheering than the idea that they had retreated to another location while their current excuse for not patrolling expired. Ironically, the kilometer from the lick to the ranger post, the one walk I did not take, turned out to be a pleasant stroll on level forest trail, the easiest going of the journey.

At the *poung* Robichaud, Simeuang, and Olay rechecked the cameras while Khamdy watched, ever amused. They installed one more camera, a fifth, on an approach trail. Almost reluctantly they shouldered their packs and filed back toward camp. The expedition's mission had been accomplished. There was nothing more to do except await the retrieval, weeks hence, of the data cards from the cameras. The time had come for us to go.

We paused for a lunch of the usual rice and fish bone, and as we ate, the sky miraculously cleared and the sun striped the land with shadows. By the time we were packed, the color of the river rocks had lightened. Above waterline, the boulders were blessedly dry.

Even so, as we proceeded downstream, I presented a spectacle to the others at every river crossing. Weaker than before, balance eroded, progress glacial, I negotiated the boulders like a geriatric mantis. Olay eyed me with pained concern. Thii smiled wryly, then danced away. After several ungainly splashdowns, I told Simeuang, with Robichaud interpreting, that I should charge him money to watch me cross the river: "I shouldn't provide so much entertainment for free!"

Simeuang hooted with delight.

And then the unthinkable occurred. Simeuang, the acrobatic master of boulder ballet, missed a step and splashed into the river. Everyone, including Robichaud, himself already wet to the hips, had a good laugh, but the fun was bittersweet. Simeuang's fall was like seeing a star pitcher lose his no-hitter to a bloop single in the ninth.

The crossings, bank scrambles, and waterfall scarps of our ascent of the Nam Mon now unfold in reverse, arduous but tamer than before. The trail hides no surprise: every steep that has been climbed can also be descended. The kilometers begin to blur. We examine otter tracks and scats, sight hornbills, and even spot a pair of fish eagles, giant straight-winged soarers, which Robichaud says are globally rare and have been recorded only a few times in NNT. I walk robotically, unanxious and relieved to be heading home, that ambiguous place of many definitions. Were my legs less wooden, I might feel a sense of elation. As it is, I try to make my mind *smooth,* a concept borrowed from Apache lore. The idea is to keep the flow of awareness open, not to let extraneous thoughts and feelings intrude, to think only *I will place my foot on that rock and will leap from it to that one.* And not to allow the dissent of countervoices, like *I haven't spring enough in my legs to do it* or *They are watching* or *I cannot bear another dunking.* The smooth mind is purged of distraction and self-consciousness. As though refusing delivery of a letter, it rejects the complaint of the inflamed knee, the empty stomach, the weary spirit. If the mind is smooth, nothing unwanted can snag on it.

Easier said than done.

On our last evening on the Nam Mon we camp by a still, deep pool. Robichaud and I place our camp stools so that we command a view downriver, gazing into the late glow, where insects hover and dart. We bring cups of wan tea to our vigil—the best our stores can provide — and the drink is warm and welcome. The evening air tastes of the forest, and the river exhales its moisture around us. We talk little, sipping our tea amid the music of barbets and a few restless owls. Before us, the silvered river vanishes in the sunset haze, and on either side, the profligate forest broods. *Breathe in.*

That night at the campfire, Olay asks about getting lost. He contemplates a naturalist's career and knows the time will come when he will lose his way in unknown country. What to do? Some say stay put. Some say follow water to people. Some wags say go home and get a GPS! Olay asks Robichaud's advice. In so many words, Robichaud says the key is controlling your mind, and although he does not use the term, he talks about making it smooth. Ever the aficionado of film, he quotes *The Edge,* a tale of travelers stranded after a plane crash in the Alaskan wilderness, in which a character asks, "Do you know what lost people die of?" In answer to his own question, he says, "They die of shame." Having lost their way, they judge themselves failures, and their sense of failure infects their decisions. They let the rescue of their pride hinder the rescue of themselves. Their minds are not smooth.

Smoothness of mind: in any kind of flow, the cobble produces less turbulence than the sharp-edged fragment. I can talk about the smooth mind better than I practice it, and I don't talk about it terribly well. Nevertheless, much can be said for a quality of smoothness that time and difficulties fail to roil. If the saola is to survive, it will have to be a smooth thing in the mind of nature, washed over by a world of difficulty. This is fanciful thinking, I know.

March 17

Nam Mon, Camp 4

Another gibbon dawn, possibly my last. A lone male on a ridge half a kilometer away calls and calls, unanswered.

Last night Robichaud said that aside from a couple of anthropologists (who rarely strayed from the villages) and a handful of biologists, we are probably the only Westerners who have probed these remote corners of Nakai–Nam Theun. If this be so, it seems less important now than it did three weeks ago, when we began. In spite of difficulties, the forests and rivers have pampered us. The weather has been kind, as have the leeches, by their absence. Our companions, with one exception, have been helpful, even if the saola, assuming they are still here, have kept a regrettable distance. Now all that remains is a one-day march of twenty-six kilometers—a long pull, the first half difficult, the second easier. After that, the modest comforts of Ban Navang will feel like luxury.

We pack under a cloud of swirling minivets, phoebelike insect eaters, the males red and black, the females yellow, all chattering in reedy voices. The temperature is mild. An infected insect bite that caused Robichaud's ankle to swell to the thickness of his knee has responded to doses of Cipro I dredged from my pack, and he is fit to travel. Khamdy, Thii, and the other guides, meanwhile, have smoked a goodly haul of fish, which they will take to their families. We are a happy camp, homeward bound.

Now begins the last gauntlet of toe trips, vine garrottings, and hat snatches, also the final medley of boulder hops and abrupt wet slides. The hypnotic call of a grey peacock pheasant warns that this

317

is also the last tour of marvels. In confirmation, we soon come to a sand-filled depression at the river's edge in which we find the hoof-print of a mouse deer, or chevrotain, the tiniest of ungulates, small enough that several would fit in a grocery bag.[1] The track is perfect, roughly oval, and no bigger than a fingernail.

Onward down blown-glass waterfalls and across the lavas of the Houay Mrro, where Simeuang mugs for his portrait, prancing on a horizontal trunk high above the rocks. Every ledge, rock ladder, and forest scramble is at least vaguely familiar, easier in reverse, and every view going down is more beautiful than going up, the mind now smoother, less worried and wearied. We spot a pair of wreathed horn-bills on a far ridge, a good find, which delights Robichaud, and he takes pains to be sure that I see them, too. The relief of having set the camera trap at the *poung*, of having accomplished that part of our mis-sion, renders him lighthearted. We stop for lunch atop the waterfall where days ago we marveled at silver fish leaping up the cascade. While the guides set out food, Robichaud records a clownish mono-logue on his tiny video camera: "I wonder what we're having. Oh, my word! Look there: it's rice and fish!"

The guides received their tips at breakfast, and with full pay in prospect, they join in the general mirth, teasing each other and pos-ing for photographs. Thii, the feral boy-man, is particularly enthusi-astic. He wears knockoff aviator shades, dangles a cigarette from his lip, and poses with his fingers contorted in hand signs borrowed from Bangkok punkdom. As soon as the camera clicks, the tough guy vanishes, and he again becomes a smiling adolescent, indulging in horseplay with his buddies.

A thousand more steps, two thousand, five thousand: the river broadens and shallows, the gradient eases. We have reached dry for-est and are no longer in saola country. We come to a copse where yellow orchids drape every tree. The flowers have just opened and are as bright as sunlight, hanging clustered like golden grapes, per-fuming the air. In the distance we hear the lullaby tolling of a water buffalo's bell. We pause for last pictures, gathering in a football huddle, arms over shoulders and heads together, looking down where Robichaud has placed his camera on the ground facing up. *Click* goes the time-delayed shutter, and now, in a babble of Lao, everyone is reaching, jostling, craning to see the curious photo.

We have come a long way, perhaps a hundred and twenty kilometers on the Nam Nyang and another seventy-five on the Nam Mon. In a small but necessary way we have tried, as best we could, to nudge forward prospects for the saola. Olay in his studies and Robichaud as both biologist and advocate still face the task of analyzing and sharing what they've so far learned and what they may yet learn from the cameras strapped to trees at the *poung*. I, too, have work to do, simple in its way, which is to bear witness to the lament of this place and also its beauty.

The lament is familiar to nearly everyone. To care about the world, we have to open our hearts, but by opening them, we make them easier to break. We mourn the depletion of species and the extinction of more of them than we can easily count. We mourn the slaughter of tens of thousands of elephants for their ivory and the grisly toll of the wildlife trade. We mourn the loss of a forest here, a river there, and, if we are paying attention and if our hearts are the least bit open, our lives become a vigil at the bedside of an ailing planet. To be sure, we grieve at least as much for the suffering of fellow humans in war, poverty, and tempest—the many afflictions that make up "the thousand natural shocks that flesh is heir to"— but the two categories of sorrow are different. The woes to which flesh is heir are an ancient and evidently immutable collection, the immortal contents of Pandora's box. Notwithstanding our unending efforts to cure, comfort, and bring peace, they have dogged humankind forever.

The diminishment of the planet, on the other hand, is a new thing, and it is *our* thing. Whether by snare, bullet, chain saw, or pollution, whether because of carbon-induced alteration of the climate, ocean trawling, upset of the nitrogen cycle, or any of a thousand other *unnatural* shocks, we relentlessly diminish the vigor of the evolutionary epoch that brought our species, *Homo sapiens,* into being.

Oh, sure, it can be argued that we humans are part of nature and so whatever we do is natural, or that nature itself is a human intellectual construct and has no objective reality (Wallace Stegner, in another context, called such academic quibbling squidlike: the quibbler flees a problem by squirting ink at it). Others will say that the divinity that created the world so favors a single species—us—that our diminishment of the rest of creation is fine with Him or Her or It.

But these parsings and counterstories deflect us from the rude fact that, pythonlike, we have wrapped ourselves around the creation that made us and are squeezing out its life.

To say that Earth will recover and the diversity of life will bloom again is technically correct but commits an error of scale. Of course there have been waves of extinction before, some of them as sudden as the one we are producing, and of course Earth, an ever-dynamic crucible of life, has carried on. Evolution will continue; it cannot *not* continue. But the inexorable emergence of what Darwin called "forms most beautiful and most wonderful" proceeds at a nearly geological pace, compared to which our human tenancy of Earth is a fleeting breath. Within the time frame of what we call civilization, the injury we do in causing extinctions is as eternal as any human accomplishment.

And so, witnessing the death of things we love, we grieve, and our hearts ache. And aching, they open more. If the saola goes extinct, some hearts may break. But nearly all of us, if we've lived with any kind of engagement in the world, have suffered heartbreak before. Our hearts mend, mostly. We keep on, going forward through the thousand shocks, toughened in mind and heart, and more resolved.

The Nam Mon flattens, growing wider, and the forest stands back. The trail is clear, the going easy. I taste a new freedom in letting my mind wander, in thinking about something besides the next step I will take, the next boulder or bank that must be climbed. Robichaud, as ever, is at the head of our line, setting the pace. I hear him talking to Simeuang and Khamdy. His voice is buoyant. I have fallen a little behind, with Olay ghosting protectively behind me. Our journey now feels like a walk, not a march, and the distances — and reveries — stream by. I think back to the gear we left at the *poung* and the camera traps of twenty years ago, encumbered with stinky, burglar-mat triggers and bulky battery packs. Today's equipment is infinitely more sophisticated, and the results are often spectacular. At some reserves in India, camera traps enable biologists to keep track of individual tigers, whose stripes can be scanned from photographs and identified as easily as bar codes at a supermarket checkout.

What works for tigers, however, may not suffice for the study of creatures as cryptic as saola. Twenty years hence, if saola still exist, the methods used to find and monitor them will likely have changed not once but several times. The perseverance of people like Robichaud and the serendipity of innovation guarantee it. New possibilities pop up in the most unexpected ways, as Robichaud himself has experienced. Not long ago, he told me a story from a survey he and Will Duckworth carried out in NNT in the mid-1990s. They were in the protected area when they heard reports from a nearby village that a tiger had killed a pig. Thinking the tiger might return to feed on the pig a second night, they rushed to the place and hired villagers to build a platform in a tree near the kill site. Then they bought a live pig and led it, using a rope for a leash, into the forest and tied it within view of the tree. They intended to spend the night on the platform, waiting for the tiger to kill and feed on the pig while they observed the great cat or, if moonlight failed, listened to it crunch and purr.

Luck was not on their side. When they reached their stakeout, they saw that the platform was too small. Worse, a fierce wind came up at nightfall and whipped the slender tree back and forth.

Nevertheless, Robichaud shinnied up the tree with Duckworth close behind. More bad luck: a regiment of red ants barred the way. Robichaud struggled both to cling to the tree and contend with the ants. A gust of wind bent the tree over and lifted a squad of ants into the air. One of them landed in Robichaud's eye and bit him, sinking its pincers into the soft tissue of the eyeball. The shock and pain were overwhelming. Robichaud almost lost his grip. Duckworth, meanwhile, knew nothing of the ants and pressed Robichaud to keep climbing. "I can't hang here forever," he said. "My arms won't last."

Exhausted, they gained the tiny platform and swatted away the remaining ants. Robichaud was all but blinded by pain and tears. Although his tears had drowned the ant that bit him, the body of the ant still clung there, its mandibles buried in the white of his eye. It felt like a cheese grater on his sclera. First in fading twilight, then by headlamp, Duckworth tried to pluck out the ant. He poked and tweezed with his fingernails while Robichaud squirmed and the wind rocked their platform as though it were a dinghy in a squall. But Duckworth's thick fingers could not immediately grasp the ant, and they knew they could not continue with the headlamp. They had to blend completely with the quiet darkness lest they spook a returning tiger. Without delay they had to become immobile and utterly silent. Robichaud resigned himself to a night of misery. The "infinite passion of expectation" gave little comfort as he tried not to blink his weeping, angry eye, and he and Duckworth took turns keeping watch through twelve wretched hours of darkness.

The tiger never showed.

In the morning a group of villagers came out to see how they had fared. The pig was still alive, although traumatized by its night as predator bait. As it was untied, someone's grip was slack, and it bolted for freedom. Several men dove vainly after its rope, but the pig vanished in the undergrowth.

Another man took a look at Robichaud's red and swollen eye and, without a moment's hesitation, plucked a hair from his own head.

He tied the hair in a loose half hitch. Then, with Robichaud rigid as a board, fingers holding open his eye, the man dropped the loop of hair over the dead ant, drew the knot closed, and pulled away the ant. Treatment complete.

Suddenly the agony was over. The cheese grater was gone, the torturing splinter withdrawn. Robichaud's relief was immense. He'd been saved by the apt idea, the unimagined technology.

As we tramp the trail toward Ban Navang, it is pleasing to imagine that a metaphorical loop of hair may yet be found for the saola. Yes, of course the thought is far-fetched, possibly absurd, but no one can know for sure. Maybe luck will intervene. The essential thing is not to give up. Not ever. Surprise happens.

We again cross dry paddies where the soil is purple. We pass the bomb craters where the wrinkled crone blessed us on our outbound journey. Slow-witted buffalo eye us with hostile incomprehension. Khamdy, in his oversize camo tunic, walks ahead, carbine slung on his shoulder, like a soldier of the last war. Days in the future, we will

Rice paddies on the approach to Ban Navang.

cross the great reservoir and the drowned plateau and resume connection to the rest of the world. Somewhere in that distant realm news of loved ones and a bath, a soft bed, and a belly-stretching meal await. But now we traverse paddies and climb fence stiles, and our path soon joins a rutted two-track through cutover forest. We hear a tractor ahead. We again cross the river, but this time the crossing is shallow, the water is warm, and the river runs on a bed of firm small stones.

Epilogue

Obliged to report on our trip up the Nam Mon, we met with Sai, the headman of the Ban Navang village cluster, in the shack behind his house, where his wife operates a store. Khamdy was there when we arrived, beaming with pride at having brought his charges home and even happier now that Robichaud, the possessor of kip-filled pockets, had appeared. Khamdy soon scurried to the main house, where the beer and other valuable goods were stored. He returned with an armload of bottles.

The ritual drinking commenced.

The glass was filled and passed and filled and passed again. Simeuang, in his modest, low monotone, made the usual statement on behalf of the WMPA. He explained his intention of returning to the *poung* ten weeks hence to change the batteries and memory cards of the cameras. Sai listened gravely. Robichaud also delivered a report, including many expressions of gratitude, in which he described his impressions of the country, the condition of the wildlife, and his recommendations for its protection. Through all this, Khamdy muttered a running commentary, not omitting his contribution as head guide.

The reports were long and the beers many. Sai asked thoughtful questions about what we'd seen and how we'd fared. Khamdy offered more commentary. The beer rounded the circle again and again, and

Khamdy became more animated. His lower lip lost altitude. His words verged on Dada: "Simeuang says stop and I stop; go and I go!" He disappeared briefly, soon returning with a second, even larger, load of beer plus several packs of cigarettes and a vial of cologne, all charged to Robichaud's account. The cologne, a remarkable commodity for a rice and beer shop in the hills of central Laos, proved to be the pièce de résistance of Khamdy's performance. He extracted the atomizer from its box and went around the circle, blasting a cloud of scent into the face of each of us and turning it frequently on himself with extra vigor. Instantly, the room smelled like a French elevator. Robichaud gasped, "What are you doing?"

Khamdy laughed, his lower lip flapping. "Because we have not bathed in days!"

Even the solemn Sai cracked a smile.

Robichaud's report on snaring in the Nam Nyang, the latest in a fifteen-year succession of dire warnings, led to a modest foundation grant to the Saola Working Group that placed a young Lao conservationist, Dr. Chanthavy Vongkhamheng, as an adviser to the WMPA. Dr. Chanthavy (as the Lao refer to him, using his first name) was charged with energizing the WMPA's law-enforcement and anti-poaching efforts. His services were deemed valuable, and, after the grant ran out, the WMPA began to pay him from its own budget. His achievements include a thorough reorganization of the agency's enforcement staff, an increase in guide wages, and an overhaul of the frequency and discipline with which patrols are conducted. Snare collection in NNT has increased dramatically, but many snares still remain, and potentially *any* snares represent a threat to the survival of saola.

Dr. Chanthavy has also joined the Saola Working Group and commenced his own surveys at what is believed to be the northern limit of saola range, in Xieng Kouang Province, interviewing villagers about their knowledge of the species.

The Panel of Experts, which advises the WMPA, has formally

"recommended" (which is to say, mandated) that the agency shift the greater part of its programmatic energy to conservation. The WMPA, meanwhile, has acquired a new director, a somewhat iconoclastic leader who professes to have taken the POE's recommendation to heart. Apart from the new director's genuine support of Dr. Chanthavy, the jury is still out on the translation of words into performance. At this writing, continued concerns about the WMPA's performance have prompted a comprehensive review of the agency and a possible overhaul of its management.

Olay has enrolled at King Mongkut's University of Technology Thonburi in Bangkok to pursue a master's degree in biology. His thesis focuses on the ungulate community in part of the saola's range in Laos, and as part of his fieldwork, late in 2013 he accompanied Rob Timmins on an expedition in Bolikhamxay Province to collect leeches near where villagers captured a saola in 2010 (recounted on pages 218–19). There has been no word whether the leeches contain traces of saola blood—they remain in the analysis queue. Olay subsequently deployed more than eighty camera traps in the same general area and continues to monitor the traps as part of his thesis research. He, too, has now joined the Saola Working Group. Touy, meanwhile, completed a master's degree in natural resource management at the Asian Institute of Technology in December of 2013, also in Thailand.

Simeuang has taken on a new challenge. In addition to his regular job with the WMPA, he now commutes weekly to Savannakhet to continue progress toward the equivalent of an undergraduate degree and an eventual master's in forestry and natural resources.

William Robichaud continues to lead a dual life in and out of the field, recruiting partners and raising funds for surveys, enforcement, leech detection, meetings of the Saola Working Group, and related projects while also paying periodic visits to Nakai–Nam Theun and its wonders.

The last time Robichaud saw Viengxai he was working as a watchman at the Wooden Guest House, managed by Olay's uncle.

As an increasing number of young people have done, Viengxai has moved his family and himself to Nakai, leaving the forest for opportunities in town.

Simeuang collected memory cards from the *poung* of the Nam Mon in late May of 2011 and again in July, at which time a couple of the cameras remained in working order. He left them there until mid-2012. The various harvests of memory cards yielded many pictures of muntjac—multiple clear images of the common and large-antlered species and less certain images of a third species, probably *truongsonensis,* as well as one or two shots of a possible fourth species, which Rob Timmins continues to puzzle over.

There were also shots of sambar, serow, macaques, and a few humans.

There were none of saola.

My friend Mary lasted until June. I was beside her when she died. Joanna and everyone else at home were all right. We continue.

The forest of Nakai–Nam Theun continues.

And surprise continues. In September of 2013, a WWF camera trap in a remote forest in Vietnam, close to the Lao border, captured multiple images of a saola, the first tangible confirmation of the species in Vietnam in fifteen years. The hour of the photograph is shortly past sundown. The saola is at the edge of the frame, its head already out of the picture, the horns barely visible. It is as though the saola were walking out of present view, into the future.

A future that, we pray, includes saola.

Breathe in.

Camera-trap photograph showing body and horns of saola in lower right, September 7, 2013. (Courtesy WWF Vietnam)

ACKNOWLEDGMENTS

First thanks, emphatic and enduring, go to Bill Robichaud. He didn't know what he was getting into when he allowed a writer to join him on a trip into NNT, and this writer didn't know, either. Bill's leadership in the field and his dedication to saola conservation remain an inspiration. I am honored to know him.

Thanks also to Soukphavanh Sawathvong (Touy), Chamthasome Phommachanh (Olay), and Simeuang Phitsanoukan for fellowship and helpful kindness on the trail. May our paths cross again often. I am also indebted to Khamdy, Thii, Mok Keo, Bone, Meet, Phaivanh, Sone, and all the guides who labored with us in the forest. *Khop chay* as well to Kong Chan, Chan Si, and the many people of NNT who allowed us into their homes and extended their hospitality.

Other help in Laos came from Akchousanh Rasphone, Steve Duthy, Roland Eve, Mark Hedemark, Michelle Smith, Lee Talbot, Phoukhaokham Luangoudom, and Thong Eth Payvanh.

Latsamay Sylavong, Chris Muziol, and their colleagues at IUCN–Laos in Vientiane gave immeasurable assistance, and Jim Chamberlain was a patient and generous teacher.

In Hanoi, Jonathan Eames of BirdLife International could not have been more helpful or hospitable, and I am also very grateful to the personnel of the Critical Ecosystem Partnership Fund (CEPF) who were based there, including Pham Thi Bich Hai, Long Nguyen

Hoang, and particularly Huong Tran Thanh, who, in spite of a heavy workload and pressing family priorities, guided me to and from multiple interviews, which she interpreted as well. Thanks also to those who granted the interviews: Vu Van Dung, Pham Mong Giao, Le Van Cham, Le Trong Trai, and Nguyen Cu. Le Duc Minh also kindly guided me through a number of difficult issues. In Vinh, Cao Tien Trung was a gracious, entertaining, and knowledgeable host who shared his intimate understanding of saola.

My thanks also to correspondents who generously answered my queries: Nick Enfield, Bob Dobias, David Hulse, Sulma Warne, Mike Baltzer, Chng Soh Koon, Ingo Wiederhofer, and John Mac-Kinnon. Will Duckworth's assistance, although provided at a distance, went far beyond correspondence, and the book is much better for his close attention. Rob Timmins, Eleanor Sterling, Joe Walston, Barney Long, and Nicholas Wilkinson generously consented to be interviewed. So did the incomparable George Schaller, who provided key files and documents, encouragement, and advice. William Conway also lent a hand when one was needed, and the support of Messrs. Schaller and Conway, together with that of other colleagues at the Liz Claiborne Art Ortenberg Foundation, has been immensely important in multiple ways. I am especially grateful to Art Orten berg, to whose memory *The Last Unicorn* is dedicated.

Jack Tordoff, a grant director at CEPF, launched this project by sending me to a meeting of the Saola Working Group in Vientiane in 2009 and followed up with a small grant that allowed me to accompany Bill Robichaud to Nakai–Nam Theun NPA in 2011. Jack's help extended to several other areas and has been invaluable.

CEPF, incidentally, likes its grantees to acknowledge formally the partnership's sources and purpose, and I am happy to do so: CEPF is a "joint initiative of l'Agence Française de Développement, Conservation International, the European Union, the Global Environment Facility, the Government of Japan, the John D. and Catherine T. MacArthur Foundation, and the World Bank. A fundamental goal is to ensure civil society is engaged in biodiversity conservation."

My old pal Jack Loeffler, along with Suzanne Jamison, kindly made available the not-for-profit Lore of the Land for grant administration. Catherine Baca, ally of many years, transcribed the scrawl of my field notes, a task I could not imagine confiding to anyone else. Yvonne Bond did likewise for many hours of recorded interviews, and Deborah Reade, in our fourth collaboration, produced the wonderful maps. Another longtime pal, Don Usner, reworked the photographs to bring out all they could offer.

Don Lamm, friend and agent, believed in the project from early on and, together with the wonderful Melissa Chinchillo of Fletcher & Company, found a home for it at Little, Brown and Company, where John Parsley greatly improved the manuscript and deftly guided it into print. His colleagues, Malin von Euler-Hogan, Barbara Clark, and Karen Landry, as well as others, also lent their talents to the improvement of this work. My thanks to all.

It should go without saying that any errors in these pages are my responsibility, and mine alone.

And finally, from start to finish Joanna Hurley was rock-steady in her support of the project and of me, acts for which I remain both profoundly grateful and amazed at my good luck.

APPENDIX

Pronunciation, Nomenclature, and Acronyms

Readers of this book will meet Bone and Sone, guides who participated in the expedition to the Nam Nyang. If those readers want these names to ring correctly in their mind's ears, they will teach themselves to hear them as "Bawn" and "Sawn," as the text encourages them to do. They might ask, however, why not write the names phonetically in the first place?

It's a good question, and the simple answer is that I have tried to follow conventional practice for transliterating Lao into English, a process that has been shaped in interesting ways. Many Lao words were translated into French before they became known in English, and so traditional transliteration has a bias toward French. For this reason *poung* (mineral lick) is not written with a double *o*—*poong*—although that is how it sounds. The double *o* does not exist in French, and so *poung*, the closest French spelling, is how the word has come down.

Another complication is that Lao has more consonant sounds than English (or French) does. *T*, *th*, *dt*, and *d*, for instance, are used to denote various Lao consonants along the progression of sounds from "t" to "d." Thus Thii, the name of another guide, is effectively pronounced "Tee" in English, but it is not spelled that way. One might think of it as another Gallicism, like the name Thierry, pronounced with a hard *t* in French.

Place names present a special challenge. Nam Nyang, for instance, is the spelling favored both by Bill Robichaud and by James R. Chamberlain, a linguist on whose advice I have relied. On the standard 1:100,000 maps approved by the Lao government, however, the name of the river is given as Nam Yang. Similar issues exist for village names. Chamberlain, emphasizing etymology, endorses Ban Na Meo; most maps, including the government's, give Ban Nameo. My choice of one system over another is essentially subjective, but in this case I side with the more conventional usage: Nameo, Nameuy, Makfeuang, Thameuang, and so on.

The rendering of Vietnamese also required a number of choices. Like Lao, Vietnamese is a tonal language. It uses a modified Roman alphabet in which vowel tone is indicated by diacritical marks. Because most English readers would not understand these marks, and on the advice of others better informed than I, I have eliminated them. Thus Nghê An Province is given simply as Nghe An. Additionally, there are two *d*'s in Vietnamese: *đ*, pronounced "d" in English, and *d*, pronounced close to "z" in English. In the case of Vu Van Dung, lead author of the scientific paper establishing saola as a new species, it is the "z"-sounding *d*. Some writers in English will spell his name Dzung, but Dung is more common. The name Do Tuoc, belonging to one of the original discoverers of saola, uses the other *d*.

Readers will note that many Lao words (like many words in English) have consecutive vowels. Often these represent blended sounds, or diphthongs, *eu* being one of the most common, as in the case of Nam Theun, which sounds roughly like "nam tŭn."

Some English speakers debate how to refer to the country of Lao PDR. Should they say Lao or Laos? The Lao people call their homeland either Meuang (or Muang) Lao or Prathet (or Pathet) Lao, both of which translate as "Lao country" or "Lao nation." Laos is the name the French gave to the colony they ruled, beginning late in the nineteenth century. They derived the word by pluralizing the name of the colony's dominant ethnic group. Some English speakers prefer to refer to the country as Lao, not Laos, because the shorter word avoids colonial overtones and conforms better with Meuang Lao, Lao PDR, and similar terms. I have elected to use Laos because of its greater familiarity for English readers. For an excellent discussion of the two terms and their relative merits, I recommend a short essay by Nick Enfield, a scholar at the Max Planck Institute for Psycholinguistics, which originally appeared in the *Vientiane Times* in 1998 and which can be accessed at http://laobumpkin.blogspot.com/2008/07/of-laos-and-laotians.html.

Finally, following is a glossary of abbreviations used in the text:

ADB: Asian Development Bank, known to its critics as Asian Dams and Bridges

FIPI: Forest Inventory and Planning Institute, Hanoi

IMA: Independent Monitoring Agency (evaluates the WMPA; can order the NTPC to withhold funding)

IUCN: International Union for the Conservation of Nature

NGO: Nongovernmental organization

NNT: Nakai–Nam Theun National Protected Area

NT2: Nam Theun 2 Hydroelectric Project

NTPC: Nam Theun 2 Power Company (operators of NT2)

PDR: People's Democratic Republic

POE: International Environmental and Social Panel of Experts (advisers to the NTPC)

TCM: Traditional Chinese medicine

UXO: Unexploded ordnance: bombs, "bombies," and land mines remaining from the American, or Second Indochina, war as well as other conflicts

WB: World Bank

WCS: Wildlife Conservation Society

WMPA: Watershed Management and Protection Authority

WWF: World Wide Fund for Nature ("World Wildlife Fund" in the United States)

NOTES

February 24, Nam Theun Reservoir

1. Because the word *Annamite* carries connotations of "conquered south" and constitutes a reminder of centuries of Chinese hegemony, the preferred term for the mountains in Vietnam is *Truong Son*, which translates as "Long Mountain." The Lao name for the range, *Sayphou Louang,* has a similar meaning, but since neither name is a suitable descriptor for the other country's uplands, one returns to *Annamite Mountains.*
2. Some will argue that the Nam Et–Phou Louey protected area in Laos is larger than NNT, but Nam Et–Phou Louey actually consists of two adjacent but separately gazetted protected areas. It is only larger in the aggregate, if then, and calculations of land areas vary. The same distinction applies to the extensive complex of protected areas within Cambodia's Cardamom Mountains.
3. *Vientiane Times*, August 20, 2013.
4. Ronald H. Pine, "New Mammals Not So Seldom," *Nature* 369 (April 14, 1994): 593.
5. Edward McCurdy, comp., *The Notebooks of Leonardo da Vinci* (Old Saybrook, CT: Konecky & Konecky, 2002), 223. Or see: Item 1232, on "Incontinence," accessed at www.universalleonardo.org/work.php?id=438.
6. William Robichaud, "Notes on a Remarkable History: Cedar Grove Ornithological Station," *Passenger Pigeon* 72, no. 3 (Fall 2010): 215–18.

February 25, Ban Tong

1. Much of the information on the wildlife trade presented herein is derived from interviews, unpublished reports, and grant proposals. Among published books, none is more valuable than Hanneke Nooren and Gordon Claridge, *Wildlife Trade in Laos: The End of the Game* (Amsterdam: Netherlands Committee for IUCN, 2001). Also recommended is Richard Ellis, *Tiger Bone and Rhino Horn: The Destruction of Wildlife for Traditional Chinese Medicine* (Washington, DC: Island Press, 2005).

The leading worldwide authority on illegal trade in wildlife and plants is TRAFFIC, a joint program of WWF and IUCN founded in 1976. TRAFFIC's extensive body of publications, including material written by TRAFFIC staff but published by other organizations, can be accessed at www.traffic.org.

2. Some authorities differentiate the Vietnamese three-striped box turtle as a separate species, *C. cyclomata,* but for the purposes of traditional Chinese medicine, the turtles are identical.

3. Jack Tordoff, a biologist experienced in Vietnam, reports that he has visited villages where the entire male population was absent—gone to Laos on turtle-hunting missions lasting a month or more.

4. Moreover, if the NTPC and the government of Laos differed in their interpretation of the Concession Agreement, the Panel of Experts would step in and arbitrate the dispute. Their power was intended to be draconian, their word final.

5. In Lao, *nyang* signifies "tree resin" and refers also to various dipterocarps that produce it, but, as place names tend to be ancient, the river's name more likely derives from a similar-sounding word in a language that was spoken in these parts before Lao became the lingua franca of the region.

6. Outside the United States, the World Wildlife Fund subsequently renamed itself the World Wide Fund for Nature. In either case, it remains known as WWF.

7. John MacKinnon, "Apocalypse Yesterday," *BBC Wildlife,* February 1994.

8. Vu Van Dung and Do Tuoc, "The Discovery of the Saola (*Pseudoryx nghetinhensis*) in Vietnam," in James Hardcastle et al., eds., *Rediscovering the Saola— Proceedings of Rediscovering the Saola: A Status Review and Conservation Planning Workshop* (Hanoi: WWF Indochina Program, SFNC Project, 2004).

9. The village name is given by Do Tuoc in the WWF film formerly referenced at http://wwf.panda.org/about_our_earth/species/profiles/mammals/saola/saola_video/ but seemingly no longer accessible. It is also given in Eugene Linden, "Ancient Creatures in a Lost World," *Time,* June 20, 1994.

10. "Journey into Vietnam's Lost World," *Time,* August 10, 1992. This account was derived from the original WWF announcement, of which no copy appears to be extant.

11. Placement of saola in the evolutionary progression of bovid species remains a subject of research. Robichaud's efforts to collect samples of bone from saola trophies in Nakai–Nam Theun were an expression of this. See, for instance, John Gatesy and Peter Arctander, "Hidden Morphological Support for the Phylogenetic Placement of *Pseudoryx nghetinhensis* with Bovine Bovids: A Combined Analysis of Gross Anatomical Evidence and DNA Sequences from Five Genes," *Systematic Biology* 49, no. 3 (2000): 515–38.

12. Vu Van Dung et al., "A New Species of Living Bovid from Vietnam," *Nature* 363 (June 3, 1993): 443–45.

13. Barbara Basler, "Vietnam Forest Yields Evidence of New Animal," *New York Times,* June 8, 1993.

February 26, Ban Nameuy

1. One of the master documents for the Nam Theun 2 project is the Social and Environmental Management Framework and Operational Plan, known as SEMFOP, available at www.namtheun2.com (see under the home-page heading DOCUMENTS). Part 3 of SEMFOP is the Ethnic Minorities Development Plan (January 2005), which summarizes the relatively scant ethnological information then available concerning the people of the Nakai–Nam Theun National Protected Area.

2. Eleanor Jane Sterling, Martha Maud Hurley, and Le Duc Minh, *Vietnam: A Natural History* (New Haven, CT: Yale University Press, 2006), 54–56. If we look back deeper in time, forty million years or so, we see that other, slower geologic processes have also caused emergence or submergence of land bridges at the periphery of the modern mainland and by so doing have influenced the evolution of life-forms and the development of the region's biota.

3. *Cervus canadensis.* The term *elk* can be confusing, as in northern Europe and Asia it connotes moose, *Alces alces.*

4. Sarah Lyall, "Rhino Horns Put Europe's Museums on Thieves' Must-Visit List," *New York Times*, August 26, 2011.

February 27, Ban Nameuy

1. In the summer of 2013, the Wildlife Conservation Society estimated that perhaps five tigers still roamed the forests of Lao PDR, all of them in the north of the country, far from Nakai–Nam Theun. Some of these tigers may periodically range across the border into Vietnam, but none is resident there and Vietnam is otherwise bereft of the great cat that figures so prominently in its mythology and traditions. Barring intervention of a vigorous program to eliminate poaching and rebuild populations of both tigers and their prey (which is not currently in sight), prospects for the survival of tigers in Laos are bleak.

2. One deconstruction of the legend holds that *phi kong koy* represents a deep memory of orangutans when they inhabited mainland Asia during the Pleistocene.

February 28, Thong Kouang

1. Barely out of his teens, Timmins predicted that if the Cebu flowerpecker, a Philippine bird unseen in many years, still existed, it was likely to be found in a certain remnant patch of forest. So he went to the patch, and sure enough, flowerpeckers flitted about the treetops. But Timmins has limits: the Cebu flowerpecker is distinguished by red and green patches on its back, and Timmins has what he calls "a color vision deficiency." Basically, "red or green on small birds in the tops of trees is just something that I can't see." So he had to send someone back to confirm the colors. The confirmation was made: Timmins had rediscovered the Cebu flowerpecker.

2. A Russian team scooped Timmins on publication of the species description. They named the rabbit *timminsi* in what might be read as a scientific apology. A. O. Averianov, A. V. Abramov, and A. N. Tikhonov, "A New Species of *Nesolagus* (Lagomorpha, Leporidae) from Vietnam with Osteological Description," Zoological Institute, St. Petersburg, Russia, 2000.

3. The *kha-nyou* is also known as the Laotian rock rat, a dreadful name on two counts. *Laotian* is a colonial construction deplored by defenders of Lao culture, including Robichaud. *Lao,* as noun or adjective, is always preferable. And *rock rat* belittles an extremely rare and enigmatic creature that, in the final analysis, is not a rat.

4. The same question might be asked regarding the leaf muntjac (*M. putaoensis*) and Roosevelts' muntjac (*M. rooseveltorum,* named in honor of Theodore Jr. and Kermit Roosevelt, sons of the American president). For additional details, see discussion of these species written principally by Rob Timmins and Will Duckworth at www.iucnredlist.org.

5. A species of *Lagerstroemia*, possibly *angustifolia* or *macrocarpa,* members of the crape myrtle family.

March 1, Thong Sek

1. George B. Schaller and Alan Rabinowitz, "The Saola or Spindlehorn Bovid *Pseudoryx nghetinhensis* in Laos," *Oryx* 29, no. 2 (April 1995): 107–14.

2. The "self-styled veterinarian" worked for an NGO, the Carnivore Preservation Trust, which had settled in Lak Xao under General Cheng's protection. The trust kept a few bears and small cats in cages, but its operations were the work of enthusiasts, not professionals. One of its several harmful practices, which caused Robichaud and his colleagues to nickname it the Carnivore Decimation Trust, was to feed its captive carnivores wildlife bought at the Lak Xao market, thus boosting demand for locally killed animals and depleting the prey base for carnivores in the wild. After General Cheng fell from power, the trust teetered for a while, then folded its tent and departed Laos.

March 2, Nam Nyang, Camp 1

1. Eleanor Jane Sterling, Martha Maud Hurley, and Le Duc Minh, *Vietnam: A Natural History* (New Haven, CT: Yale University Press, 2006), 224.

2. In the early days of saola research some authorities reported that *thien nien kien,* or *Homalomena aromatica* and other *Homalomena* species, were vital food for saola, but this now appears to have been a misidentification.

March 5, A Tributary of the Nam Nyang

1. Philip Shenon, "An Indochinese Goat Is Imperiled by Its Year of Fame," *New York Times*, November 29, 1994. See also "Greed Hastens Demise of New Mammal," *Bangkok Post*, July 2, 1995.

2. Professor Jack Rutledge of the University of Wisconsin–Madison received the following fax on August 1, 1994, from Bi Xuan Nguyen at the National Centre of Science and Technology in Hanoi:

Dear Prof. Rutledge,

...Enclosed you find the photographs of living Saola (Vu Quang pseudoryx and some informations about new jungle deer [large-antlered muntjac]. Last days, there are two other new young Saola females have been captured by montain hunters. I'm regret haven't money to by them (they have asked for about 2000 US$). So the hunters are being forced to give back these animals into the forest.

I am looking to hear from you soon.

Kindest regards.

3. Shanthini Dawson, "Saola (*Pseudoryx nghetinhensis*) Studies in Nghe An and Ha Tinh Provinces, Vietnam," consultancy report for World Wide Fund for Nature Indochina Programme, National Wildlife Federation, and World Conservation Union, Hanoi, Vietnam, April 1995. Dawson mentions seven saola killed or captured (and eventually dead) in 1994. I reduced the number by one to reflect the juvenile taken to FIPI. The second FIPI juvenile probably came from Pu Mat.
4. Saola Working Group, "From Plans to Action: Proceedings of the First Meeting of the Saola Working Group," Vientiane, Lao PDR, August 17–21, 2009: 13.
5. Malcolm W. Browne, "Vietnam Finds First Live Example of Rare Ox," *New York Times*, June 23, 1994.

March 11, Nakai

1. Appendix 1 of a 1995 preliminary report by Shanthini Dawson ensuing from "a field trip which ended in February 1994." Dawson delivered the report directly to the minister of forestry, recommending that the ministry "liaise with the People's Committee of Ha Tinh province to pass an interim decree which would make any form of hunting/trapping of the Vu Quang ox illegal." The decree appears to have been issued soon after Dawson's meeting with the minister.
2. The last strong evidence of rhinos in Laos is a report of a rhinoceros being shot on a remote headwater of the Nam Theun in 1990. This could have been a lesser one-horned or an Asian two-horned rhinoceros, both species being native to the region and both now presumed eradicated from Laos (see J. W. Duckworth, R. E. Salter, and K. Khounboline, *Wildlife in Lao PDR: 1999 Status Report* [Vientiane: IUCN, 1999], 201). Intermittent reports of rhinos in NNT continued until at least 2004, but none was confirmed.
3. A third subspecies, *R. sondaicus inermis,* known from the area that is now Myanmar, Bangladesh, and northeastern India, was presumed extinct by 1925.

4. Rhishja Larson, "Rhino Horn: All Myth, No Medicine," *National Geographic News Watch*, July 7, 2010. Accessed at http://newswatch.nationalgeographic.com/2010/07/07/rhino_horn_and_traditional_chinese_medicine_facts/.
5. This incantatory list of illnesses is borrowed (save for the addition of "hangover") from "Rhino Horn Use: Fact vs. Fiction," at the website for the PBS program *Nature*: www.pbs.org/wnet/nature/episodes/rhonoceros/rhino-horn-use-fact-vs-fiction/1178/, accessed May 25, 2012.

March 12, Nakai

1. Andreas Reinecke, "Bi-Cephalous Animal-Shaped Ear Pendants in Vietnam," *Bead Study Trust Newsletter* 28 (Winter 1996): 5–8.
2. According to linguist James R. Chamberlain, Guignard compiled his dictionary in a town on the upper Song Ca, in Nghe An Province, Vietnam, near today's Pu Mat National Park. It was at Pu Mat that Nguyen Ngoc Chinh of FIPI confirmed the presence of the "Vu Quang bovid" in 1993 and learned that local Tai villagers called it *saola*. Chamberlain says that the Guignard dictionary is "in fact a dictionary of the [local] Phouan language, not Lao proper."
3. *Antiaris toxicaria,* a member of the Moraceae family, which includes mulberry and fig. In Atel, the name is *tanaong*.
4. The Atel are one of many small groups among the cultures of central Laos. Perhaps a dozen languages are spoken in NNT alone — two dozen if one enlarges the area by a few kilometers — making central Laos one of the most diverse linguistic regions on the planet. Analysis of the Atel language suggests that it is at least two thousand years old, perhaps considerably more. Its proximity to other ancient Vietic tongues — Kri, Thémarou, Malang, and others — suggests that the Vietnamese language was born in the central Annamites, a conclusion much at odds with the traditional model of Vietnamese cultural development, which points to China as the source of Vietnam's linguistic and social character. (More than 60 percent of the vocabulary of contemporary Vietnamese consists of borrowings from Chinese, a result of many centuries of interchange and domination.) James R. Chamberlain, who was instrumental in putting together the new family tree of Vietic languages, expected the keepers of Vietnamese historical tradition to rebuff the theory of an Annamite origin for Vietnamese. But the opposite happened. Vietic tribal languages in Vietnam are especially concentrated in Nghe An Province, somewhat north of NNT. Nghe An also happens to be the natal home of Ho Chi Minh. That Nghe An is the birthplace of both the nation's language and its greatest hero has proved to be a highly acceptable revelation.

   A vital source on Vietic linguistic history and on Atel ethnology is Chamberlain's "Eco-Spatial History: A Nomad Myth from the Annamites and Its Relevance for Biodiversity Conservation," in Xu Jianchu and Stephen Mikesell, eds., *Landscapes of Diversity: Indigenous Knowledge, Sustainable*

Livelihoods and Resource Governance in Montane Mainland Southeast Asia, Proceedings of the III Symposium on MMSEA 25–28 August 2002, Lijiang, P.R. China (Kunming: Yunnan Science and Technology Press, 2003), 421–36.

5. Chamberlain, "Eco-Spatial History," 431.

March 15, Nam Mon, Camp 2

1. It is unlikely that giving exact latitude and longitude would do harm, for the location of the *poung* is well known locally, but exact information would also make possible the criticism, even if false, that after the coordinates of the *poung* were published all the animals were hunted out.
2. Interestingly, the small-toothed ferret badger of the Annamites (*Melogale moschata*) can be distinguished from its large-toothed cousin (*M. personata*) only by physical examination of dentition, a potentially traumatic experience for badger and examiner alike. By contrast, the leech-survey method should allow the badgers' presence to be detected without capture or handling, a benefit to all. For the process to work, however, there must first be baseline sets of DNA sequences from animals of verified identity. At present some researchers question whether the genetic sequences purported for the Annamites' two types of ferret badgers are entirely reliable.
3. Should *M. truongsonensis* prove to be distinct, its detection in the Saola Nature Reserve, Quang Nam Province, where the revealing leech was collected, would be an important datum in the map of its range.
4. Ida Bærholm Schell et al., "Screening Mammal Biodiversity Using DNA from Leeches," *Current Biology* 22, no. 8 (April 24, 2012): R262–63. doi:10.1016/j.cub.2012.02.058.

March 16, Nam Mon, Camp 3

1. J. W. Duckworth et al., "Why South-east Asia Should Be the World's Priority for Averting Imminent Species Extinctions, and a Call to Join a Developing Cross-Institutional Programme to Tackle This Urgent Issue," *S.A.P.I.EN.S.* 5, no. 2 (2012). Online since August 12, 2012, at http://sapiens.revues.org/1327.

March 17, Nam Mon, Camp 4

1. *Tragulus kanchil*, the lesser Oriental chevrotain, is found throughout much of Southeast Asia. The IUCN Red List classifies it as a species of "least concern."

INDEX

Page numbers in *italics* indicate maps and photographs appearing in this book.

ADB (Asian Development Bank), 244
agriculture, swidden. *See* swiddens
American Friends Service Committee, 187
An, Mr. (Lao headman), 37–38, 43, 49, 54
   An's son, 43, 49, 53–54
Annamite Mountains (Sayphou Louang), 20, *336*
   biota of, 23–24, 56, 116–18, 304–5, 311; endemic to area, 76, 162; lack of knowledge of, 119; saola, 3, 24, 75, 103, 117, 161, (as "flagship species") 313, (searched for) 93
   culture groups living in, 62, 165
   as Laos-Vietnam border, 4, 15, 206, 258 (*see also* Laos [Lao People's Democratic Republic, Lao PDR])
Annamite striped rabbit (*Nesolagus timminsi*), 117, 304–5, 339
Annona (custard apple), 210
Apache, 74, 315
Apocalypse Now (film), 204
Arctander, Peter, 66, 337
Asian Wild Cattle Specialist Group, 3. *See also* International Union for the Conservation of Nature (IUCN)
Atel people, 73, 269–73, 311, 341

Bach Ma National Park (Vietnam), 68, 258

bamboo, 182–83
   cut (*tok*), 70
Ban Beuk (village), 70, 86, 214, 230
   "porters" from, 53–54; boatmen, 240, 241–42; teenagers on expedition, 101, 127, 150, 166, *190*, 206, 222
Ban Fangdeng (village), 253–54
Bangkok. *See* Thailand
Bangkok Post, 20, 65
Bangladesh, 311
Ban Kounè (village), 86, 101, 127, 223, 232
   as border post, 234, 239
   as habitat for saola, 72, 113, 163, 238; camera traps near, 214
   meetings with villagers of, 74, 76–79, 236–40, 261
Ban Maka (village), 72, 107
Ban Makfeuang (village), 11, 35, 43, 94
   Brou people of, 33, 72
   rendezvous at, 231, 240, 242
   technology arrives in, 28, 45
Ban Nachalai (village), 134
Ban Nahao (village), 268, 275
Ban Namee (village), 196
Ban Nameo (village, "Cat Paddy"), 70, 86, 93, 122, 126, 230
   clinic in, 237
   rendezvous in, 100–1, 103–4
   Sek people of, 70–71

Ban Nameuy (village, "Gaur Paddy"), 93, 160, 241
  as expedition starting point, 11, 40, 85–86, 99, 103, 144, 167; boats to, 37, 43, 49, 53–54; return to, 230, 240
  Kong Chan as headman of, *see* Kong Chan
  and saola, 231–32
  Sek people of, 70–71, 127; census figures, 72
Ban Navang (village), 215, 268, 275, 280, 285, 287–88, 307
  electricity comes to, 274–75
  final visit, 317, 323, 325
  headman of, 276, 282
Ban Peu (village), 43, 49, 52, 243
banteng (wild cattle), 14, 22, 243
Ban Thameuang (village), 249, 268–74
Ban Thongnoy (village), 240
Ban Tong (village), 40, 42–43, 45
  Phong people of, 72; children photographed, *44*
  trek to, 4, 11, 28, 32, 35, 240; arrival, 37
bare-faced bulbul (bird) (*Pycnonotus hualon*), 117
barking deer. *See* muntjac
beauty, 245–46, 313
Beijing Olympics, 46
binturong (animal), 293–94, 312
Bolikhamxay Province (Laos), 134, 218, 231, 302, 327
  governor bans saola studies, 217
Bone (guide), 127, 149–50, 166, 167, 189, 210, 213
  and aluminum water bottle, 169–70, 174
  bitten by dog, 225
  in photographs, *190, 224*
Borneo, 3, 76
Bounchan (member of Atel tribe), 270–71
Bounthai (member of earlier expedition), 89–90, 94, 99
Bounthavy, 153
BPKP (Bolisat Phathana Khet Phoudoi, the Mountainous Areas Development Corporation), 118
Brazil, 17

Brook, Sarah, 256–57
Brou people, 72, 127, 273
  encounter saola, 236; native term for, 137–38
  language of, 33; and Lao language, 239
  swidden agriculture of, 77, 269

Cambodia, 15, 20, 22, 131, 194, 268, 290
  language of, 72
camera traps, 166, 169, 300, 307, 314, 318–19
  animals caught: muntjac, 118–19, 215, 327–28; "python," 221, 261; tigers, 108, 321 (*see also* saola [*Pseudoryx nghetinhensis*])
  memory cards, 214, 220, 301–2, 325, 327–28
  plans for setting up, 25, 56, 80, 214; Robichaud's proposal, 231–32, 277
  testing, 113–16, 305–6
Cat Tien National Park (Vietnam), last rhinoceros in, 256–58, 304
cattle. *See* wild cattle
Cedar Grove Ornithological Research Station (Wisconsin), 36–37
Cham, Le Van, 58–59, 61–64, 209–10
Chamberlain, James R., 334, 341–42
Chanphan (village headman), 253–54
Chan Si (wife of Kong Chan). *See* Kong Chan
Chanthavy (Vongkhamheng), Dr., 326–27
Cheng Sayavong, General, 22, 118, 133–34, 136, 140–42, 254, 339
China, 13, 17
  Kinh migration from, 62
  population and wild populations of, 290, 311
  qilin and unicorn myth in, 27
  trade with, 18, 106, 191, 194, 195, 254; smuggling, 46–47
  traditional medicine (TCM) of, 47, 81–82, 84
  western, conservation in, 313
Chinh, Nguyen Ngoc, 67
Christianity, 245
  Christian iconography, 26–27
CIA (Central Intelligence Agency), 156

colugo (animal, *Cynocephalus variegatus*), 76, 117, 312
Communist governments, 13, 39, 134, 260. *See also* Soviet Union
crested argus, 56, 65, 76, 312
Cuba, 13

Darwin, Charles, 284, 310, 320
da Vinci, Leonardo, 25
Dawson, Shanthini, 208
deer
    Eld's, 14
    mouse deer (chevrotain), 318, 342
    See also muntjac; sambar (deer)
dhole (wild dog), 85, 160
Dictionnaire Laotien-Français, 267
DNA (genetic) analysis, 176, 184
    of last Vietnamese rhino, 257
    of leeches, 304–5, 327
    of saola horns and skin, 23, 25, 66, 80, 237, 253
Dobias, Bob, 133
dogs
    "detector," in rhino census, 256, 304
    hunting with, 84–85, 207, 216, 218, 238
dog trucks, 196
Doi Moi (Vietnamese "renovation"), 59, 61, 106
Dong Son people (Vietnam), 267
douc (monkey), 164, 173, 205, 312
    red-shanked (douc langur), snared, 197–99; photograph, 199
Duckworth, Will, 119, 179, 215, 321–22
Dung, Vu Van, 61, 64, 66
Duvall, Robert, 294

eaglewood (*Aquilaria*), 106–7, 165, 191
    poaching story, 186
Eames, Jonathan Charles, 59–61, 68
ecotourism, 44, 74, 291, 302
Edge, The (film), 316
Edwards's pheasant. *See* pheasant
Eld's deer, 14
electric fish, 249–50
electricity, 12, 28, 45, 274–75, 277
    Thailand's consumption of, 15, 17
    See also TV
elephants, 14, 65, 196, 290–91, 312

on Red List, 256
    slaughtered for ivory, 107, 195, 319
Enfield, Nick, 335
environmental services, 244
Erysichthon (mythical Greek prince), 196–97
Etter, Matt, 133
evolution, 320
    of saola, 23, 66, 117
    of wild cattle, 80
extinction, 14, 18–19, 289–91, 311, 320
    politics of, 313

ferret badger, snared, 175, 176, 224, 342
Fitzgerald, F. Scott, 178–79
"Flowerpot" (boatman), 51–52
folk medicines. *See* medical care
France, 102
    French colonialists, 14–15, 52, 62, 78, 117, 194, 334
    French language, 333

gaur (wild cattle), 14, 22, 65, 70, 213, 256
genetic analysis. *See* DNA (genetic) analysis
Giang, Mr. (owner of trophy), 237
giant forest hog, 22
giant squirrel. *See* squirrel, black giant
Giao, Pham Mong, 208
gibbons (*Nomascus siki*), singing of, 65, 112–13, 130–31, 152, 220
Glass, Philip, 129
Golden Mountain. *See* Phou Vang
golden turtle. *See* turtle, box
Goodall, Jane, 61
Greek myth, 26, 196–97
Guignard, Théodore, 267, 341

Haiphong, Vietnam, 156
Hanoi, Vietnam, 58–63, 135, 142, 194, 210, 276
    U.S. bombing of, 156
Ha Tinh Province (Vietnam), 58, 67, 206, 255
Hmong people, 77, 118, 137, 253, 273
    market hunting by, 18, 277–78, 302
    saola captured by, 134; Martha, 138–42, *139*
Ho Chi Minh, 59

Ho Chi Minh City (formerly Saigon), Vietnam, 256, 276
Ho Chi Minh Trail, 25, 61, 156. *See also* Vietnam
Homalomena aromatica, 208
Homo sapiens, 66, 320
Hoover Dam, 17
Houaphou Restaurant (Nakai), 248
Houay Kanil tributary, 270, 271, 274
Houay Mrro tributary, 287, 318
Hue, Vietnam, 216
hunter-gatherers. *See* nomadism
hunting with dogs. *See* dogs

Independent Monitoring Agency (IMA), 48, 201, 244
India, 17, 321
  population and wild population of, 290, 311
Indochina, 15, 22, 116, 194, 256
  war in, 55
Indonesia, 76, 146, 256, 311
Institute of Ecology and Biological Resources (Hanoi), 62
International Crane Foundation, 20
International Environmental and Social Panel of Experts. *See* POE
International Union for the Conservation of Nature (IUCN), 61, 217
  Asian Wild Cattle Specialist Group, 3
  IUCN Red List, 184, 199, 256

jaguars, 195
Japan, 207
  kirin and unicorn myth in, 27
Java, 76, 256
juju, 120. *See also phi kong koy*

Ka, Mr. (Lao woodsman), 74, 78–81, 79, 83–84, 232, 234, 237–38
Kambai (villager), 217
Karesh, Billy, 138–42, 162
Keo, Mr. (restaurant proprietor), 259, 261
Ket, Paa (villager), 29–32
Khamdy (guide), 280–82, 284–89, 288, 307–8, 314
  homeward bound, 317, 321, 323, 325–26

Kham Laek (guide), 127, 169–70, *190*
Khammouane Province (Laos), 274
kha-nyou (Laonastes aenigmamus) (animal), 117, 339
Khum (guide), 281, 282, 288
Kim Quang (Vietnamese village), 62, 65, 210
Kinh (largest Vietnamese ethnic group), 62–63, 254
Kong Chan (headman), 72, 77, 127, 240, 242
  and expedition manpower, 57, 86, 167–68
  house of, 54–58, 69, 80, 88, 103, 230, 241; photograph from porch of, *235*; porch dog, 85, 223–25
  knowledge of saola, 58, 163
  meetings with, 230, 231–32, 236–37; lobbies for road, 57, 101, 233–35
  wife of (Chan Si), 57, 72, 107, 229
Korea, wild populations in, 290
Korean War, 187, 281
kouprey (wild cattle), 22
Kri people, 72, 107

Lak Xao (town), 117–18, 196, 217, 276, 305
  captive saola at, 21–22, 132–41, 162, 274
Lao language, 71, 157, 239, 293, 333–34
  Dictionnaire Laotien-Français, 267
  Lao script, 189
  as lingua franca, 70
  and place names, 13
  spoken with guides and boatmen, 28, 53, 123, 127–28, 143, 165, 167, 185; counting mistake, 190
  spoken with villagers, 250–51
  word for *saola,* 19–20, 138; word for turtle, 47
Laos (Lao People's Democratic Republic, Lao PDR), 102
  Concession Agreement with NTPC, 48
  Department of Forestry, 45, 133

development issues of, 73–74, 268–74 (*see also* ethnic groups in, *below*)

ecotourism planned, 44, 74, 291, 302

ethnic groups in, 13–14, 29, 33, 70–73, 135, 217; living standards, 45; medical care, 88; nomadism among, 72–73, 269–70, 273–74; oral culture, 70

flag of, 101

gross domestic product, 17

language of, *see* Lao language

maps of, 5, 145–47

protected area, *see* Nakai–Nam Theun National Protected Area (NNT)

rice varieties grown in, 38

Robichaud meets with villagers of, *see* Robichaud, William "Bill"

royalty of, 11, 14, 39

saola discovered in, 132; captured, 133–43, 218, 254; further captures banned, 142; photographed, 231; studies of, 302, 326–27, (banned) 217; as unique to, 103, 253–54 (*see also* saola [*Pseudoryx nghetinhensis*])

Thai conquest of, 71

-Thailand border, 13

UXO (unexploded ordnance) in, 156; "bombies," 157

Vientiane, 45, 218; authorities at, 60, 260; expeditions start from, (French colonial) 52, (Robichaud's) 4, 14, 92–93, 125

-Vietnam border, 3–4, 11, 15, 206, 258; border posts, 107, 234, 239, 307–8, 314, (Border Defense Unit 567) 62, 65; forest villages of, 20, 239; saola photographed near, 328 (*see also* Annamite Mountains)

Vietnamese in, 165, 260; trade with, 107 (*see also* poaching)

wild population in, 290; last tiger photographed, 108 (*see also* tigers)

See also Nakai; Nakai–Nam Theun National Protected Area (NNT)

Lao Women's Union, 29

laughingthrushes (*Garrulax*), 65, 124, 132, 220

leeches (Haemadipsidae), 74–75 DNA sequencing of, 304–5, 327

leopard, clouded, 310

Louey, Mr. (Lao owner of trophy), 237

Luangoudom, Phoukhaokham, 74, 302

Luang Prabang (Lao village), 52, 105, 125, 214

MacKinnon, John, 20, 61, 64–68, 206

Madagascar, 76

Malay Peninsula, 76, 256

Mang, Mr. (villager), 90–91, 93, 95–96, 104, 126, 144

Man Tran (Vietnamese village), 64

Martha (saola), 138–43, 274 cast of front hoof, 162 death of, 141–43 photograph of, *139, 160* post-capture myopathy, 137

Mary (friend of author), 40–41, 120, 177–78, 266, 328

medical care, 88, 91–92, 237 folk medicines, 18, 47, 208, 290; rhino horn, 191, 196, 257; traditional Chinese (TCM), 47, 81–82, 84

Meet (militiaman), 126–27, 132, 144–48, 158–60, 180–81, 183, 210 finds new trail, 168–69, 171–74 in photographs, *159, 190*

Mekong River and delta, 11, 13, 20–21, 62, 71, 133, 196, 249

Metamorphoses (Ovid), 197

Millennium Development Goals (UN), 45–46, 260

Miocene epoch, 24, 66, 160

Mok Keo (guide), 104, 122, 126, 189, 223, 265 and food supply, 125, 152, 167–70, 176, 184–85, 213 in photograph, *190*

Mon-Khmer languages, 72

mountain goat. *See* serow

mouse deer (chevrotain), 318

Mu Gia Pass (Vietnam), 156

muntjac (*Muntiacus vuquangensis, M. truongsonensis, M. muntjak, M. phuhoatensis*), 80, 84, 160, 312
  barking deer a species of, 23, 103, 111, 118
  captive, 137
  DNA sequence in leeches, 304–5, 327
  eaten by expedition crew, 184–85, 265
  photographed by camera trap, 118–19, 215, 327–28
  protection of, 48
  snared, 114, 119–20, 122, 175–76, 213, (photographed) *177, 190*
  taxonomy of, 116–18, 339
Myanmar, wild population of, 290

Nakadok (village), 133
Nakai (town), 4, 21
  food from, 38; restaurants in, 247–48
  as market town, 12, 50, 234
  as rendezvous point, 14, 32, 215, 240–41, 242; ferry from, 43, 243; resupplies expedition, 231
  WMPA offices in, 249–50 (*see also* WMPA [Watershed Management and Protection Authority])
  young people moving to, 327
Nakai–Nam Theun National Biodiversity Conservation Area, 133
Nakai–Nam Theun National Protected Area (NNT), 4, 117, 163, 327, 336
  biodiversity protection in, 16, 244–45, 260, 302, 311–12; lack of, 18–19, 108, 201, 291 (*see also* poaching in, *below*)
  ethnic groups of, *see* Laos (Lao People's Democratic Republic, Lao PDR)
  habitat of: changing, 27; climate, 75; decline of species, 128, 213, 261; vines, 171
  map of, 6
  poaching in, 19, 46–48, 74, 105–8, 252; patrols against, 78, (deficiency of) 258; snare collection, 326
  saola sightings in, 83–84, 133, 214–15, 219
  size of, 15; proposed extension, 217
  during Vietnam War, 156

  Westerners' explorations in, 248, 317, 321
  wheeled vehicles arrive in, 191
  See also Nam Theun (river); Nam Theun 2 Hydroeletric Project and Reservoir (NT2, Laos)
Nakai Plateau, 13, 14–15, 20–21, 48, 132
Nam Kading (river), 13–14, 249
Nam Mon (Mulberry River), 287, 292
  animals of river canyon, 310; hunted, 302; otters, 289, 312; saola, 214–15, 219
  expedition to, 241, 242, 248–49, 259, 268, 289, 315; camera traps, 214, 327; on the river, 266, 277, 319, 320; report to villagers on, 325
  photographs of, *295, 309*
Nam Nyang (river)
  expedition to, 4, 53–54, 121, 124–25; arrival at, 144–47, 150, 265, 319; camera traps considered, 25, 214; fishing in, 266; manpower, 57, 74, 90, (friction with) 282; return, 168–69
  flora in watershed of, 162 (*see also* rosewood)
  origin of name, 337
  and poachers from Vietnam, 251, 281; camp destroyed, 212
  as saola habitat, 110, 162–66, 219; saola sighted, 83
  side streams (tributaries) of, 91, 152, 154–56, 157–59, 172, 180–81, 192; reached by expedition, 184, 292, (on way to Phou Vat), 202, 204
  snaring in, Robichaud's report on, 326
Nam Pheo (river), 4, 40, 43, 236
  loaded boats on, *50*
Nam Sapong (creek), 104
Nam Theun (river), 13, 15, 17, 48–49, 206, 249
  ethnic groups of watershed, 70, 72
Nam Theun 2 Hydroelectric Project and Reservoir (NT2, Laos), 4, *10,* 16–17, 21, 49, 250, 312
  environmental program of, 46–48, 260; betrayed, 252
Nam Theun 2 Power Company (NTPC), 48, 244, 259

INDEX

Nam Xot (river), 268, 269, 270,
    276–77
National Geographic, 297
Native Americans, 73–74, 274
Nature (British journal), 67
New Mexico, protected areas of, 128
New York Times, 201
New York Zoological Society. *See*
    Wildlife Conservation Society
    (WCS)
Nghe An Province (Vietnam), 67, 84,
    216–17, 255, 289, 341
Nghe Tinh Province (Vietnam), 67
nomadism, 72–73, 269–70, 273–74
North Korea, 13
Notre Dame de Chartres, 24
NTPC. *See* Nam Theun 2 Power
    Company

observer effect, 303
okapi (animal), 22, 137
    captive-breeding program for, 140
Olay (expedition member), 11, 32–33,
    43, 48, 58, 70, 153–54, 180, 191
    and camera traps, 114, 305–6, 314
    clothing, 114, 122, 145, 222, 305,
        308
    documents saola sightings, 219
    education of, 327, Robichaud as
        mentor, 316, 319
    innkeeper uncle of, 248, 265, 327
    leaves, returns, 248, 259
    and meetings with villagers, 236,
        276–77
    in photographs, *190, 288*
    protectiveness of, 294–95, 321
    writes full name, 128
oryx, Arabian or African, 67
ospreys, 27
otters, 289, 312
Ovid, 197

Pakxe (city), 11, 306
pangolin (animal), 82, 83, 310
Pathet Lao, 39, 185
Phaivanh (guide), 127, 175, 184, 191–93,
    210, 212
    gathers snares, 197, 200, 202
    in photographs, *190, 199*

pheasant
    Edwards's, 76, 313
    gray peacock, 65, 113, 152, 317
    silver, snared, 175, 197, 211
Phiang (guide), 127, *190*, 222
phi kong koy (folkloric creature), 110–11,
    220, 311
Philippines, the, 267, 311
Phok (villager) sights saola, 277, 299, 307
Phomvihane, Kaysone, 39
Phone (village headman), 237–39
Phong people, 72
photographs
    of animals, *see* camera traps
    of crew, *190*, 318–19 (*see also* names
        of individual crew members)
Phou Hone Kay (Chicken Comb
    Mountain), 165
Phou Vang (Golden Mountain), 102,
    156, 165
    ethnic groups near, 71
    expedition to, 53–54, 109, 111, 146,
        154, 182; earlier expedition, 87–89
    as saola habitat, 205; saola sighted, 163
Phou Vat (mountain), 202–4, 206,
    210–11, 212
Phouvong, Mr. (Olay's uncle), 265–66
Phudoi Guest House (Lak Xao), 134
Phung, Phan Dinh, 62
Platoon (film), 186
Pleistocene epoch, 161, 213
poaching
    impact of, 18–19, 49, 74, 110, 194–95
    "most wanted" list, 290; and prices,
        46–47, 106, 168, 290
    protection against, 48, 78, 108;
        guards, 130, 281; lack of, 252, 258;
        WMPA efforts, 19, 46–48, 123, 326
    snares used in, *see* snares
    Vietnamese in Laos, 18, 46–47, 74,
        78, 105–8, 110, 213; poacher
        murdered, 289; poachers' camps,
        125, 132, 251, (abandoned) 105,
        122, 150, 155, 158, 184, 191,
        (destroyed) 171, 203, 212; story
        about rival gangs, 186
POE (International Environmental and
    Social Panel of Experts), 48, 201,
    244, 261, 326–27, 337

349

pollination, 245
Polo, Marco, 26
Pone (Lao villager), 232
porcupines, 83, 191, 203
post-capture myopathy, 137
Predator (film), 187
Pu Huong Nature Reserve (Vietnam), 84–85
Pu Mat Nature Reserve (Vietnam), 67, 208, 216, 254, 258
python, 312
    "photographed," 221, 261

Quang Nam Province (Vietnam), 258
Quy Chau, Vietnam, 84

rabbit, Annamite striped (*Nesolagus timminsi*), 304–5
Rabinowitz, Alan, 132–34
Rasphone, Akchousanh, 125
rattan, 123, 125
Red List, IUCN, 184, 199, 256
Red River delta (Vietnam), 62, 267
rhinoceros (*Rhinoceros sondaicus annamiticus*), 14, 26, 310–11, 340
    death of last, 256–58, 304
    on "most wanted" list, 290
    rhino horns, 26; demand for, 82, 191, 196, 257
road-building, 57, 101, 233–35
Robichaud, William "Bill," 37–38, 42–43, 53–54, 125, 142–47, 167–68, 180–81, 223, 280, 282, 285, 327, 334
    birds studied or noted by, 17, 27, 35–37, 275; "Genghis" the hawk, 36
    early expeditions, 19–22, 78, 108, 152–53, 321; bitten in eye by ant, 322–23
    and Vietnam War, 187
    AS EXPEDITION LEADER, 3–4
    camera traps set by, *see* camera traps
    camp rules, 9–10, 14, 110, 280
    departs from Vientiane, 4, 14, 92–93, 125
    field notes, 176, 189–90
    food supplies, 125, 152, 167–70, 176, 185, 213
    as head of line, 109, 124, 132
    hires guides and boatmen, 99–101, 110, 126–28, 242 (*see also* camp rules, *above*)
    meets with villagers, 236–40, 253–54, 261, 270–78, 325–26; celebration, 30–32, 89–90, 93–96; Kong Chan and Ka, 55–58, 74, 77–81; proposed camera traps, 231–32, 277; road-building, 57, 101, 233–35
    and poachers, *see* poaching
    photographs by, *139, 159, 206, 218, 224, 319* (*see also* camera traps)
    photographs of, *10, 34, 190, 288*
    reconnaissance by, 129, 192, 211, 221–22, 292
    and saola, 24–25, 65–66, 163; continuing hunt for, 165–66, 191; observes captive, 19, 21–22, 118, 132–38, 140–42; quoted on, 102–3, (describes) 135–36
    specimens collected, 175–76, 265
    and technology, 92–93
    as WMPA adviser, 261; meets with managers, 249–52, 259; reports on snaring, 326
robin, American (*Turdus migratorius*), 299
Robinson, John, 67–68
rosewood (*Dalbergia cochinchinensis*), 56, 105, 107–8, 165, 193, 239
    lack of protection of, 47–48, 78, 280; road-building and, 234
    phone number on stump of, 122–23, 251
    price of, 46, 168
    Rosewood Highway, 145–47, 150, 173, 194
Ruggeri, Nancy, 133

Sa Huynh culture (Vietnam), 267
Sai (guide), 281–82
Sai (village headman, member of earlier expedition), 87, 276–78, 299, 325–26
Saigon, Vietnam. *See* Ho Chi Minh City
sambar (deer), 115, 160, 174, 211, 312
    antler trophies from, 80
    camera trap shots of, 215, 328

extinction of, 18
Vietnamese hunters snare, 83
Sang, Nguyen Van, 62, 64
saola (*Pseudoryx nghetinhensis*), 3
in camera trap, *see* photographed,
below
captive, 19, 21–22, 118, 132–43, 218;
described, 135–36 (*see also* Martha)
capture banned, 142, 254 (*see also*
protection of, *below*)
discovery of, 19–24, 58–68, 132, 206,
215; animals killed, 207; known to
first millennium BCE people, 267;
named, 19, 67, (*souphap,* "polite
animal") 138, 208
elusiveness/scarcity of, 53, 56, 82–83,
102–3, 238, 303–5; population
estimate, 119
evolution of, 23–24, 66, 117, 160–61,
337
fate of, 313, 328
habitat of, 23–24, 72, 75, 214, 236,
326; and diet, 140–41, 161,
162–63, 165, 208, 210; expedition
reaches, 152, 205; inaccessibility
of, 53, 84–85, 215–16, 303; on
Nam Nyang, 162–66, 219,
(potential) 110; "protected" in Laos,
258; as unique to Laos and
Vietnam, 103, 253–54
horns (frontlet) of, 24, 163; as trophy,
20, 59, 63–68, 79, 81, 83, (genetic
analysis of) 23, 25, 66, 80, 237, 253,
(photographed) 20, 65
hunted by dogs, 84–85, 207, 216,
218, 238
as liability to villagers, 231
only complete specimen of, 143
photographed, 133, 209; camera trap,
215–19, 218, 231, 328, 329 (*see also*
camera traps); Martha, 139, 160
predators of, 162
protection of, 48; government poster
about, 39, 83; lack of, 78, 102–3, 258;
meetings about, 236; Vietnamese
efforts, 258, (capture banned) 142,
254; WMPA efforts, 302
sightings of, 133, 214–15, 219, 277–78,
299, 307; difficulty of, 303–4; rarity

of, 25, 83–85, 162–63 (*see also*
photographed, *above*)
size and color of, 135–36, 207–8
snared, *see* snares
studies of, 327; governor bans, 217
Saola Working Group (SWG), 3–4, 102,
304, 326–27
sarus crane, 20
Saykham (villager), 217
Schaller, George, 93, 132–33, 161–62,
179, 256, 313
Schismatoglottis (plant browsed by
saola), 163, 164, 193
Schwartz, Martha, 138
Schwarzenegger, Arnold, 187
Secret War (CIA), 156
Sek people, 70–72, 127, 189, 236
language of, 70–71, 137, 165
swidden agriculture of, 77, 269
wheeled vehicles introduced to, 191
serow (*son duong,* mountain goat), 84,
134, 137, 304, 328
saola mistaken for, 63–65, 68
Shurter, Steve, 140
Siengtho (villager), 253
Simeuang (expedition member), 14, 28,
53, 183–84, 225, 268, 281–82
allots gear, 50, 99, 100, 104; monitors
supplies, 152–53, 170, 202, 259
and camera traps, 300–2, 306, 314
and camp rules, 110
clothing of, 122, 195, 222
fishes, 266, 296; cooks fish, 69–70
ignores smuggler, 280
in photographs, 190, 288; mugs for
camera, 318
sets pace, 32–33, 35; and river
crossings, 292–96, 314, (falls) 315
as WMPA representative, 11, 16, 78,
276, 302, 325; further education,
327; manpower sought, recruited
by, 57, 242; and meetings with
villagers, 101, 232, 236, 238, 253,
277, 325; and poaching, 203;
reports to post, 240, 249–50 (*see
also* WMPA [Watershed
Management and Protection
Authority])
writes full name, 128

smuggling, 46–49, 78, 165, 193, 234, 251
  guide ignores, 280
  See also poaching
snares, 18, 197–200, *199, 224*
  army patrols for, 78
  collected by expedition, 175, 189–90,
    197, 200, 202, 326; bounty for, 225
  destroyed, 114, 197, 211
  porcupines snared, 191
  Robichaud's report on, 326
  saolas snared, 3, 207, 218–19; avoid
    snares, 56; incidentally snared, 83;
    placement of snares, 161
  snare lines, 174–76, 182, 210;
    abandoned, 173; destroyed, 197,
    211; labor required to build,
    193–94
  Vietnamese, 83; government removes,
    258
  wire, 119, 174–75; introduction of,
    107; steel cables, 108, 114, 202–3,
    254
Sone (militiaman), 126–27, 132, 148,
    165–66, 176, 180, 183
  in photograph, *190;* house shown, 235
Souphanouvong "Red Prince," 39
South China Sea, 267
Soviet Union, 134, 233, 281
  equipment and weapons from, 22, 59,
    104, 159
  See also Communist governments
squirrel, black giant (*Ratufa bicolor*),
    122, 165
Stegner, Wallace, 320
sticky rice, 38, 110, 170
Stone, Oliver, 186
Sumatra, 76
swiddens, 28, 32, 72, 76–77, 81, 269,
    272–73

Tai-Kadai family of languages, 70–71
Tai language, 19
Taxol (anti-cancer drug), 244
TCM (traditional Chinese medicine),
    47, 81–82, 84. *See also* medical care
technology, 92–93
  wheeled vehicles arrive in Nakai–
    Nam Theun, 191

  See also electricity; TV
Thailand, 103
  Asian Institute of Technology in, 327
  Bangkok, 45, 61; University of
    Technology Thonburi in, 327
  as consumer of electricity, 15, 17
  dog trucks from, 196
  -Laos border, 13
  Laos laid waste by, 71
  Thai language, 71
  U.S. air bases in, 156
Thakhek (provincial capital), 29, 88, 91
Thii (guide), 281–82, 284, 286–89, 308,
    317
  photographed, *288, 318*
Thong Dam (guide), 127, *177,* 189, *190*
Thong Kouang (Grand Grassland),
    113–14, 167, 169–70, 202, 211, 220
  burned, 124, 131
  expedition arrives at, 108–11;
    crossing, *109*
  "python" at, 221, 261
Thong Sek (grassland), 121, 124–25,
    129, 131, 143
Thua Thien–Hue Province (Vietnam),
    258
Tibet, 313
tigers, 107, 310, 338
  and bad luck, 70
  as "most wanted" animal, 290;
    extinction of, 14, 289–90
  photographed by camera traps, 108,
    321
Timmins, Rob, 116–19, 152–53, 179,
    215, 303, 305, 327, 338–39
Tordoff, Jack, 3, 337
Toum ethnic group, 217
Touy (expedition member), 32–34, 45,
    225
  education of, 327
  and food, food rations, 69, 167, 170
  guards gear, 43, 153
  in photographs, *126, 190*
  returns to Vientiane, 146, 248, 259
  of royal lineage, 39
  writes full name, 128
Touy (village elder), and Touy's niece,
    270–74

traps. *See* camera traps; snares

Trung, Cao Tien, 84–85

Trung's restaurant (Nakai), 247–48

Tu, Nguyen Thai, 62, 64

Tuoc, Do, 61–66, 207

turtle, box ("golden") (*Cuora trifasciata*), and turtle blood, 47–48, 86, 106–7, 191, 290, 337

TV, 45, 63, 90, 247, 259, 269
  Japanese, 207
  See also electricity

UK (United Kingdom), 102

UN (United Nations) Millennium Development Goals, 45–46, 260

unicorn, the, 24–27

United States, 102
  Vietnam and Laos bombed by, 61, 156–57 (*see also* Vietnam War)
  Western, early days of, 73–74, 274

UXO (unexploded ordnance), 156–57

Vieng (guide), 281–82, 288

Viengxai (guide), 115–16, 127–28, 152, 180, 202, 221–23, 282, 327
  complaints by, 100–1, 103–4, 146–47, 168–69, 214
  in line of march, 109, 124, 145, 171–72
  older brother of, 229–30.
  photographed, 190, 205–6
  searches packs, toys with equipment, 113–14, 143, 153–54, 220

Vientiane. *See* Laos (Lao People's Democratic Republic, Lao PDR)

Vientiane Times, 335

Vietic people and language, 72, 268, 341–42

Vietnam, 13, 84, 102
  Doi Moi ("renovation") in, 59, 61, 106
  ethnic groups in, 62, 267
  Forest Protection Department, 208; removes snares, destroys camps, 258
  highways to, 117, 196; "Rosewood Highway," 145–47, 150, 173, 194
  indomitable people of, 255; work ethic of, 99, 143–44, 194
  ky lan and unicorn myth in, 27

-Laos border, *see* Laos

last rhinoceros in, 256–58, 304

map of, 5

Ministry of Forestry/Forest Inventory and Planning Institute (FIPI), 61, 63, 67; saola acquired by, 135, 162, 207–10, 267

saola discovered in, 20, 58–68, 132, 206–8; camera-trapped, 216–17; captured, 142, (further captures banned) 142, 254; hunted by dogs, 84–85, 207, 216, 218 (*see also* saola [*Pseudoryx nghetinhensis*])

smuggling into, 234, 251

United States bombing of, 61; UXO (unexploded ordnance) in, 156 (*see also* Vietnam War)

Vietnamese in Laos, 83, 165, 239, 276; poacher murdered, 289 (*see also* poaching)

Vietnamese language, 333

wild population of, 290

See also Hanoi; Ho Chi Minh City

Vietnam War, 147, 187–88, 254, 256
  UXO from, 156–57

Vinh (Vietnam) and Vinh University, 60, 62, 84, 208

Vlad the Impaler, 175

Vong, Mr. (owner of trophy), 237

Voy, Mr. (guide), 285, 288

Vu Quang Nature Reserve/National Park (Vietnam), 118, 161, 258, 267
  saola discovered in, 58–68, 206–8, 216; capture banned, 254

"Vu Quang ox," 20, 66–67, 206

Walston, Joe, 312

Western United States, settlement era, 73–74, 274

wheeled vehicles, first use of, 191. *See also* technology

White Oak conservation center (Yulee, Florida), 140

wild cattle:
  Asian Wild Cattle Specialist Group, 3
  evolution of, 80
  kouprey discovered, 22
  See also banteng; gaur

Wildlife Conservation Society (WCS),
    68, 92, 132–33, 138, 142, 153,
    217–19, 244
  Asia Program of, 312
Wilkinson, Nicholas, 304–5
WMPA (Watershed Management
    and Protection Authority), 17, 201,
    215, 244, 260
  guides' wages set by, 86, 168
  offices, 249–50, 274, 276; ranger
    station, 277
  Panel of Experts (POE) and, 261,
    326–27
  Robichaud as adviser to, 261; meets
    with managers of, 249–52, 259
  saola research and protection:
    antipoaching efforts, 19, 46–48,
    123, 326; ecotourism program,
    74, 302
  Simeuang as representative of, see
    Simeuang (expedition member)
  villagers' view of, 101, 233, 239
World Bank (WB), 16, 201, 233,
    260–61
World War II, 60, 187
World Wildlife Fund (WWF), 61, 244,
    256, 258, 313, 337
  and saola, 207–8; announces
    discovery, 20, 65, 68; photographs,
    328

Xieng Kouang Province (Laos), 326

Yellow Leaf People, 269, 273, 311

ABOUT THE AUTHOR

WILLIAM DEBUYS is the author of eight books, including *River of Traps: A New Mexico Mountain Life*, a *New York Times* Notable Book of the Year and a finalist for the Pulitzer Prize in general non-fiction in 1991; *Enchantment and Exploitation: The Life and Hard Times of a New Mexico Mountain Range*; *The Walk* (an excerpt of which won a Pushcart Prize in 2008); and *A Great Aridness: Climate Change and the Future of the American Southwest*. An active conservationist, deBuys has helped protect more than 150,000 acres in New Mexico, Arizona, and North Carolina. He lives in New Mexico.